AFTER GOD

Peter Sloterdijk

After God

Translated by Ian Alexander Moore

polity

Polity Press
65 Bridge Street
Cambridge CB2 1UR, UK

Polity Press
101 Station Landing
Suite 300
Medford, MA 02155, USA

ISBN-13: 978-1-5095-3350-3
ISBN-13: 978-1-5095-3351-0 (pb)

A catalogue record for this book is available from the British Library.

Library of Congress Cataloging-in-Publication Data
Names: Sloterdijk, Peter, 1947- author. | Moore, Ian Alexander, translator.

Title: After God / Peter Sloterdijk ; translated by Ian Alexander Moore.
Other titles: Nach Gott. English
Description: Cambridge, UK ; Medford, MA : Polity, 2020. | First published in
  German as Nach Gott: Glaubens- und Unglaubensversuche, Suhrkamp Verlag 2017.
  | Summary: "After God is dedicated to the theological enlightenment of theology.
  It ranges from the period when gods reigned to reveries about the godlike power of
  artificial intelligence"-- Provided by publisher.
Identifiers: LCCN 2019034770 (print) | LCCN 2019034771 (ebook) | ISBN
  9781509533503 (hardback) | ISBN 9781509533510 (paperback) | ISBN 9781509533534
  (epub)
Subjects: LCSH: Death of God theology. | Philosophical theology.
Classification: LCC BT83.5 .S5613 2020 (print) | LCC BT83.5 (ebook) | DDC
  210--dc23
LC record available at https://lccn.loc.gov/2019034770
LC ebook record available at https://lccn.loc.gov/2019034771

Typeset in 10.5 on 12pt Times by Fakenham Prepress Solutions, Fakenham, Norfolk
Printed and bound in Great Britain by TJ International Limited

For further information on Polity, visit our website:
politybooks.com

Contents

Translator's Note

I would like to thank Ben Acree, Myron Jackson, Oliver Berghof, and especially Manuela Tecusan for their helpful comments on the translation.

1

TWILIGHT OF THE GODS

"Every world of gods is followed by a twilight of the gods"*

Rest now, rest, you god!

Richard Wagner, *Die Götterdämmerung*

I

The intelligentsia of our culturally forgetful days still remembers, partially, that the Greeks of the classical era used the term "mortals" to refer to human beings. Human beings bore this name because they were conceived of as earthly counterparts of the gods, who were called immortals. Immortality was in fact the only eminent feature of the Greek gods. Their behavior hardly differed from that of humans, with their all-too-humanness.

A century ago, amid the convulsions of World War I, Paul Valéry extended the attribute of mortality to high cultures. We should now know, he assured us, that even the great collective constructs (*nous autres, civilisations*), those integrated by language, law, and the division of labor, are mortal. We should regard it as a happy accident if this immense statement has left behind a trace here and there, in the memory of a culture that bears the old European stamp. "We civilizations" are indeed mortal and, after everything that had happened, we should have taken note of this. No longer should mortality be predicated only of Socrates and his ilk. The term leaves the domain of syllogistic exercises and inundates a

---

* Gotthard Günther, "Seele und Maschine," in Gotthard Günther, *Beiträge zur Grundlegung einer operationsfähigen Dialektik*, vol. 1 (Hamburg: Felix Meiner, 1976), p. 79.

continent that does not grasp its Great War. Mortality acquires this new valence not only from the fact that, within four years, more than nine million men were sent to their deaths. What is decisive is that the countless fallen soldiers and civilian casualties seemed to result from the internal tensions of the cultural events themselves. What are cultural nations, and what do civilizations amount to, if they allow such an excess of casualties and self-sacrifices, indeed not only allow it but provoke it from their ownmost [*eigensten*] impulses? What does this mass consumption of life say about the spirit of the industrial age? What could this unparalleled recklessness toward individual existence possibly mean? When applied to civilizations, the word "mortality" also hints at the possibility of suicide.

The shock to which Valéry's note bore witness reached deeper than his contemporaries could have known. For once, our insight that civilizations could fall was not relegated to distant worlds such as Nineveh, Babylon, or Carthage. It now applied to great civilizations close at hand: France, England, Russia ... These were names that, until yesterday, still resonated with us. They were spoken of as though they were metaphysical universals in the form of peoples. They stood for the supertemporal stability that used to be attributed to clans and to their associations into peoples. Since time immemorial, clans were ruled by the law of ancestry. They embodied the duration that flows through the generations, no matter how much individuals come and go. Valéry: "And now we see that the abyss of history is big enough for all."[1]

The twilight of civilization begins at the moment when the inhabitants of the great cultural enclosures suspect that even the most established human systems of the present have not been built for all eternity. They are subject to a fragility that also goes by the name "historicity." Historicity means for civilizations what mortality means for individuals. In the philosophy of the twentieth century, this idea was applied to individuals under the description of "being toward death." When related to cultures, it is called historical consciousness.

As a rule, members of the historically affected nations have ignored the idea that their historians are at the same time their thanatologists. *Ex officio*, thanatologists make the better theologians. Relying on a local point of departure, they leap ahead and assume God's standpoint at the end of the world and at the end of life. As a rule, historians don't realize that they are indirectly practicing the perspective of the end when they recall early beginnings.

From a divine perspective, history means nothing but the process of converting what has not yet been into what has been. Only when all being has entered into a state of having been has the "omnipotent god"[2] of classical metaphysics reached its goal. Only when it is certain that nothing new will happen any more may God discard the initially intoxicating, but later on compromising attribute of "omnipotence"; this attribute had indeed become increasingly embarrassing and superfluous. At the actual end of history there is neither anything to create nor anything to preserve. Everything that is is there for the sake of what ultimately will be. The dossier of creation is closed. The end God drapes himself in the robe of omnipotence. As soon as knowledge that has become complete is no longer confronted with new tasks on behalf of creativity (or of the "event"), God surveys the universe in its totality. He serenely looks straight through everything that was the case.

In the old European tradition, "apocalypse" designates this moment of looking through things in a comprehensive retrospection. In the strict sense, this means: uncovering all things from the perspective of the end. If everything is complete, everything becomes transparent. The so-called revelations that were available to mortal observers in certain high cultures in the guise of "holy texts" are like vistas into the static beyond that have been fixed at the halfway point. They testify to the fact that higher religions don't work without rushing things.[3] Such pre-haste [*Vor-Eile*] is subject to the temporal schema of impatient faith: already now, but then all the more! Yet, as a rule, religious apocalypses do not deal with real "ultimate concerns." They wallow in the depiction of tumults before the advent of the great tranquility.

Whoever accepts such messages as truths is able to imagine leaping ahead and partaking of the total view from the end of time. The spheres of such representations are called "worlds of faith." They are created in order to bridge the gap between nowness [*Jetztzeit*] and eternity. The believer nevertheless remains subject to the law of being on her way, in the realm of the temporary [*im Vorläufigen*]. She knows she can catch up with God only by attaining the same ontological rank in death. This is the case for the ancient Indians as well as for old Europe, and for the domains of Islam no less.

There was a name for those groups of believers who were convinced they could achieve the apparently impossible task of catching up with God *media in vita* [in the midst of life]. They were called mystics. Thanks to their efforts, transcendence has not remained a completely empty word. These virtuosi of self-renunciation attempted to eschew every sort of separate life outside of God. In this way they devoted themselves to the idea that they had already entered into the beyond here, in this life. Indeed, to die means to give back one's soul – as the French idiom *rendre l'âme* expresses it in such a metaphysically fitting way. Yet only when everything has in fact died – whether in advance, or whether at the proper or improper time – will everything that was destined to exist be freed from the compulsion of becoming and of innovation. If we had to say in one sentence what classical metaphysics had in mind, it would be this: it wanted to convert the "world" into participants in the stasis of God's omniscience. This end was served, among others, by the Stoic and Christian doctrines of providence (Greek *pronoia*, Latin *providentia*), which were supposed to secure for the future God's exposed flanks.

*

The modern world exists because this attempt at conversion failed. Included in modernity is anyone who rejects the idea of a complete emptying of the future into the past and votes for the inexhaustibility of the future, even if this vote excludes the possibility of an omniscient god who, "after all time," bends back, in a comprehensive retrospective on creation.

The "world" – a word that, as Nietzsche knew better than anyone, was for a long time a "Christian insult"[4] – resisted the invitation to empty the future into total pastness, because it renounced the ontological precedence of the past. It offered resistance because, in its struggle with itself and through an autodidactic exertion of remarkable coherence, it had learned to give time its due. Ironically, this new attempt at a deeper understanding of time was carried out on European soil, of all things, the homeland of resolute stasis metaphysics and convulsive apocalypticism. In the philosophical thought of modernity, the fundamental openness of the future was appropriately grasped for the first time. At the intersection of will and representation, the world assumed the form of a project and undertaking. It is not the merchants and seafarers who are responsible for reforming the world into an ensemble of projects, but rather the thinkers who undid the metaphysical paralysis of the future. Thus figures such as Schelling, Hegel, Bergson, Heidegger, Bloch, and Günther, perhaps even Cusa, too, all assume prominent positions in the pantheon of "contemporary" philosophy. Above all others, it was these authors who put an end to the eviction of time and novelty from being. They burst the dead enclosures of ontology by placing time and the new at the heart of being.

II

Ancient Greek mythology had, from afar, anticipated the revenge of time against eternity. It did so when it took the liberty of suggesting that even the immortal gods must reckon with a disaster of a higher order. The Greeks called this power of destiny *moira*. It embodied an unspecified variable in the background of structural being. Working from the invisible realm, it allotted to all variables what was proper to them. It possessed complete power over the arrangements, the portions, the lots, the destinies. It "prevailed" as a power prior to power, as justice prior to justice, as destiny prior to destinies. It allowed the regime of the Olympians to come into being by effecting a division of powers at the level of the absolute; it demarcated each of the jurisdictions of the chief gods from one another. Hades is appointed ruler of the underworld, Poseidon ruler of what is covered by water, and Zeus ruler of the visible realm under the heavens. When each is allotted his portion from the whole, a decisive step has been taken in the civilizing of the gods.

Look how far removed we are, already at this stage, from the crude power monsters of the pre-Olympian forces, which always wished to dominate everything en bloc! We are still just as far removed from the god of the philosophers and his cyclothymic, now merciful now wrathful doppelganger, the god of theologians! Little is known, even today, about the damage that theologians caused when they elevated "the One" at the expense of "the many." With their disastrous distinction between God and idols they gave rise to a theodicean epidemic that has still not died away. Didn't Isaiah already deal with the gods of other peoples by depicting them as painted pieces of wood?[5] Didn't Nietzsche remark, still in the tonality of monotheistic religious satire, that "[t]he world has more idols than realities"?[6] After the One had pushed the others to the margins, the gods faded into the twilight of exile. The appointed theologians nevertheless continue to believe that they have done the world the greatest service by making a large portion of humanity dependent on an intrinsically riven god, whose uniqueness was paid for by the cleverly masked incompatibility of his highest attributes.

In their supremacist zeal, the religious theologians had insisted on garbing God with the most radiant attributes: omnipotence and omniscience.[7] They did not consider that their simultaneous procla-mation of these attributes implanted a real and highly explosive contradiction into the Highest. Either God is omnipotent, in which case his creative will is always free to introduce novelty and can be mirrored by his knowledge only after the fact; or he is omniscient, in which case he must have used up all his creative power. Only in the latter case can he take an eternal holiday and look back on the universe of what has been.

Old European thought needed one and a half thousand years to detonate the contradiction concealed in the monotheistic concept of

God. The bursting of this contradiction, which had been disguised for so long, was for the most part misunderstood as the atheistic crisis of the modern age. In truth what happened was that power and knowledge, both the higher and the lower forms, were interwoven and reconfigured. However, while the younger theologians, the Protestants above all, embraced modernity's openness toward the future and, more or less tacitly, reconciled themselves to the loss of God's omnipotence,[8] contemporary Islam continues to make much ado about Allah's omnipotence. Yet, because even Allah has long since become incapable of novelty and remains fixed in his past as creator, he can allow his allegedly still virulent omnipotence to be proven exclusively through the will to obliterate unrighteous creatures.[9] The young murderers and suicides who break out into open jihad have grasped without any theology to what extent a god like Allah cuts an impossible figure as soon as he is observed against the backdrop of a modern world – that is, a world that has been rendered dynamic by *human* creativity. Nota bene: the fact that all human beings sooner or later die may be chalked up to nature or fatality, far from any idea of God. Yet the fact that individual mortals engage in premature obliteration and that the obliterators often sacrifice themselves in the process, in a dull and heroic sort of way, is now, in all seriousness, supposed to show evidence of the spirit and power of Allah. The young fanatics do not suspect how much they, through their actions, stand proof of the sterility of a decrepit theological culture. It will be a while before more people realize that the terror practiced by Islamists against the "unfaithful" within and outside the "house of Islam" is a demonstration of how the twilight of Allah is enacted. Assassinations are wayward proofs of a god who no longer understands the world.

The unresolved question of creativity stands at the center of the theological crisis of Islam. It is at once a question about technology and a question about the right to make images. The problem cannot be solved by means of the Qur'an. The Islamic nations, in total, do in fact take part in the creativity of modernity, especially in its advanced technological accomplishments, but so far only from the standpoint of the user. They have not proceeded to the level of "technological existence."[10] They do not produce what they use; they do not generate what they take by the hand. They have neither accepted the principle of *translatio creativitatis* [transfer of creativity][11] nor grasped it as the task of our times.

*

It would be an exaggeration to say that, in the implicit theology of Greek mythology, there is an underlying premonition of what other mythological traditions called a "twilight of the gods." *Moira*, after all, implies the thought of a regime that grants gods their "constitution." (Rousseau's claim that a nation of gods would inevitably govern itself democratically is metaphysically ignorant; for, to judge by everything we know about the gods, they tend to pick out a sovereign on the spur of the moment.) *Moira* says nothing about a possible end of the immortals.

Nevertheless, in some of the dramas about the titan Prometheus attributed to the poet Aeschylus, we can glimpse the anticipation of a post-Olympian state of affairs. By virtue of his farsighted intelligence, Prometheus is thought to have looked beyond the regime of Zeus. Legend has it that he offered to share his menacing visions with Zeus if the latter would free him from his eternal torment on the rock in the Caucasus. Zeus – obviously quite far from being omniscient when it came to his own affairs – is supposed to have entered into the deal and "unbound" Prometheus. He did this in order to find out whether a virtual son of his could threaten him with the same fate that he had prepared for his own father Cronus when he, Zeus, emasculated him while Cronus was having sex with Gaia. Zeus subsequently refrained from producing a son capable of imitating his father. He relinquished the spicy nymph who was standing by as the possible mother of his murderer.

Up to this point, the premonitions of unrest in the houses of the gods remain confined to dynastic phase changes. Without further ado, the Greeks of the classical centuries could imagine a palace coup in the Olympian realm; a twilight of the gods in the Indo-Germanic or Nordic style is foreign to their temperament. The Stoic doctrine of *ekpurōsis* (world conflagration) is a later exoticism imported from the Middle East.

Germanic mythology gives us more fecund material for approaching the question of the sort of event that the "twilight of the gods" is. Admittedly, up to the present day scholars have had various reasons to debate whether the poets of the gods in Old Norse had already thought up the idea of a consuming fire at the end of times independently, or whether it was exposure to Christian apocalypticism that gave them an understanding of what it means to take an interest in downfall.

Let us remember that the idea of *Ragnarök* – a word sometimes translated as "the end of the world" and sometimes as "twilight of the gods" – was ushered in at a time of genealogical deregulations. In the wake of these deregulations, brothers strike one another dead, fathers strangle their sons, and parents sexually abuse their offspring. Something similar happens at the cosmological level. The giant wolf Fenris swallows the sun and moon, and the stars vanish.

After a winter of a thousand days when the summer can no longer
fulfill its task of separating one winter from next, the earth shakes,
mountains topple, the ocean floods the mainland, the world tree
trembles, and everything alive is filled with dread. In the final battle
between the Muspelheim gods and the archaic monsters, Thor dies
from the poison of the giant snake he kills, while the wolf swallows
Odin. The battle comes under the law of an almost certain mutual
annihilation. Finally, Surtr ("the Black," Vulcan's Scandinavian
counterpart) sets the world aflame and burns down everything that
exists. The only survivors to emerge from the inferno are a few
gods and a human couple. It will be their task to establish a new
cycle of life.

There is no reason here to delve into analogies between *Ragnarök*
and the *Mahabharata* or the Apocalypse of John. Nor are we
worried whether the word *Götterdämmerung* [twilight of the gods]
is a correct translation of *Ragnarök*. According to the scholarly
literature, *Ragnarök* covers a wide range of meanings, which extend
from "death of the gods" to "renewal of divine forces." Even
Richard Wagner appears not to have been entirely convinced of
the adequacy of the expression. According to a report by Cosima,[12]
while he was working on the fourth part of *The Ring of the
Nibelung*, he played with the idea of calling the piece *Göttergericht*
[*Court of the gods*], "for Brünnhilde holds court over them" (i.e.
the gods). Thus at issue for the composer who inaugurated the
renaissance of the "twilight of the gods" motif[13] was not so much
a myth of downfall in Nordic garb as the corrective to an ethical
mistake that had long ago woven itself into the fabric of the world.
His *Götterdämmerung* is a moral drama of purification; it is not
intended as a phenomenology of spirit for the stage. It recognizes no original sin – just an original mistake. There is ingenious
symbolism in the fact that the logs from the fallen world tree make
Wagner's location for the gods, Valhalla, go up in flames. The finale
of the stage performance exceeds all proportions. It is as though
the profane fragmentation of the world's organism into pieces of
wood were the spiritual and material cause for the dying down of
the gods.

The twilight of the gods on stage reveals a marked pessimism.
Wagner's libretto puts up with the fact that the old gods have
become metaphysically worn out. Seen from a cultural perspective,
even Brünnhilde's sublime suicide is no more valuable than Emma
Bovary's. A certain anarchic vandalism has the last word. There is
no talk of a new cycle of creation. The "estrus of downfall"[14] seizes
everything. The reasons for this cannot be found in the work of art
itself.

III

We can invoke Richard Wagner's contribution to the portrayal of the agony of the gods as evidence of the fact that the freedom of the will migrated to the domain of art some time ago. In today's turbulent world, the human being can experience a trace of freedom, that is, an openness toward what is to come, only by drawing on his "own" creative potential – and on that of his companions who share in the same fate. There is an epochal significance in the immigration of creativity to the realms of art and technology. Without this immigration, the word "modernity" would be mere sound and fury. The first thinker of Europe, Giambattista Vico, conceptualized this movement by distinguishing the age of the gods from the epoch of heroes and from that of human beings. This sequence can be rewritten as a progressive incarnation. Where there were gods, human beings should come to be. Where there are human beings, artificiality increases.

Wagner's work is so philosophically remarkable because it brings these three spheres very close to one another. It evokes a demanding near simultaneity of gods, heroes, and human beings. Wagner's meditation on the power of time can be seen in how he presents the heroes after the gods and the human beings after the heroes – without offering any further justification for this sequence. Wagner's new mythology is a hermeneutics of fate. It purports to make us understand by means of pure presentation. Matters of fate can only be shown, not explained. Fate refers to what happens without allowing any questions as to why.

From the perspective of philosophy, Wagner is not just chronologically situated between Hegel and Heidegger. As a reader of Feuerbach, he knows that human beings have an innate god-making ability. As a reader of Schopenhauer, he understands that action incurs debt from blind will. As a reader of Bakunin, it is clear to him that whoever wants something new must lay his torch on what is flammable, that is, on what the critical spirits call the "existent." No purification without passing through the fire. No phoenix without ashes.

The *Götterdämmerung* constitutes evidence of Wagner's insight that the old set of gods has become obsolete. They "are able only to watch this ending approach and do nothing to prevent it."[15] At the same time, Wagner's speculations only provide an indirect contribution to our understanding of the process that, with regard to ontology, can be called *translatio creativitatis* [transfer of creativity]. This expression refers to the fact that it is not only God who is a creator; nature and human beings have creative qualities too. There are obviously a multiplicity of creativities and a multiplicity of reflexivities in the world that a divine authority cannot reclaim, let alone monopolize. The earth is a place of polyvalent intelligence. It forms the only known point in the universe where one can really say: there is thinking, in manifold ways.

From a philosophical perspective, what mythological discourse called the "twilight of the gods" amounts to nothing but the symbolic condensation of the consequences that result from the thesis that there is thinking. Precise thinking establishes a new reality. Descartes's fallacy consisted in reclaiming thinking for his ego. Yet the ego is nothing but the place in which we first take note of the discovery that there is thinking. The fact that an ego ascribes its thinking and what is thought to itself is secondary. Descartes' primary thought that, when I think, I thereby certainly am, turns out to be sterile from the beginning. The cogito builds an unshakable foundation without any structure on top of it. Every substantially fruitful thought belongs to the sphere of the "there is thinking" – or in any case to the sphere of the "there is thinking in me." (Parenthetically: Fichte's greatness comes from the fact that in his late work he emphasized the "there is" in the ego. If we are to think, we do need an ego first, but behind the ego that I immediately know – because I am the one who posited it – there is another ego rearing up; I do not know this latter ego, which uses me as its eye, as it were. This unknown ego that looks through me is called God. God is the will to substance, the will to non-sterility, the will to non-exhaustion in empty self-relation, in short, the will to world.)

Mythological aids are not sufficient for grasping the phenomenon of the "twilight of the gods." Yet the word "twilight" does correctly indicate that God and gods don't die, but instead fade away. This happens whether a brighter light consumes their own light or whether obfuscation makes them invisible. Lessing's parable of the ring in *Nathan the Wise* (1779) – which he borrowed from Boccaccio's *Decameron* (1356) – marks one stage in the process of their fading away. After it an aura of amiable undecidability surrounds the god of the once sharply contoured monotheisms.

Fading away as such need not be fatal.[16] As the present shows, a god can recover from pallor when the times are favorable, even if the color he or she regains is for the most part questionable. Fading away is essentially irreversible because modern civilization has produced so much artificial light with its art, its science, its technology, and its medicine that God's light seems faint in comparison. One can only let it shine on Sundays and holidays by turning off the machines of artificial light.

This last point can best be explained by turning back to the thanatology of classical metaphysics. According to old Europe's authoritative story of creation, it was divine breath that lent human beings their feeling and reflecting soul. As long as the soul preserves its community with the body, the human being is still alive – or, as the German language puts it so profoundly, the human being is still *am Leben*. In the universe of Genesis, the pinnacle of reflection is located in divine intelligence, which can do what it wills and wills what it knows. (This is the case in most creation myths that are acquainted with a demiurge, a maker,[17] a first author.) Individual human intelligences are loans that have been portioned out from the stock of the total intelligence. These gifts are repaid to the creator upon the death of the creature. The myth of the Last Judgment suggests the logic of a loan agreement: when the soul that has been borrowed is taken back, there is an examination of whether the refund is whole and sound. If it is not, the lender enacts his revenge on the dead ones who bring their souls back damaged, defaced, and darkened.

It is obvious that the classical model of transactions between God, the soul, and the world does not allow any other intelligent being to enter the world. Nor does this seem necessary to allow it, since God has drawn from his unsurpassable abundance and given to creation or nature as much order as they need for their existence. Not even the intelligently animated human being can arrange the world any more cleverly than it is as he finds it to be according to its primordial arrangement. For this reason, it is not uncommon for him to feel that the world is an "external world." He is its guest, not one who should change it. Within this metaphysical model, the reflexive communication plays out only between God and the human being. The one who bestows intelligence brings souls into being and grants them enough revelation to lead them to believe in him; for the rest, human beings live "in their time," after which they give back their animated intelligence, at death's door. Once again we recall the subtle turn of phrase in French: *rendre l'âme*. The Protestant hymn knows this too, in its own way: the world is not my "proper home."[18]

The suggestiveness of these ideas may remain unaffected. Yet one cannot fail to recognize that they, too, breathe the spirit of a sublime sterility. This spirit gives the events of the world and creation the form of a zero-sum game. In this respect God gains nothing in the end. Human beings, by contrast, risk damnation if they have lived in a problematic fashion. An influx of intelligence into the world is unthinkable on the classical model of communication between God and souls. Under these circumstances, Post-Babylonian humanity, which has been dispersed into different cultures, can do no more than produce sufficiently similar offspring.

At this point modernity raises its objection to classical metaphysics. Owing to the matter under discussion, this objection must take the form of an alternative interpretation of death. One cannot rule out the possibility that the human being "gives the soul back" upon death. Yet it no longer corresponds to the experience of symbolically and technologically active human beings in higher civilizations to assume that the world remains unaffected by the departure of an intelligent soul from it.

Indeed, wherever one looks, one sees that human beings have been active as god-making animals. Yet as soon as they invested in their god creations, their god-making frenzy revealed them to be the sort of animal that raises monuments. In high cultures, they act as producers who fill the "hall of memory" with material. They operate as collectors of sacred and profane memorabilia. They function as administrators of "cultural heritage" and as wardens of patrimonies. These observations can in no way be aligned with the basic idea of classical thanatology, namely that in death human beings give their soul back to God without any deductions. Rather it seems that, to the extent that they have become "creative," humans have gained the ability to leave behind, in the world, something of their intelligent soul. They do, admittedly, give "themselves" back in death. Yet they also frequently create a "work" that is preserved in the world and can become the point of departure for further creations and for renewable legacies.

*

The phenomenon of the "twilight of the gods" thus has practically nothing to do with transcendent fatalities at the divine level. Rather it concerns only the relation between creative intelligences and the world. If we want to keep making use of the concept of fate, we could say that this concept pertains to the fact that higher cultures become beholden to the backlash of their creativity. The more they advance in accumulating artificial effects – and the more these effects succumb to the law of self-intensification (or, in cybernetic terminology, to positive feedback) – the more intensely can we notice culture's overshadowing of nature, and the more relentlessly does the fading away of the divine side take place.

It is no accident that the pious have always suspected that large cities were hotbeds of atheism. And they were right to do so, for city dwellers have always been surrounded by proofs of the mind and of the power of purely human environment formations. Since the days of the Tanakh (in Christian language, the Old Testament) the name "Babylon" has stood for the funfair of artificialities. This inevitably turns people's attention away from the one thing that is necessary. The artificial environment of the city directs its inhabitants more toward themselves and toward the architectonic ambitions of their predecessors than toward the work of the gods or of God. The fact that metropolises such as Jerusalem, Rome, and Benares survived as holy cities proves only that certain priestly elites were able to mystify their cities as theaters of constructed proofs of God. In Chicago, Singapore, and Berlin, as well as in other urban agglomerations around the earth, such a maneuver would have failed beforehand.

If we wish to use terms from philosophy and cultural studies to interpret what is going on with the dynamic of the twilight of the gods, it will be necessary to revise the classic metaphysical image of giving back one's soul. We need not infringe on the noble idea of the soul's returning home to a transcendent source. However, it will be essential for us to rethink the figure of the testament or of the "legacy," from the ground up. In the civilization of modernity, which is animated by creativism and where artificiality is raised to ever higher powers, we can no longer ignore the fact that human intelligence flows out into "works" or artifacts. And this is so even if, today as always, their creators succumb to mortality. (The secondary outflowing of mass culture into trash is another theme.)

In this respect, the necrologist is the key figure when it comes to understanding the process of civilization. When a creative type passes away, the agitated world pauses for a second and meditates on the conveyance of a work in progress[19] into the global archive. During this meditative second we are closer to the phenomenon of the twilight of the gods than we would otherwise be.

It was Hegel who, with his concept of "objective spirit," first took note of the outflowing of intelligence into informed structures with relative stability. His concept was too laden with metaphysical presuppositions to be integrated into the vocabulary of the human sciences without suffering compromises. It was discreetly replaced by the noncommittal term "culture." Yet, even in the often unbearably vague concept of culture, there is an unmistakable echo of the basic phenomenon: what is invariably at issue is the entrance of living reflexivity into objectivized and materialized structures, whether they be signs, rituals, institutions, or machines. As soon as they stand the test of time, they all take on the quality of a legacy or bequest that no longer presupposes the presence of the living originator. The thanatological significance of books, houses, artworks, administrative bodies, and machines can be seen in the fact that their "functioning" – as readability, as inhabitability, as usability, as sustainability – has become detached from their originators and emancipated for a sort of independent life. The durable artifact often outlives its creator's lifespan many times over. In time, the light of the legacies, taken together, outshines the idea of a transcendent originator and plunges beings as a whole into the artificial light of civilization. It was with good reason that Gotthard Günther spoke of the "historical frenzy of high cultures."[20] It arises from evolutionary acceleration due to the combined effects of writing, schooling, technology, art, empire building, archives, and askesis.

Historians of ideas have designated the seventeenth century as the key period of burgeoning modernity, because ever since then it has not been just individual, unconnected inventions that have caught sight of the light of the world. This period was epoch-making because it was in this period that invention was invented as the universal method of innovation. The engineer is an invention of the seventeenth century – even if his name already appeared two centuries earlier, at the same time as that of the virtuoso. It was at that time that the evening twilight of God stirred the morning twilight of human creativity. In the following three centuries, this changed the world more starkly than millions of years of natural evolution could have done.

*

In order to understand the present as a time of growing complexities and intricacies, we must gain insight into the proliferation of twilights. At issue now is no longer merely this or that twilight of the gods, which gave mythologists, theologians, and artists pause. If twilights of the gods follow from the very dynamics of cultures of invention, it stands to reason that future twilights won't stop at the mysteries of the human power of invention either.

Since the early twentieth century we have been able to recognize how an earthly twilight of souls has overlain the metaphysical twilight of the gods. There is a certain consistency here, insofar as God and the soul formed a pair in classical metaphysics. The fading away of one authority cannot be easily conceived without the fading away of the other. The arrival of depth psychologies around 1800, of Viennese psychoanalysis around 1900, and the sublation of both in the neuro-cognitive sciences around the year 2000 are unmistakable signs of this occurrence.

Consistent with this twilight of souls is a concomitant twilight of intelligence. In the course of the latter, numerous accomplishments of the human mind are increasingly transferred to the "second machine" – to use a term that Gotthard Günther coined in 1952 (in a commentary on Isaac Asimov's novel *I, Robot*). In the processual universe of the second machines, the remainder of the old Indo-European concepts of the soul become secularized.

In view of this evidently inexorable event, the question arises, what remains of the eternal light of the soul once the artificial lights have been turned on? What remains of it after the soul has ceded a good part of its former luminosity to the more and more clever artifacts of the world, to computerized objects? The first machine empowered the soul; the second forces it to question itself.

Must we really entertain the suggestion that the inventors of artificial intelligence had thrust themselves into the vacant position of God the maker? But then shouldn't they have followed God's lead and banked on the resistance of their creatures? Is there an original sin for machines? Should machines believe in their humans, or will we have an ahumanism of robots?

What should we say to the antimodernist hysteria that has been blazing for centuries, now that it alleges that the human being would like to "become like God"? And if the answer were that, according to basic Christian doctrine, God wanted to become human, should anyone be surprised then that humans' certainty of their distinguished provenance from a maker leads them to want to become a second machine?

We cannot foresee the consequences of this ever faster emptying out of human reflections into machine reflections. Countermovements make their stand against it. Dams are built to resist the floods of externalized intelligence. To speak in traditionalist terminology: we no longer live merely in the midst of the first *analogia entis*, between God and human being, but also with the second one, between human being and higher machine. Being is intrinsically constituted as a scale of powers and intelligences. Not a few of the shrewdest among our intellectually virulent contemporaries – here I will name Hawking and Harari, but many more are worth mentioning – express their spiritual worries by envisioning humans as taken over by their digital golems.

Perhaps the distinction between God and idols will soon reemerge here for the citizens of modernity – but this time in a technological and political register. For them, theological enlightenment – which is completely different from an instinctive rejection of religion – will be a fateful task.

For the time being, let me leave the last word to the thinker who reflected on the phenomenon of artificial intelligence earlier and more incisively than all of our contemporaries. At the end of his 1956 essay *Seele und Maschine* [*Soul and Machine*] (1956), Gotthard Günther writes:

The critics who lament that the machine "robs" us of our soul are mistaken. There is a more intensive interiority that lights up on a deeper level. With a sovereign gesture, this interiority thrusts away its forms of reflection that have become indifferent and reduced to mere mechanisms, in order to affirm itself in a more profound spirituality. And the doctrine of this historical process? However much of its reflection the subject cedes to mechanism, it only becomes richer. For it thereby acquires ever-new powers of reflection from an inexhaustible and bottomless interiority.[21]

2

IS THE WORLD AFFIRMABLE?

On the Transformation of the Basic Mood in the Religiosity of Modernity, with Special Reference to Martin Luther

2.1 The eccentric accentuation

"The rays of the sun drive out the night, / The surreptitious power of hypocrites annihilate." This celebratory, incontestable declaration by the priest-king Zarastro, with which Mozart's opera *The Magic Flute* (first performed in September 1791) ends, condenses the two primary motifs of the theological and political Enlightenment into a compact threat. Whenever the Enlightenment takes the stage, whether it is inspired in a rational–religious fashion or filled with the pathos of a movement of liberation, it undertakes to expel the despotism that is allied with "the night" and to unmask the systems of established hypocrisy. The protagonist in this drama can be none other than the sun itself.

Schikaneder's childish, folksy Enlightenment did not do a bad job of striking the critical nerve in the psycho-political construction of the ancien régime. Since time immemorial, a problem of constitutional hypocrisy has indeed accompanied the alliance between throne and altar in the monarchies of old Europe, supported as they were by clerical power. Its reflections entered into the popular image of the medieval church; they are just as inseparable from it as is the old, tacit conviction of humbler people that hardly one of the greats of the world can be trusted. From the late Middle Ages on, the hypocritical priest and the dissolute monk functioned as standard figures of popular realism. Starting in the sixteenth century, the consultant to the prince, the trickster who teaches deception in order to prevent his listeners from falling prey to it themselves, was added to their number. In the literature of the baroque period, worldly wisdom and masked existence closed ranks to the point where they could no longer be distinguished. Indeed, wasn't it a time-honored necessity to view the entirety of the world as the epitome of falsehood, guile, and dissimulation? Wasn't Lady World considered to be the hypocrite par excellence – at the front, the voluptuous harlot who promises happiness, but at the back the gruesome skeleton? Since the advent of the bourgeoisie, the hypocrite, alongside the bastard and the actor, was portrayed as a key figure in the emerging sciences of humankind. As long as you failed to take the omnipresence of Tartuffe into account, you did not know enough about how the human being was among her own kind. Whenever you encounter idealists making pleas, plaster saints won't be far away. The French moralists had set the tone: as soon as altruism dolls itself up, the petticoat of egoism peeks through.

The roles of criminal and secret agent have often been depicted since the late nineteenth century. This attests to the typically modern interest in phenomena of disguised behavior, far beyond the motif, widespread since the eighteenth century, of unmasking the deception of priests. The basic mood of "bourgeois society" resounds in the motif of "lost illusions." It betrays how much the battle lines between hypocrisy and enlightenment had shifted. From the nineteenth century on, the critique of hypocrisy receded into the background. Yet this was only in order to make room for its expanded edition as critique of ideology. The great power of concealment was thereby transposed one octave lower, as it were, into class-conditioned systems of illusion and half-automatic self-deceptions.

*

One year after the first performance of *The Magic Flute*, the theatrical skepticism against the hypocrisy of the powerful came to a head on the streets of Paris. There was now an armed fervor against the new masks of hypocrisy. During *la Terreur*, which raged from 1792 to 1794, it was the "annihilation" of the "surreptitious power" that took the helm. Its protagonists, Jacobins above all, were steeped in the conviction that they alone, plenipotentiaries of the light, were in a position to see through hypocrisies, both new and old. They dedicated themselves to the self-appointed mission of preserving the purity of the revolution and of tearing off the masks of both the feigned patriots and the secret partisans of earlier conditions – or of tearing off their faces from their torsos.

*

The course of events after 1789 revealed that the activists had conceived of the practice of "driving out" and "annihilating" in a crudely simplistic fashion. What was supposedly snuffed and driven out, namely hypocrisy and nightshades of older times, asserted itself as a recurrent phenomenon. Hardly had the militancy taken up its work of driving out the night when an irony came to the fore: the expelled reappeared at the very heart of the expellers. The traditional subreption of power irrepressibly reemerged in the following generations of public characters. The delegates of good newness were mustered as politicians of light, only to fall into the old twilight themselves, shortly afterwards.

In more recent times, people have attempted to tell the story of the Enlightenment as a story of inevitable inversion into its opposite. People have also wanted to understand its trajectory as an increasingly manifest realization of its cleverly masked totalitarian impulses. Meanwhile such generalizing interpretations can be considered over and done with; a charitable reading may put them to rest, as discarded exercises in exaggeration.

It could be more in line with the facts of the history of ideas and more fruitful for the self-understanding of human and social sciences to count the course of the Enlightenment from the time of Spinoza and Voltaire to postmodernism, as a history of resigning to hypocrisy – more generally as a growing insight into the commandments of dissimulation that adhere to culture as such. Nietzsche's words about the "reverence for the mask" indicate the direction of movement.[1]

From a moral perspective, what is called resignation in psychology refers to the neutralization of disputes. This makes mediating options available. In front of a steep choice between all-reprehensible dissimulation and completely praiseworthy true confession, it may be advisable for the present to shrink back into the realm of overtones.

Philosophical anthropology, as it has taken shape since the third decade of the twentieth century, has played a towering role in the neutralization of hypocrisy. It was above all Helmuth Plessner who constructed a platform for the relaxing and leveling of the critique of hypocrisy. He did so through his doctrine of the "eccentric positionality" of the human being which he first presented in 1928 and then subsequently developed.[2] It was on this platform that overtones could first be heard as explicit compositions.

Plessner capitalized on the discourse about the difference between human and animal, as was common in his time. While Nietzsche had defined the human being as the "unestablished [*nicht festgestellte*] animal," Plessner took the step of positing that the human being is the animal "placed" [*gestellte*] beside himself. Animals live without exception in a "concentricity" proper to their nature, and are thus sheltered in a permanent state of being at home with themselves in the midst of their environments (although even tortured animals can be "put out of sorts"). "The human being," by contrast, is characterized by an existential eccentricity. This does not indicate any tendency to odd demeanor or mannered comportment, except in the sense that humankind qua humankind occupies an eccentric pole of the universe: ever since "human beings" buried their dead, negotiated with the beyond, attended balls, and contemplated the series of prime numbers, they have been ontologically derailed, off-track creatures.

Eccentricity, as a positional value in the Plessnerian sense, marks "man" through the structure of his consciousness. It is as though, by virtue of his reflexive constitution, he – and here the naive masculine predominates – were a priori transposed from the middle of existence into the surroundings. For him, to exist means as much as falling outside the borders of an environment. No matter what his environment presents, the human being goes beyond the enclosing effect of the horizon, even when he stays put. He is not here without being there. Having always already run away from the borders of the immediate environment, he must, in the attempt to come to himself, discover himself as a being that is essentially moved beside itself. As if wounded by an inevitable beyond, he is alienated from himself from close range. Nevertheless, he is capable of being "himself," insofar as he succeeds at coming back to himself from standing beside himself. Being a human takes, accordingly, the form of a task never to be entirely accomplished: in order for existence to succeed, it requires that the individual shape the tension between eccentric and concentric tendencies.

One may, with all due respect, object that Plessner's artfully elaborated doctrine of the positionally redoubled existence of "man" put a half-price version of German idealism on the market. His doctrine was original insofar as it presented a spatialized interpretation of "self-reflection." It struck a surprising chord by revealing a hitherto unnoticed depth to the horizontal realm. Up until then, "men" had negotiated with an upwardly transcendent world; now and in the future they were to clinch the deal by dispensing with it altogether, as creatures of a displaced proximity to themselves. If we wished to characterize Plessner's impulse in a word, we could say that he transposed Feuerbach's anthropology from the vertical into the horizontal. Eccentricity is offered as a successor figure of transcendence. "Man" is the animal that not only places a heaven above itself, but also bears within itself a remoteness from which it returns to itself.

With his theorem of "eccentric positionality," Plessner took the conception of the human being as an actor on the stage of the world, which had been in circulation since the Renaissance, and brought it to bear once more, in a terminology of the twentieth century. All men and women are merely players,[3] and all have their entrances and exits. Shakespeare's maxim inaugurated the age of theater anthropology. According to it, the human being is the animal that acts *as if*. Hypocrisy and hysteria should not be missing from the portrait of the being that is endowed with dissimulation; they furnish the traits of an existence that is histrionic and thoroughly cued in on the gazes of others. What is called "identity" is the self-illusion of the actor, who would like to be, even in the wings, what he portrays on the stage. There is no outside the stage. Resting in the image of what is proper to one can ever emerge only from the antagonism between the perception of the foreign and the positing of the self. At best, it's a resting in the restless. Phantoms nest in the space of this antagonism. These phantoms lead "man" astray by leading him on. They make him believe that he is himself so long as he looks into the fun-house mirror that others put before him. Today it is, above all, respect and recognition – as well as their negative counterparts – that serve as mirrors. When these cast their reflections, we will inevitably become frustrated with our attempts to find anchorage in what is proper to us. No search for lost naivety can help combat the expectations of shipwreck as we work on mediating between our own perspective and another's.

*

What Nietzsche wanted to elucidate with the example of Richard Wagner, in order to reject it as a mistaken development, was the "advent of the actor type" in the arts. In reality, this was an event of much older provenance. Its trajectory could not be gleaned from the perspective of the polemics that surrounded art in the nineteenth century. Even Shakespeare – who flourished barely two generations after Martin Luther and eight generations before Nietzsche – only touched in passing on the real origins of the pull toward an eccentric positionality, even if his dictum was destined to be remembered. The entire world is a stage and men and women together mere players: with this thesis he proclaims what will be interpreted philosophically three centuries later – that being and being seen converge. The element of discontent in civilization cannot be attributed solely to the compulsory renunciation of the drives; it stems even more from the feeling of being burdened by the gaze of the unfriendly other. The human being cannot become what and who she is so long as she does not produce herself before the eyes of observers. Existence implies a permanent test of whether one can let oneself be seen.

Regardless of whether this thesis was presented around 1600 or after 1900, we must derive the excentering of the human being, his removal from the center, from much more remote events. Shakespeare and Plessner make some essential points, but both come millennia too late to bear witness to the real beginnings. In a nutshell, the impetus to establish and solidify the "eccentric positionality" that Plessner would have wanted to interpret as a supratemporal constant was due to the emergence of higher powers, typically called gods, which had already driven the human being out of his animal centering early on. The gods of the first hour are entities that are interested in the existence of human beings in an uncanny, ambivalent, and for the most part interventionist fashion. In the beginning, gods appeared to be beings that had to settle an outstanding balance with humans. Even Dante still speaks of God's vendetta (*Inferno* 16, 16–18; *Inferno* 24, 119). The resentment of those who no longer exist against those who do is condensed in these beings. At the same time, they hold all the power, because their chapters have been closed, while the living still flounder about in incompleteness.

Accordingly, Nietzsche's sentence "God is dead" contains an element of perspectival deception: whatever truth it may express, that truth pertains less to the end of the history of the human being's relation to what lies beyond the world (for this has largely faded today)[4] than to its beginning. Dead is the god who looked over the shoulders of the living with an eye of ontological envy – but also the one who looked through the lenses of compassion for those who still had to exist. From the fact of his own deadness, the early god staked out claims against the living. Debt wove the cord that connected the here and the beyond.[5] Indifferent gods formed a very late chapter in the history of transcendence: with an everlasting smile, they prefigure the mysteries of a releasing being, which does not insist on getting revenge in the present or in the future. Not without reason does Aristotle emphasize God's lack of envy; he is not jealous of the human being's knowledge. The loving god was a later addition, although, admittedly, his love was often a sort of compulsory contract filled with threats. For the time being, we must continue to wait for gods who are loving beyond ambivalence, and until they arrive human beings would do well to look after the shape of their own relationships.

The morning twilight of the gods takes place in a half-archaic period, when the heavenly ones don't yet know the virtues of indifference and equanimity. Human beings of the twilight period had to grapple with such invisible and not indifferent gods, who hovered over the collective like embittered ancestors in a vengeful mood. Human beings learned from these gods to fall outside themselves. Already in very remote times, human beings hit on the idea that their fates depended on powers that were incomprehensible for sacred reasons, terrifying, and occasionally benevolent. They did so independently of one another, in the most diverse cultures, owing to the similarity of their situation.[6] These powers, whether they bore names that could be appealed to or not, allowed themselves not only to be moved by petitions, but to be bound by means of cleverly negotiated contracts. The most radical form of a binding petition is blood sacrifice on the altar of a beyond that is not too remote. *Les dieux ont soif* [The gods are thirsty]. In a universe pervaded by the law of reciprocity, fascination-generating sacrifice, whether in the form of human or animal life, compels the otherworldly addressee to answer with a rich return gift of existential goods. The first macroeconomy develops in the system of sacrifice.

What we call today the "pressure to succeed" formed the first article in the system of terms of trade[7] between the executors and the recipients of sacrifice. Ever since these terms have been established, the gods have shared the business risks with the cultures that worship them. They represent transcendence in the state of manipulability. The gods are dependent on human beings who believe that they are dependent on gods. The Latin term *religio* points to this schema of reciprocal neediness: initially it signifies nothing less than the anxious care to safeguard the protocol when dealing with the higher powers.

We have thus introduced a first phase of excentering. It implies the tendency to take on a certain role; here the human partner puts herself in the position of surrendering to the expectations of a strong superworld. Entrance into the eccentric position came about for the first time only when ethnic groups became willing to respond to adversity by jointly taking the path that leads from anxiety to ecstasy. At the beginning of cultural evolution, it is of course not the individual who ends up in a position beside himself. It is rather the collective that consolidates itself: as a group sacrificing together in the common experience of horror, it takes responsibility for the death of a living being – whose equality as a bearer of life is deeply felt.[8]

*

We give the name "high cultures" to what was at first a very small number of civilizations. These civilizations sublimate archaic transcendence by keeping the burden of blood sacrifice at bay. Indeed, they elevate the superworld into higher spheres by removing it entirely from the effective domain of human manipulations. "High culture" is a code name for three inseparable movements. First it designates the hypostatization of an unmanipulable super-world, whose incorruptibility is condensed into pathos concepts such as "truth," *kosmos, universum, brahman*, and *tao*. Second it signifies the civil war that selected individuals launched against all-too-humanness – and *eo ipso* against every form of trivial religiosity, which now gets called "superstition." Lastly it refers to the liberation of death and the progressive easing of the burdens of threats, debt collection, and revenge.

Karl Jaspers used the phrase "cultures of the axial age" to refer to the groups that instigated these campaigns against the rest of the world.[9] The campaigns were begun by enlightened individuals; but, once begun, they could not be stopped. Among these cultures Jaspers counted the Chinese of the Confucian and Taoist age, the Indians from the time of the Upanishads, the Persians of the Avesta, the Jews of the high period of the prophets, and the Greeks of the tragic theater and the first philosophy. At that time – around 2,500 years ago, give or take a few centuries – a "breakthrough" occurred worldwide; note the military metaphor, which this time has been employed correctly. Worldviews that were more abstract and tended toward universality came into being, as did ethical doctrines that pertained to everything. All of a sudden, the gateway to the age of excessive demands was pushed open. Here begins the world history of an exclusivity that paints universal inclusions on the wall. The superworld began to code itself in concepts of truth that one could no longer live up to through externalized rituals. From then on, communication with higher powers and with the Highest was much more likely to take place in thinking souls and in literacy-demanding schools than on sacrificial stones and in sacral slaughterhouses. What later gets called "culture" designated, already at this time, work toward devulgarizing the superpowerful.

Among rare and circumspect individual human beings, as they were to begin with, the sublimating tendency led to the (premature) insight that the absolute owes them not even the slightest of things; rather they owe everything to it. The emergent spiritual elite launched a subtle, unattainable, and thus unending civil war against the uncircumspect, as they arise everywhere from everyday life. This was a civil war that could be fixed as a permanent mission.

Right from the beginning, four almost invincible groups stand against the few who have knowledge: the haughty, whose pride prevents them from gaining insight (given that insight cannot be gained without humiliation); those with entitlement, who want to persist in their received *religio* (given that knowledge is not possible without change); the miserable multitudes, whom everyday life has numbed into resignation to their shackles (given that they have not yet been awoken by the counter-resignation power of wonder); and the reserve army of the jealous, who lie in wait for their cue to bring everything down to their level.

*

From the perspective of the present day, we can hardly avoid noting that Jaspers's doctrine of the axial age represents one of the last among the outsized confabulations that western historians of ideas and of religion have concocted to make sense of humanity's past. The boldness of this epochal fairytale, as it comes from the pen of the newly appointed Basel professor, consists in the fact that he backdates the Enlightenment – which has advanced since the eighteenth century, along with the cockade of contemporary reason – to 2,500 years ago.

One can get an idea of the space-making effects of this maneuver once one realizes that it is now no longer necessary to be modern at all costs in order to take part in the Enlightenment. Not only did this maneuver create a freedom of movement for ecumenical exchanges, as they manifested themselves since then, in the dialogue between cultures. Above all, it lessened the fanatical tensions between the avant-garde of the European Enlightenment – whose voice has been raised ever since the seventeenth century – and the heritage conservationists, who reject any progress of questioning and testing that takes place beyond the preserved holdings. If the trial conducted by the light against the night already began two and a half millennia ago, then we should be able to recognize the bearers of the extended enlightenment above all by their evolutionary patience. The distinction between esotericism and exotericism, which, significantly, is as old as the high cultures,[10] helps us be patient – or, in modern parlance, tolerant.

*

Doctor Martin Luther, who is often labeled a rebel, indeed a religious precursor of the Enlightenment, would in no way have been able to comprehend this wide-ranging construct of the philosopher Karl Jaspers; Luther would have indignantly put it to the side. Indeed, he would have rejected it as a dubious bow to the reason of unbelief. For it only examines cultures whose age indisputably precedes Christianity. So long as truth is to be allied with seniority, any attempt to assign a pre-Christian date to ways of approaching the highest insight – alias revelation – will remain suspect. Luther would have sensed in Jaspers's theorem a fabrication from the spirit of humanist paganism, calculated to dissuade the person of the "now" time from worrying about the salvation of her soul. What is more, he would have rejected the concept of "culture" as a heretical suggestion. It expects Christianity to subordinate itself to the comparative study of worldviews and robs it of its character as the absolute "religion."

Luther would have shuddered at the widespread and well-argued fact that, obviously, the "whore of reason" did not speak only through the immeasurably overrated Aristotle – that retrovirus of paganism inside *corpus Christi*, and the advocate of the unbearable thesis that human beings are able to display the virtue of magnanimity, *megalopsuchia*, through their own efforts. She also expressed herself through previously unknown figures with exotic names such as Confucius, Shankara, and Zarathustra. Even a familiar name such as Isaiah, who we believed was the first to prophesy the coming of the savior, would all of a sudden look like a colorful piece of cloth in the globalized whorehouse of reason.

*

Jaspers's doctrine of the axial age rests on the offensive universalization of the supposition that "the human being" exists under permanent transcendent supervision. Like no philosophizing psychologist before him – Nietzsche excepted – this philosopher perceived the shift in mood that took place in the first millennium before Christ and continued to resonate throughout the religious actualities of the next two millennia. We can characterize the "axial age" not only by the more or less synchronous emergence of all-encompassing cosmologies and precursors of post-conventional ethics. There is more: the axial age distanced itself in the first place from everything that came before it. It did so by means of an unparalleled overshadowing of the existential moods of the time – to the point of a complete negation of world and life. We need not discuss here whether this incursion of a disgruntled mood was a reverberation of cosmic catastrophes like the Flood or an undesired aftereffect of the emergence of holy texts and promissory notes. In terms of the atmosphere of belief, it does not seem to be unproblematic when a god that allows himself to be paraphrased with the cipher JHWE threatens his "own" people more than eighty times, in writing, with obliteration. Alongside the risky predicate of "omnipotence," the potential for total negations is also gathered in the Highest. In 1946, Jaspers noted: "We are guilty of being alive."[11] The tremor of the National Socialist catastrophe and the era of mass murders reverberate in this sentence. Yet it still belongs, undoubtedly, in the global resonance chamber of the disgruntled mood of the axial age.

At any rate, "high culture" refers to the epoch of growing anxiety about being touched. Whoever turns toward the One or *to agathon* [the Good], whoever strives for *moksha* [release from incarnations] and desires sanctification, must be in a position to rescind his membership in profane spheres. As long as the rays of the sun have not driven out the night, the adepts of purity do well to avoid entering impure precincts. The "world" is everything that the soul courting true knowledge keeps at a distance. In the future, wisdom and world contempt are to be unified by more than alliteration.

*

In order to trace the beginnings of the compulsion toward dissimulation, it is then necessary to trace the eccentrification of the human being back to the revolutions in the world picture that took place during the "axial age." Hypocrisy is not merely vice's bow to virtue, as La Rochefoucauld once remarked. Rather it marks the human being's embarrassment about the omnipresence of a transcendent observer. It corresponds to the need not to be always seen. From this need emerge various strategies for circumventing unbearable scrutiny. Even the invention of the "unconscious" in the late eighteenth century belongs with the maneuvers of escaping an all too invasive scrutiny. The excessively observed human being is driven to hypocrisy the more she is held to the belief that the observer misses no detail, no matter how small. God, who is all eyes, surrounds me from without and vets me from within – all according to the Augustinian spatial schema of double transcendence: *interior intimo meo, superior summo meo*, "more inward to me than my most inward part, higher than my highest part."[12]

Accordingly, the establishment of the eccentric position of the human being on the stage of existence results from an internally fixated reaction to high cultures' impositions of always being watched by an observer who can see through everything. The excesses of the Genevan city of God revealed just how far the attack of rigorous scrutiny on daily modes of life can go. The church of Calvin employed its own watchmen, spies, and executioners, in order to transform the city into a concentration camp of the elect.

The majorities, which remain in their world childishness, count on the fact that God for the most part does not see them. Like Tartuffe, they think that anything that is not seen is not a sin. The god of the people is to be exempted from the burden of having to register everything in his logbook. Since time immemorial, the people has therefore voted for the oblivion of being – that is, for the obfuscation of the presence of constant scrutiny from both within and without. Nor has the people ever warmed up to the clerical elites' attempt to enforce permanent self-control through universal confession. By contrast, those spiritual minorities that have been seized by the revolution in the world picture [*Weltbild*] feel overwhelmed by the lofty suggestion that they produce themselves relentlessly in the face of a super-clairvoyant observer.[13]

2.2   And they saw that it was not good

In what follows, let us hold fast to the assumption that the altered mode of human existence in high cultures can be explained as a result of the increasing stress placed on human beings by the idea of permanent external scrutiny. This state of affairs is reflected in a risky compulsion toward self-scrutiny – risky because chronic attention to one's inner states can mark a stage on the path to discovering one's own nothingness. When such a path is followed to the end, it leads almost inevitably to the misery of self-rejection. Individual experimenters have managed to traverse the entire stretch and put down their results in writing, as doctrines of wisdom. Later guides of the soul built on their predecessors by claiming that not liking oneself is the beginning of salvation. Still in 1843, Kierkegaard was able to reason in a sapient–depressive tone about "[t]he upbuilding in our always being in the wrong in relation to God."[14]

Against this background we can ask how it was possible for a young man, laden with complexes, bearing the name Martin, christened after the patron saint of wayfarers and horsemen – how it was possible for this man to feel so fiercely lost in angst and misery as to release himself from his previous, "worldly" *modus vivendi* after the crisis of the legendary storm in Stotternheim in July 1505. Obviously, being a twenty-two-year-old at the time, he belonged in a cultural context in which renouncing one's belonging to the "world" had long been available as an established option. What was called *religio* at the end of the Middle Ages was identical with the offer to immigrate, in the midst of the world, to a counterworld. The counterworld existed as a spiritual "estate" with its own autonomy vis-à-vis worldly estates. On the basis of his accomplishments as a creator of metaphysical legitimacy, the "cleric," that is, the ordained elite of the visible church, knew how to reserve the rank of the highest estate for himself – above the nobility, the bourgeoisie, and the peasants. (Let me note that, in their day, estates, as degrees of status in the social realm prior to political states, obeyed the imperative to create livable arrangements within segmental societies by means of hierarchization.)

To the extent that Martin Luther's despair was bound up with a western-style world denial that could be encoded in high culture, we can see him as a distant heir of the exaltations and overshadowings of the axial age. Already in his era, the monastic topos of *contemptus mundi* [disdain for the world] served as leitmotif in an immeasurable body of literature. To write contemplative books and at the same time not to have contempt for the world: that was almost a matter of impossibility at the beginning of the modern age, namely before Boccaccio. The modern intellectual does not originate in the Dreyfus affair. He emerges from the fourteenth-century literature against being dependent on a world that could not be affirmed.[15] An unhappy consciousness is embodied in this individual. He knows how much the world deserves contempt, yet he remains bound to the contemptible through his striving for fame (*gloria*) and search for love (*amor*).[16]

The young monk Luther learned through his own experience that evading the worldly sphere by entering into cloistered counterworldliness was not qualified to brighten up the disgruntled mood of his existence. It did not matter what he read, whether it was the rather sympathetic mysticism of the *Theologia Deutsch* or Aristotelian ethics, which was distasteful to him owing to its lack of contrition; it was only through the serious climate of a *religio* behind cloister walls and the passion he felt from his engagement with contemporary theology (namely that of the Augustinian persuasion) that his youthful disorientation was able to mutate into a systematically grounded metaphysical despair. If up to that point the adolescent Martin had experienced the drama of the lost and unloved child, the young monk and theologian Luther – *doctor theologiae* since 1512 and professor at the young regional University of Wittenberg since 1514 – now developed into an exorbitant case of high-culture eccentrification: as he attempted to compose himself *coram deo* [before God], the unfathomable extent of his lostness came undone.

*

The Augustinian term *peccatum originale* [original sin] – in German *Erbsünde* [inherited sin] – summarizes this state of affairs as an anthropological urfact, without making reference to the individual case. In looking inward, the young monk experienced himself as the object of a transcendent scrutiny. Under its effects, he is at first unable to do anything other than petrify into a statue of despair.

Luther's early spiritual struggles carry the echo of the supremacy of 2,500 years of denying the world and life. This supremacy was defended by the bizarre, always renewable band of ascetics, hermits, penitents, self-dissolvers, dolorists, flagellants, and other character masks of holy extremism. In their ranks we find remote figures such as Gautama Buddha, whose basic saying *sarvam dukha* – "everything is full of suffering" – resonates throughout more than 2,000 years. Among them we must also count the Greek Silenus, with his tragic piece of wisdom according to which the best thing for human beings would never to have been born and the second best is to die soon. The greater age of anxiety[17] includes the lamentations of Job and the discourses of the preacher Solomon, the apocalypticism of the Near East and the tears of Augustine; it extends from the zenith of world denigration – which was reached by Lotario di Segni (1160–1216),[18] the future Pope Innocent III (from 1198 on), in his treatise *De miseria humanae conditionis* [*On the Misery of the Human Condition*], composed in 1189 – to the nadir of philosophical resignation in Schopenhauer's doctrine of the denial of the will to live. They all contradict God's self-praise at the end of each day of creation: they see that for the most part it was not good, and at no time was it *valde bonum* – very good. With the "breakthroughs" of the axial age, the scope of the denial grows alongside the affirmations.

Within this darkened space, every instance of despair is related to all the others; for millennia, the despisers of the world and of their own world-proximate selves live simultaneously: "Every human being is Job."[19] We are all subject to *turpe naturale* [what is natural and base] and must continue to pay tribute to the abomination of being caught up in bodily necessities. The sayings of the desert fathers reverberate in the Russian love of beauty; the agony of Golgotha echoes again in *devotio moderna* [the modern devotion]. It is no accident that the penitential struggles of the young Luther are so directly connected to the salvational uncertainty of the old Augustine that it is as though eleven centuries did not lie between them.

In Lotario's miserabilistic *Summa*, nothing that could be deployed against human existence on Earth has been forgotten. It reaches unerringly, from the "misery that is bound up with the entrance of the human being into the world," though the "guilt that human activity and striving incur," to the "wanton denouement of human existence," which risks ending up in the "unspeakable plight of the damned" after the Last Judgment. In its attempt at completeness, this text on the murk and gloom of *conditio humana* can be read as a masterwork of pious hypocrisy. Already in the first lines, the author recognizes a grave objection to his opusculum, namely that it entertains the idea of an opposite exercise, in which, with the aid of Christ, the "dignity of the human being" should be emphasized. These lines articulate the constitutional hypocrisy of the cleric, who affirms his baseness the more he climbs the bureaucratic ladder. It may have been an accident that Innocent III never found the occasion to write a rebuttal. From a cultural–psychological perspective, it is more plausible that this omission classifies him as a prisoner of the persistent and momentous mood of world renunciation.

Nearly three hundred years were to pass before Pico della Mirandola's *Oratio de hominis dignitate* [*Oration on the Dignity of the Person*] (1486). Measured against this text's cosmophilic tendency toward cheerful optimism, Luther's life and work mark a recursion to the society of the somber bishop of Rome, who reveled in images of human misery. Lotario's hypocrisy, which is betrayed by the pleasure he took in exaggerating on the dark side, was not necessarily merely a feature of extreme Catholic Tartuffery. It mirrored the ambivalence of transcendent scrutiny. Those who were affected by it were never able to know whether it brought salvation or damnation.

When Nietzsche gave the earth a new name, he was thinking about the spheres of a broken participation in the "existent" – these spheres that, from an evolutionary perspective, were relatively new:

> The ascetic treats life as a wrong path that he has to walk along backwards till he reaches the point where he starts; or, like a mistake which can only be set right by action – *ought* to be set right: he *demands* that we should accompany him, and when he can, he imposes his valuation of existence. What does this mean? Such a monstrous method of valuation is not inscribed in the records of human history as an exception and curiosity: it is one of the most wide-spread and long-lived facts there are. Read from a distant planet, the majuscule-script of our earthly existence would perhaps seduce the reader to the conclusion that the earth was the ascetic planet *par excellence*, an outpost of discontented, arrogant and nasty characters who harboured a deep disgust for themselves, for the world, for all life and hurt themselves as much as possible out of the pleasure in hurting – probably their only pleasure.[20]

In his studies on Byzantine Christianity, Hugo Ball found the appropriate terms when he called the early friars of Upper Egypt "athletes of mourning" and the anchorites "athletes of despair."[21] His portrait of John Climacus stands under the motto: "It is good to disintegrate and to be with Christ."[22]

Max Weber seized upon Nietzsche's intuitions when he ascribed the faintly parodic title of "religious virtuosos" to the spiritual heroes of the axial age, the protagonists of world renunciation, of self-rejection, and of resettlement to a blessedness that was not of this world. With their exercises that were eccentric in every possible sense of the word, these artists of a high-culture *religio* set standards by which subsequent generations had to direct themselves if they wished to learn from the claims of the masters. Indeed, only now does the concept of master acquire its pregnant meaning: that of teacher of something nearly impossible.[23]

Whoever is taken by the evidence that being a human among humans is no longer sufficient can train to be a virtuoso of *religio*. In the future this will come down to reworking the raw materials found in the human being in the direction of a conformity to the cosmos, a conformity to nirvana, and a conformity to God. The individual who is humbled and spurred on by the absolute will thereby experience herself as the being who has a relation to what is without relation. The adventure of individualization begins with such alterations. Above the door to the world there is now the inscription: "Know thyself!" Under it are the lines: *Etiamsi omnes non ego*. Even if all run in one direction, I will not.

Everything that comes after the "axial age" is therefore, spiritually, an age of "virtuosos." It forms the laboratory in which acute despair is distilled from a vague disgruntled mood. Psychic efforts extending beyond all rational measure grow from the concentration of despair. Ultimately, with the discreet help of the Highest, the effort turns into a relaxation beyond trivial humanity. This relaxation is sometimes called wisdom, sometimes holiness, sometimes illumination.

Martin Luther does not clutch the peaks of despair so tightly for the state of the soul. He contents himself with the conventional term "faith" (*fides*); yet he removes from the word its tone of relaxation. He redeploys it as if he were standing at the source of its meaning. He thereby recommends that the following be held for certain, beyond any established *religio*: that God, who sees human beings from without as from within, will in the end not only judge them according to the records, but also be merciful to the remorseful, in accordance with the promised grace.

2.3   The derivation of the Reformation
from the spirit of tempered despair

It has often been noted, correctly, that Luther's intervention reduced the ostentatious Roman Catholic papal church to a church that was, if not invisible, then at least inconspicuous.[24] In this new church the priestly class was to be thoroughly disempowered. It offered as little space for a self-serving clerical apparatus as it did for an instituted theology that was right ex officio. It was based on the fundamental experience that had spread among the spiritual elite after the high-culture revolution – namely that the soul, in its insufficiency, stands alone and unarmed before the Highest.

Through the pathos of its *sola gratia* [by grace alone] credo, the Lutheran doctrine pushes to the extreme the eccentric positionality of the faithful. It demands of them an extreme degree of remorse-fulness, which it explains to them at the same time that they cannot accomplish on their own. By urgently holding them to an ultimately impossible repentance, it forces them on the path toward a new version of hypocrisy. Being able to regret is, itself, already a work of grace. You should be lost, as if you were saved. Reformation thus essentially rhymes with reduction. This holds consistently for the Lutheran sphere, and even more so for the Reformed (whence it turned out that, in the long run, the Wittenbergians were not a patch on the Genevans when it came to hypocrisy). The vanishing point of the reduction consists in nothing but the question of how the faithful discover the Archimedean point at which despair over one's salvation passes over into the certainty of having attained it. In Luther's language, what has to be discovered is called "justification."

Nota bene: systems of belief can be passed on so long as they are successful in making invisible the paradoxes from which they draw their power.

The basic figure of the axial-age revolution is hereby repeated; it should be made explicit once and for all how matters stand with the human being who realizes that he is dealing with a superworld that cannot be manipulated. Once the Highest has become incor-ruptible, the minds that wish to take seriously the idea of existing "in the truth" are forced to consider the initially prerevolutionary, then revolutionary question of what to do. Luther cast his vote on the matter long before Chernyshevsky and Lenin; and the decisive thinkers of the axial age did so long before Luther. It is not just the Enlightenment that can be predated by two and a half millennia; in point of fact, the Reformation, too, began around the middle of the first millennium before Christ.

*

In the reductionism of the fledgling Reformation during the Luther era, energetic activity and the extreme ability to do nothing became entangled in a manner almost unparalleled in the history of ideas and of the soul. The reduction proceeds from the now firmly internalized evidence that sacrifices and courtesies cannot sway the incorruptible Highest. The only method of drawing the absolute to one's side consists in delivering oneself to him wholly, as the mystics teach – in the West and East alike. Yet, as long as the gesture of self-deliverance remains a self-conscious act, it would be, for its part, nothing more than a speculative transaction with an increased wager: it would trade blood sacrifice for self-sacrifice. It would seek to domesticate the absolute by fusing with it. This diagnosis would, however, be accurate only so long as one were dealing with an inert absolute. A communicative absolute could have preempted the human attempt at encounter. In the linguistic space of western ecumenism, such a scoop is called "Christ." His love would be the unmerited thing that cannot be compelled, no matter how great the effort.

Following the Augustinian schema of revolt in heaven, Protestant reductionism is content to simplify the issue of God into an eccentric love story. In a nutshell, one day human beings stopped placing God above all things, because they decided to emulate the example of Satan and chose themselves as the object of their predilection. In doing so, they warped *ordo amoris* [the order of love] to a point beyond repair. In contrast, God continues to love human beings, albeit not without placing certain conditions on them. If they turn back with enough remorse, they should be welcome. If they remain as they are, their damnation is irreversible.

Whoever espouses this screenplay as an interpretation of her being in the world must brace herself for complications. The young Luther read himself into this scenario, under pressure from his pre-religious, existential mood of disgruntlement. He could not guess that the schema of the troubled love story was elaborated without exception within high cultures. According to this schema, the lovers originally belong together, but must become estranged and fail for some unknowable reason. The young Luther obviously brought into play a high potential that was set up for estrangement and failure. In modern parlance, one would call his point of departure a severe neurosis. It became historically decisive that Luther's disturbed state was suited for a recoding of religion, and even more for a religious–political translation.

We should not see it as an accident that Luther first made a name for himself by handling the question of how to deal with the facts of guilt, penance, and despair. All in all, the October 1517 theses on indulgences represent no more than zealous – and, seen from a historical distance, hairsplitting – statements on questions about the external and internal administration of penance.

Luther drops the air of nitpicking in three of his theses, however. They concern the human's acute despair of himself, a despair that does not allow him to assume two positions at the same time. Some of the theses read as though they were a proleptic answer to Plessner's theorem on the eccentric positionality of the human being: when the individual, once compacted into a single point, hears that human existence and doing penance should become the same, he feels subject to Jesus's saying, *Poenitentiam agite* etc. [*sic*] [Repent etc. [*sic*]].[25] Technically and from the perspective of the disputation, Luther had already won with his first thesis. In the form of a dominical saying (from Matthew 4:17), it recalls the price one must pay for God's accommodation. If the Highest steps toward you, everything else is just padding.

The entire program of the Reformation is contained in the reference to unpurchasable and unmanipulable penance, in which no one can stand in for another. From then on Luther has the privilege of being certain of his orthodoxy. What remains is formalities. It requires almost no effort to dismantle the industry of indulgences in the papal church as a suspect fabrication, concocted by hypocrites for the use of hypocrites.

"Man" is even more starkly reduced to a single point when he experiences how *horror* [the horror] of dying anticipates *horror* of the purgatorial fire. In the terror of the last hour, the otherworldly flames encroach upon this world. Here Luther indirectly picks up on the motif of humans gaining wisdom when it is too late. The fifteenth thesis leaves no doubt about the gravity of the situation: *Hic timor et horror satis est se solo … facere penam purgatorii, cum sit proximus desperationis horrori.* "This fear or horror is sufficient in itself … to constitute the penalty of purgatory, since it is very near to the horror of despair."[26] We cannot say for certain whether, at the time of writing this, Luther had already stood at the bedside of someone dying. What is certain is that he is speaking of himself in this passage. His effort to find a strong foothold in the abyss culminates in the sixteenth thesis, where he brings the problem of penance to a head:

Hell, purgatory, and heaven seem to differ the same as despair, half despair, and assurance of salvation.

Videntur infernus, purgatorium, celum differe sicut desperatio, prope desparatio, securitas differunt.[27]

The reduction hits the target with this distinction between different grades of despair. The seemingly harmless *prope* ("near," "well nigh," "nearby") turns out to be the cardinal point in the radicalized interpretation of faith. Because near despair on Earth is distinct from complete despair in hell, even if only slightly at first blush, there is still a remainder of hope for later security. Whenever such hope is alive, the human being moves about in a middle zone. What one calls faith is actually the oscillation between extremes. Pastoral ministry has a term for it: *Anfechtung* [affliction, trial, tribulation]. The possibility of the human's salvation is hidden away in the inconspicuous word "near." Whoever only almost despairs can just as well undertake to be confident.

The successful reduction immediately gives rise to a dissolution of boundaries: If human existence is to become an integral exercise in penance, the purifying event will already be occurring, here and everywhere. Besides baptism no special access is needed. The cobbler, the smith, the farmer – they are all ordained priests and bishops. The spiritual privilege of the monastic form of life falls to the wayside. Luther democratizes the state of semi-despair. He indicates that the cleric is not saved a priori – not an ounce more than laypeople are. Now the motto holds: Purgatory for all, and right away at that, not after death! The extremes of heaven and hell, together with their reflections in definitive certainty and complete despair, lose all their lifeworld and everyday practical meaning. They remain the province of eschatological speculation and artistic depiction.

The Reformation is thus based on a relocation of the purgatorial function to the earlier stage of earthly existence. Concomitant with this is an expansion of penitential existence. If the cloister and the lifeworld have become one, it no longer makes sense to join a monastery. The clergy is no longer an independent estate. This is related to the observation that the later Luther still speaks of purgatory only rarely, and in the end almost not at all. In a sense, he is in a position where he no longer needs it; for it has been replaced by existence in the flames of the everyday. He no longer feels the dogmatic pressure to presuppose it as an established third location in the otherworldly realm either. Moreover, God himself would turn out to be a protector of ecclesiastical hypocrisy if he tolerated the emergence, from either–or, of an all too comfortable both–and. Purgatory is indeed a *compositum mixtum*, a mixed compound that serves as an antechamber to heaven ontologically, all the while resembling hell phenomenologically. The older Luther seems to think that, if such a place were to exist, it could only be demonstrated in human life. Human existence is in fact the intermingling of pre-hell and pre-heaven. Whoever knows the proper fear of death has no need of a transcendent purgatory. In 1928, Martin Heidegger said that Dasein means being held out into nothingness – as though, for the last time, we can hear in this an echo of Luther's admonition that, when properly conceived of, existence qua existence is a purifying fire.

In his final years Luther seemed tacitly to come closer to Calvin's positions. In his *Institutio* of 1536, Calvin completely rejected the idea of purgatory as a fiction concocted from "heresies." He thus restored the implacability of the initial either–or – which inevitably made him the honorary chairman in the world congress of hypocrisy, as the harsh either–or could be borne only with help from the self-hypnotizing fiction of belonging to the flock of the saved (keyword: "Innerworldly askesis").

It has been occasionally remarked that the annulment of monastic life in Luther's work removed the East from the western culture of religion. It would be more appropriate to say that his reductionism stripped religious virtuosity of its foundations. The loosening of eccentric tension contributed to the routinization of *religio*. Minimizing the cult led to the internalization of the interaction with the Highest. Internalization led to privatization; and privatization led to an assimilation under profane worldliness. The rest is pedagogical Christendom. The entire process was accompanied by the inevitable generalization of hypocrisy. For the model of a human existence oriented toward the command to do penance could not be sustained for long.

Luther anticipated the problem of a Protestant hypocrisy and attempted to temper it with the formula *simul iustus et peccator* [righteous and sinner at once]. His precaution turned nothing from the direction of development. It was inevitable that the condensation of existence into a single point should fail, because eccentric positionality cannot be eliminated, not even after reduction. Who would be capable of distinguishing the justified sinner from the hypocrite relocated to eternity? The penitential imperative lost its plausibility to such an extent that the expectation of the imminent Last Judgment petered out. In Luther, belief in the approaching judgment was still paired with a rock-solid certainty; it was surpassed only by his conviction about the omnipresence of the devil.

*

When we take stock of the Reformation, the first thing we are compelled to notice is that Luther's impulses were essentially restorative much more than revolutionary. His interventions in the papal church followed the schema of a conservative revolution where innovation presents itself as restoration. Luther preached a Christian salafism, as it were. He never lost the conviction that his reading of the holy text was more catholic than every Catholicism and more evangelical than all scholastic theology; and this all the more as the conceited theologians had given undue pride of place to the master thinker of the pagans, Aristotle. Luther's slogan could have been: Rise up, you Christians, onward into the past!

2.4   Protestant entropy

Luther belongs among the rare figures of cultural evolution of which we can say that they were lucky in terms of the history of ideas. In this field, being favored by luck means finding successors who are better than one deserves. In the case of Martin Luther, his unmerited successors include – and I will content myself with the shortest of lists – Gottfried Wilhelm Leibniz, Johann Sebastian Bach, Gotthold Ephraim Lessing, Immanuel Kant, Johann Gottlieb Fichte, Georg Wilhelm Friedrich Hegel, Friedrich Nietzsche, Albert Schweitzer, Gotthard Günther, and Martin Luther King: here Luther's universe resonates like a world history in first names.

When we do history of ideas, we devote ourselves to the attempt to do justice to the asymmetries of what was said "earlier" and what was said "later." Cultural evolution runs its course in a manner that is asymmetrical per se. This can be gleaned from the fact that we would find it absurd if someone said that Luther announced his theses before the appearance of Hegel's *Phenomenology of Spirit*. By contrast, it makes sense to observe that, when Hegel formulated his vision of the idea as it makes its way through history, he did so from a position that came after Luther in history.

Luther's historical effects can be described as a regression with progressive consequences. His unanticipatable and undesired progressivity is bound up with the interplay between his retrogressive tendencies and the proleptic political and media constellations of his time. From a politological perspective, Protestantism was the front desk of a squabble that took place among theologians on the terrain of princes – and within the space of provincial universities. It was the German imperial princes who took a conflict about questions of *religio* and turned it into a vector of world history. The princes (and their learned tutors at universities) were the ones who developed Luther's offensive potential by discovering how useful it would be for them and their political practice to take on the premodern, state-forming element of confession. In confessions, parties cast their shadows in advance. Seemingly marginal questions, such as whether God is present or merely remembered in the Eucharist, become a scandal of epochal significance. Europe assumed a prominent place in the history of surrealism when it began to sacrifice countless lives for invisible differences.

In order to speak further about a Lutheran difference, one must investigate whether it can still be connected with the basic moods of contemporary feelings about the world and life. The answer can be given almost without qualification: no. Luther was lucky in point of history of ideas and psychohistory; for, in and of itself, his overwhelmingly dark legacy was dubious in terms of the psychology of religion, theologically unoriginal, and philosophically regressive. It was also reshaped by ever new levels of the Enlightenment, of civilization, and of cheerfulness. Luther could not prevent a theological frenzy from becoming a sort of evening song. Here the forest had learned to fall silent in a dark, unmistakably German way, while the fog ascended from the meadows as whitely as the moonlight would allow and as wondrously as world-weary souls believed was merited. Luther was lucky to have new virtuosi appear after him. These, however, were not virtuosi of *religio* but rather grand masters of thought, language, and affirmation.

We will not sufficiently understand the history of the world, of ideas, and of the production of cheerfulness if we do not realize to what extent Luther, who preferred to invoke biblical allies, became a favorite of pagan Fortuna. The new theologians felt that they were guided by the Holy Spirit. But from this point on the Holy Spirit entered the stage wearing the mask of the goddess of luck. Success – and success equals causality plus luck – ensues only as a result of Fortuna cooperating *cum spiritu sancto*, with the Holy Spirit. Luther had such luck with Erasmus, in whom he found a contemporary opponent who knew how to articulate the universally legitimate concerns of the Reformation without making an uncivilized racket. He was lucky when, more than a century later, a Jewish dissident named Baruch de Spinoza called for the evacuation of the sad passions from the rational soul and broke with the traditions of clerical world denial. He was lucky when Johann Sebastian Bach brought jubilation back into the bleak churches with his "Jauchzet, frohlocket!" ["Exult, rejoice!"]. He was lucky, seeing that Leibniz, as an advocate of God, minimized the share of irrationality in creation. He was lucky when, in the monumental collection *Irdisches Vergnügen in Gott* [*An Earthly Pleasure in God*], Brockes taught that we should joyfully perceive the presence of the Highest even in the least of things. He was lucky, given that, as a cultural, climatic whole, the German classicism of Klopstock, Lessing, and Herder up until Fichte, Hegel, and Schelling – to say nothing of the Olympians in Weimer – was able to present a more cheerful transposition of the Wittenbergian missive to the world, three hundred years *post eventum*; the transposition was bound in cloth, with gilt edging and tail bands.

Luther was also lucky when the romantic theologian Schleiermacher made religion into a matter of talent and disposition so as to make it accessible again to the educated among those who despised it. He was still lucky when Nietzsche, the preacher's son, invented a figure named Zarathustra, who preached to his friends: "Remain true to the earth!" – and beware the teachers of *ressentiment*! He was lucky, even if he did not earn it, when Albert Schweitzer explained why the western ethics of brotherly love need not hide from the eastern mysticism of the contemplative life.[28] He had more luck than understanding when it turned out that, despite Luther's late words against Judaism, he was not responsible for that pathetic former Catholic, Adolf Hitler. He was lucky when the evangelical church in Germany issued the Stuttgart Declaration of Guilt in October 1945, taking responsibility for their lack of courage and love in resisting the National Socialist catastrophe. Finally, he was lucky when Martin Luther King declared before an exalted crowd that he had a dream.

*

If the beginning of the Reformation was characterized by the move of gaining energy through diminution, entropy remained characteristic of its development. Irrevocably and with remarkable haste, religious entropy dismantled the overexertions of the forms of world denial and life denial of the axial age. It had taken thousands of years to establish these forms; their demolition took less than two hundred. Now a life that has been flattened out comes to affirm itself. Yet it does so without specifically making much ado about its self-affirmation – leaving aside the episode of inflated philosophy of life that was inspired by Nietzsche. Eccentric positionality has advanced a few steps further: a massive quest for horizontal attention takes the place of burdensome vertical scrutiny under the eyes of God. In this situation Protestantism cannot expect its historical luck to continue. It would get off well if, five hundred years from now, one could say that it has shown itself to be an intelligent third power in the confessional war of our times, in the resistance – disguised as a campaign of the unsatisfied against the "elites" – that mass culture offers to high culture.

3

THE TRUE HERESY: GNOSTICISM
On the World Religion of Worldlessness

3.1   Where Nag Hammadi is located

A world religion has been newly discovered.
        Gilles Quispel (1951: 1) on the Nag Hammadi findings

Shortly after the Second World War, which led to the death of forty-two million people according to conservative estimates and fifty-five million according to others, a large clay container filled with numerous papyrus codices in the Coptic language, almost all extraordinarily well preserved, was found at the foot of a crag in the Egyptian desert, about fifty kilometers north of Luxor. Shortly afterwards it was rumored among intellectuals that a "Gnostic library" had been discovered that consisted of fifty-two chiefly unknown treatises in the Sahidic–Coptic language. The few who, in these dark times, kept a clear head – clear enough to register events of intellectual history – soon suspected that it was more than just one archaeological fact among others that had been uncovered here. In 1946, it was as though the reemergence of texts that had gone missing for ages was a sign, a hint from the depths of time to the survivors of the great catastrophe of the "Christian West." From the sacred desert of Egypt, an inconspicuous signal made its way to the devastated nations. From the place where the holy protest against the world and life had first been radicalized, the overpowered continent received a message that appeared to be subterraneously connected to its current state of affairs. A faint yet undiminished and active spiritual substance beamed forth from the letters inscribed on fragile paper in 1,600-year-old ink. The magic word "Gnosticism" hovered around the find – and, without knowing a single line from the lost gospels, the apprehensive contemporary of the great discovery could read into this word whatever she, in her current condition, would expect from a mystical message. That has remained the case up until this very day: the aura surrounding the Nag Hammadi finding still outshines its content – even though the impressive efforts of translators, editors, and commentators have meanwhile made all the material available to the public. Furthermore, Nag Hammadi is a mythical name – it stands for the incursion of scandalous and yet plausible countertruths into western memory. In the middle of efforts to clean up after the catastrophe, references to the manuscripts that had just opened up the desert again must have seemed like a call for a forgotten dimension of European history. When the Dutch historian of religion Gilles Quispel held his lectures on Gnosticism at the C. G. Jung Institute in Zurich, hardly five years had passed since the discovery. He was nevertheless certain about the significance of the event: with the rediscovery of authentic ancient Gnostic voices, the Jungian trend in modern psychology had received its historical sanction. He believed that a new Gnosticism could be reflected in the older one, which was now acknowledged; the recurrence of late antiquity at the peak of modernity entered into its hot stage. The phrase "world religion" signals the magnitude of the claim. From now on one would speak of the "soul" as if it were an underestimated world power. Indeed, one would have to give in to the suspicion that it was precisely this underestimating that had been a decisive factor in the fatal turn taken by the world.

Something of the discontent in Christian European culture has been linked to the name Nag Hammadi. In it there gleams the promise of the wholly other – of what had never come to be and what was never attempted. It appears to symbolize unrealized possibilities of the "western spirit." It stands for the lost opportunities and suppressed alternatives of the continent that really made world history. Nothing about this can be changed by the sober philology that has meanwhile produced a sophisticated image of the texts. Even after it has been thoroughly edited, the Gnostic library of upper Egypt will retain more of a mythical than a scientific significance: its emergence cooperates with the need for the fundamental revision of a culture that had manifested and unmasked itself in its compulsion for world war. These texts are a mixture of alternative gospels and apocryphal treatises. In the future, they will be read as lost letters to posterity, as messages in bottles stuck in the sand, as classified documents of the world spirit, hidden from the threats of Christian censorship and furnished with the invisible annotation: "Preserve for all time." They belong in the curriculum of anyone wishing also to get to the historical bottom of the current state of world war and world crisis. In the original writings of the Gnostics, we believe that it is finally possible to encounter the primordial history of all dissidence; the traces of metaphysical revolt are patent in them. The "perfect ones" of the desert had tested what it means to disobey the world to the very end – to the point of breaking with everything that binds you to the given and to the existent. The authors of Nag Hammadi and their first readers severed themselves from beings. They thereby placed themselves completely into a fanciful offside position, to the left side of creation, far from the powers of the cosmos, into the fullness of having nothing of the world and reality. "After Nag Hammadi" – this phrase has meanwhile become a sort of caesura in the history of ideas. Even Christians must begin to understand that they live after an event in whose light their faith takes on another meaning, one that is still incomprehensible to them. Is Christianity perhaps not Platonism for the people, as Nietzsche once said, but rather Gnosticism for the people?

Yet, even if the codices had not been uncovered from the desert, it would have become necessary in our century to invent them. If, then, we had to formulate a metaphysically relevant reading of this monstrous century, it would have to go as follows: evil must be more than the absence of the good. Whoever experienced the darkest aspects of our epoch cannot escape the impression that evil has an agency entirely of its own, with a lot of staying power and inexhaustible reserves. To speak in mythical terms, at the basis of the world there is a catastrophic fissure gaping wide open, from which evils burst out with wanton violence. Wasn't this what ancient Gnosticism appeared to be speaking about? When the archaeologists freed the manuscripts from the urn, they caused a surprise that was already due. Today we know: in the Egyptian papers, initially, there was nothing to be read that this era of revisionism had not already braced itself for.

The Nag-Hammadi fever had to subside as soon as people acquired greater knowledge about the texts. It turns out that the old writings mutely resist what we project on them. They continue to remain what they have been for us – hardly legible testaments to an extinct world whose foreignness we are scarcely in a position to appreciate. Perhaps this is also the reason why the interpretive spoils from the sensational archaeological story have been so remarkably thin. The great discovery has yielded no new idea among contemporary mythologists, theologians, and philosophers. So far it has not been able to inspire any new and actually outstanding interpretation of the phenomenon of Gnosticism – and I say this with all due respect to the brilliant contributions of Harold Bloom, Elaine

Pagels, and Peter Koslowski and to the encyclopedic knowledge that
has been gained thanks to researcher personalities such as Henri
Charles Peuch, Kurt Rudolph, and Simone Petrement. The situation
of research has improved dramatically after Nag Hammadi; even
so, the exegetical circumstances before and after have remained
peculiarly static. It may appear almost as though our understanding
of Gnosticism were something that no contribution from external
archeology could improve on, no matter how great it may be.
The great interpretations of Gnosticism in the last one hundred
and fifty years emerged independently of the sensational forays
into the "original texts." For the most part, they drew on indirect
sources, in particular the tendentious, albeit precise reports by
the church fathers. These interpretations were inspired by their
authors' immersion in what one likes to call the spirit of their times.
Although the literature on Gnosticism has meanwhile filled up the
libraries, profound interpretations of the tradition have remained
rare. Until today there have been only two towering works in which
the spirit of Gnosticism has been masterfully understood and
unfurled again for us: Ferdinand Christian Baur's voluminous study
*Die christliche Gnosis oder die christliche Religionsphilosophie in ihrer
geschichtlichen Entwicklung* [*Christian Gnosticism or the Philosophy
of Christian Religion in Its Historical Development*], from 1835, and
volume 1 of Hans Jonas's inspired work *Gnosis und spätantiker
Geist* [*Gnosticism and the Spirit of Late Antiquity*], from 1934. As
can be seen from the years in which these texts appeared, neither
owes anything to the more recent discoveries. Rather they appear
to prove that, in order to attain an eminent understanding of the
Gnostic cast of mind, one must have got close to one of the two
greats of modern "continental" philosophy, Hegel or Heidegger – so
close as to open stereoscopic vistas, as it were, into the past of the
most profound thinking. Thus, a few years after Hegel's delivery of
his explicit philosophy of religion, Baur discovered in the Gnostics
of late antiquity the model for a god who reaches self-awareness
[*Selbsterfassung*] by proceeding through human subjectivity. Thus,
a few years after the appearance of *Being and Time* (1927), Jonas
was also able to find the structures of Heideggerian fundamental
ontology in the documents of Hellenistic and eastern Gnosticism
that were available to him at the time, as well as in Manichaeanism
– in particular, he was able to find the basic determinations of world
alienation and the appeal to make existence authentic. In both cases,
one gets the feeling that great insights into Gnostic thought emerge
as a function of decisive philosophical self-interpretations of the
modern age rather than as a result of archeological–philological
discoveries, however impressive these may be. One could almost

conclude that Gnosticism itself is not amenable to any external discovery; nor does it need one. It is not salvaged from urns, but rather reconstructed in radical meditations on the structures of the contemporary consciousness of human existence. It can be found only when it is sought in its proper "place": in the broken containers of subjectivity – with its suffering "from the world" and its unforgotten paradises. This is where Nag Hammadi is really located. Hence, for us, spontaneous Gnosticisms take precedence over traditions. Gnosticism is understood from the hot center of current self-adherence.

Indeed, modern conjunctures of Gnosticism follow the tracks – and modes – of current interpretations of the world and of the self. This holds for Hegel's process theology as well as for Heidegger's doctrines of falling prey to the world [*Weltverfallenheit*] and of becoming authentic [*Vereigentlichung*], as may be seen clearly in the illuminated projections of Baur and Jonas. It also applies to the remaining streams of more recent thought, in which we find a renewal of interest in Gnosticisms of the most distinct variety. When, after 1870, Helena P. Blavatsky wrote her book *Isis Unveiled*, which was intoxicated with a sense of mystery, she filled the old term "Gnosticism" with the aspirations of a modern theosophy; and ever since it has stood for the tendency of the occult scene to translate matters that were once esoteric into the exoteric realm, in as direct a manner as possible. Steinerian anthroposophy took up the example of theosophy; a good part of Rudolf Steiner's productive output between 1903 and 1908 appeared in journals with names like *Luzifer* and *Luzifer-Gnosis*.

As can be seen from these examples, the positive overstraining of Gnosticism by necessity makes the term appear hollow. The same can be said – though with a minus sign – of the effect that Eric Voegelin's writings had. For decades, this author worked with the manic energy of an imprecise Inquisition, to denounce as a "Gnostic mass movement" – that is, as a vulgar self-deification of the human being – anything that tried to make do without the blessing of Aristotle and Aquinas. This included *progressivism, positivism, Marxism, psychoanalysis, communism, fascism, and National Socialism*.[1] Yet it can hardly be proved that Voegelin was actually acquainted with the authentic Gnostic literature. It looks as if the twentieth century gave rise to a general hysterical itchiness in the charismatic politologists; whoever is familiar with the circumstances will perhaps judge Voegelin's philosopher-king absurdities less harshly. In a completely different way, we can find in the school of Carl Gustav Jung the precedent for modern projections upon ancient texts studied with rigor. Jung's therapeutic Gnosticism consciously overrode the dualistic structure of most of the more ancient Gnostic systems in order to ensure that, in the battle zone of the human soul, light and darkness would in the end be unified into a "salutary wholeness." Even so, this transference of Gnostic dualisms into monistic doctrines of psychic immanence gives us a sense of how seriously Jung took the psychagogic side of psychiatry. He believed he knew that psychotherapy – especially in view of complex deep-seated disorders – does not escape the quandary of formulating a contemporary equivalent of the traditional answers to the question of redemption from evil. Here the old and venerable formula "unification of opposites" had to be brought into play once again. Finally, the current Islamic revival is partly responsible for a new interest in gnosticizing forms of spirituality.

It lies in the nature of Gnostic states of knowledge that their mode of being is not one of continuous transmission, but rather one of a sporadic rediscovery in suitable cultural conjunctures: in the most difficult crises of the world, Gnostics of every variety protect life from the temptation to adapt to what would no longer be life. Whenever it rekindled and thereby constituted itself anew, "Gnosticism" was the opposite of a world religion that would have established itself through positive institutions and canonical writings. It flared up and passed away as a non-world religion, in the double sense of the word. It remained without expansive organization in space and time and without faith in the idea that the world could adopt Gnosticism institutionally as a world religion. For this reason, the history of Gnostic phenomena is largely identical with the sequence of their repeated self-discoveries. Consequently, "Gnosticism" is dissenting from itself. The heretic hunters in the early church were in a certain sense right to bewail the inventiveness and sponta-neous mythological incalculability of the heretical systems. When it came to the older Gnosticism – and to its newer avatars – one was in fact dealing more with a species of metaphysical fiction[2] than with a firmly established, repeatable dogmatic theology. Irenaeus, Hippolytus, and Epiphanius are well aware of where they have to look for their enemy: in that polymythic insolence of heretics who take the liberty of inventing what they will "believe" in. Instinctively, the men of the church denounce all manifestations of the free spirit, which ventures to be inventive even in matters of the most holy kind. They sound the alarm when faced with Gnostic myth-making, which spins the Christian material into something that is no longer Christian. Indeed, from the angle of literary criticism, late ancient Gnosticism demolishes the standards of "classical" religious faith; a dimension of fantasy[3] presses forward into the field of dogma. The Gnostic irony toward creation anticipated the romantic irony toward the text. Wasn't, then, every pneumatic, spiritual self called to become a hero in a highly personal novel of salvation? What Christian bishops held to be substance, self-styled Gnostic authors took to be form: evangelicalism is for them a mode of writing, resurrection a style of life. Here the Catholic who worships order can only take fright; whoever experiences the connection between church and bedrock as a personal need will feel lost in the midst of the fanciful Gnostic invention of *ignes fatui* [foolish fires]. Even ancient Gnosticism had already individualized the religious need, so much that even the counterworldly world form of the church was no longer acceptable to it; hence modern opponents of every sort of churchianity[4] can find their own striving for freedom prefigured in Gnostic individualism.

3.2   How the real world finally became an error

quis audeat dicere Deum irrationabiliter omnia condidisse?
[Who would dare to say that God has constructed everything irrationally?]
                    Augustine, *De diversis quaestionibus* 83, quaestio 46

On the matter of the "authentic" nature of Gnosticism, there predominates what we would properly expect to find among scholars: disagreement. Some tried to make metaphysical dualism its criterion – and then failed when confronted with the monistic and triadic varieties of the older systems. Others tried to define the connection between animosity toward the cosmos and anti-Judaism as the distinctive feature, and thereby left aside those Gnosticisms that, without any noteworthy polemical exertions against the "existent" and its creator, knew how to climb to superworldly heights. Others emphasized the fundamentally "sapiential" feature of Gnosticism, and in doing so failed to recognize its poetic, ascetic, experimental, and cathartic dimensions. Still others sought to label it a "cult of self-salvation," and thereby overlooked the numerous soteriological doctrines in which the darkened soul caught in the prison of the world received a call from a foreign site. Up until now, those who have attempted to define Gnosticism have had no luck – as is the case with so many phenomena of spontaneous spirituality.

Its uniqueness has been best grasped by those who have applied Nietzsche's Cynicism-inspired, cultural revolution-style battle cry of a "reevaluation of all values" to the incursion of the Gnostic spirit into the ancient world. At issue for Nietzsche was an anti-Christian revision of western history; what he dreamed of was nothing less than a retranslation of the denatured human being of Christian modernity back into "nature." This image seems to be the very reverse of the Gnostic "world turning of the spirit," which intended nothing less than to carry the human being out of nature – or, to put it in Greek concepts, out of the cosmos and into the "kingdom of God," into the superworld, into the *plērōma* [fullness], into the eighth and ninth heaven. Whereas Nietzsche prophesied, to an unprecedented degree, a new human type that would be entirely of this world, ancient Gnosticism had scandalously loosened, nay rent apart, the bond between the human being and the world. When Gnostic authors dared a new metaphysical localization of the human being, they moved what was "authentic" about the human being into a radical perspective of de-worlding.

It was only in the atmosphere of burgeoning Gnosticism that this revolutionary new formula for localizing human existence would emerge: "in the world, but not of the world." This was more than a reevaluation of all values; it was a redirection of all movements, a replacement of all places, a resettlement of all settlements. One may say that the Gnostic impulse in the Johannine distinction between "in the world" and "of the world" became manifest in a manner that was at once premature and definitive. In fact Gnosticism can take place only after the discovery of a "place" that would not be of "this world" – still "here" and yet already "there," still in the world and yet already at the non-place, in what has un-become, in what is beyond being, in the pre-actual realm. The spirit of utopia awakens with the Gnostic distinction of places. With the help of the previously unthinkable distinction between "in the world" and "of the world," the human spirit gains the ability to think for the first time of the fact of its own existing; put hyperbolically, what we, in modernity, designate by the term "existence" "is given" only with the eruption of Gnosticism. *Pneuma*,[5] the Gnostic spirit-soul that comes from "above," is the organ of this logically new sort of knowledge about existing: it is *pneuma* that can see itself "in the world" as something that has entered from the outside – as something different, which does not belong and is capable of withdrawing. Gnosticism is the igniting of human self-consciousness by means of the fundamental thought of existing "in the world." Philo of Alexandria was already able to write: "for each of us has come into this world as to a new city, in which he had no share before birth, and having come into it he dwells here as a guest, until he has completed the period of life allotted to him."[6] The existential rupture of holistic idealism is announced through this image of the guest. Gnostic knowledge would thus be nothing but the self-penetration of the world guest, of the existing *pneuma*; the story of the soul, told by itself – for itself and its ilk – emerges from the *pneuma*'s initiating recollection of its "provenance." The typically Gnostic linkage of fantasy and rigor can be found in the nature of such narratives, told by and for the cognitive soul. The rigor comes from the soul's insight into the seriousness of its situation – its exile "in the world." The fantasy is inspired by the new sort of freedom that belongs to a self-conscious not-being of the world.

The logical genius of a Gnostic mode of thinking breaks ground, even at the level of mythology, through the distinction between "in the world" and "of the world." We can see how ingenious this new distinction is – one might call it, point-blank, "the Gnostic difference" – when we consider the sort of operations it made possible. As long as being in and of the world had to be thought of as a homogenous complex, it was logically and linguistically impossible to negate all beings completely. Initially, as the comprehensive concept for all beings, the world can be negated as little as being in the world can. The fact of the world always already precedes every negation. The thesis that something *is* cannot be disempowered by any antithesis. Yet, from the moment when the Gnostic difference between "in the world" and "of the world" is accomplished, a field of deniabilities at the highest level of generality opens up. Vast mythological and theological energies enter into this field right away. Now the symbolic levies behind which psychological negativity was dammed up can break. The Gnostic difference creates a new language of dissatisfaction with the world – it loosens the tongue of the mute spirit of the great negation. Insofar as the soul reckons that it "authentically" belongs to a worldless sphere, it attains, from the undeniable place "in the world," the possibility of negating everything that is "of the world."

In this regard, the emergence of Gnostic forms of thought is epoch-making, above all in the history of the development of negativity. Negativity is, obviously, not just a matter of logic; on it depends the weightiness of higher self-interpretations of human "existence." Indeed, without the revolution in the possibilities of denial in the early Gnostic and early Christian space of thought, the word "existence" would be meaningless to us. A religiously and philosophically fruitful dimension of distance from the world emerges from the Gnostic discovery of a possibility of total negation – not "of the world," but of that which is "of it." Minds critical of the world, from John the Evangelist to Heidegger, from Simon Magus to C. G. Jung, from Basilides to Adorno, are – forgive the expression – *at home* in this new dimension.

Only at this point does it make sense to ask about the religious–historical "origins" of Gnosticism and about the psycho-historical conditions of its emergence. What can be said about the ostensible clouding and darkening of attitudes to life in the "age of anxiety" of late antiquity? What's to be done with the rumors that the Greeks' life-affirming universal piety was toppled in one fell swoop, in Gnostic and early Christian despair about the world? How could denial come from affirmation, anxious contempt from marveling reverence? How were human beings allowed to hit on the idea of incinerating what they had only just worshipped? Where are we to look for the pivot of this negativistic "world turn" of the spirit? The answer to these questions must be ontological rather than psychological. Only since the soul has understood itself as an entity opposite to the world – more precisely, surrounded by the world, yet not reducible to it – has it been possible for the "world" as a whole to be displaced and exposed as a superobject. Gnostic anti-cosmism is, originally, the result of a grammatical achievement: a logical novelty becomes manifest in the early Gnostic–early Christian idiom "this world." "World" becomes a possible object of universal deixis; suddenly one can point to it with one's finger, at least linguistically; take a look at "this" world. Is there anything that will make you wonder from now on? Gnosticism develops with the systematic unpacking of this effect: it articulates a structural change in astonishment – from philosophizing to being horrified, from being horrified to parody. It lives out of its virtual distance from the darkened whole, from which there is at the same time no distance to be taken. Its mode of being is the self-conscious shattering of reality, its passion the incineration of the earthly ship, its ethos the responsibility of ascending to heaven. Its place of thought is a being inside as if one were not inside. The Pauline *ut non* [so as not to] already belongs within the field of this *epochē* [suspension], this taking distance from what cannot be taken distance from. To possess as if one did not possess; to be here as if one were there; to have women as if one had none; to be in this outland as if one were "authentically" already back home: Gnosticism is a philosophy of the "as if not."

But, before the total object "world" could be taken distance from and criticized, the whole had to be dissembled into parts that could be negated – or, in modern parlance, into bad partial objects – and represented as such. The development of a position of animosity to the world is in fact accomplished through such steps both at the level of the history of affects and at the mythological level; it goes the whole way, from one bad aspect of the world to the badness of the whole of the world. Now, from year one, the shopwindow in which bad things in the world have been spectacularly displayed has been political power – as perceived from the angle of those who suffer

injustice in the form of repression and exploitation. A fierce critique
of power is played out as a sort of intermezzo, halfway through, on
the one hand, the positive cosmologies of the Greeks and Romans,
where observations about nature always function, simultaneously,
also as paradigms of harmony for the use of the city – *polis* and
civitas – and, on the other hand, the negative cosmologies of the
Gnostics. The negation of the "world" emerges from being appalled
by the world powers. Initially these powers can be identified with
precision – only then do they become mythologically reformulated
as ministers of beings, archons, tyrants of the celestial bodies. The
world – that is, in the first place, the lords of Rome, the Antonine
emperors, the provincial governors, the tax collectors, the solicitors,
Pontius Pilate and company, all with their whores, their encomiasts,
their astrologers – the world is the vogue of ancient consumerism. In
"this world" a picture of Juno performing fellatio on Jupiter hangs
above the emperor's bed; their gods are no different from them. In
"this world" everything does indeed hang together, but the principle
of this interconnectedness is the most common of villainies: the
self-celebration of successful predators, the self-preservation of
wickedness – the system-building force of evil, the transformation
of the fear of annihilation into sovereign sadism. From this moment
on, "this world" will appear to be perverse and completely without
light, a place that demonstrates best the equation of sovereignty with
criminality. Hence the significance of judicial murder for gaining
insight into the true "essence" of such power. In judicial murder,
the lords of the world lay their cards on the table. One cannot
overestimate the role that the two great myths of judicial murder in
antiquity – the Socratic–Platonic and the Jesuanic–Pauline – both
play in the emergence of a spiritual distancing from the world. Just
as the *polis* had sinned toward philosophy in the case of Socrates,
so had Roman *civitas* as a whole unmasked itself as a huge harbor
of injustice in the case of Jesus. Yet when it comes to the murder of
God, the degree of wrongdoing extends beyond the limits of what
can be forgiven. The Gnostic critique of the world had the courage
to draw from the extreme crime the following conclusion about the
essence of the perpetrator: the nature of the perpetrator called "the
world" – the Pharisaic–Roman coalition – is demonic all around. In
the "ultimate" jurisdiction, a world that has made itself guilty of
murdering the savior already stands under the sign of the highest
guilt. Ontologically, it is prejudged as alienated; religiously, it is
prejudged as possessed; and, cognitively, it is prejudged as incapable
of recognizing its guilt. After the event at Golgotha, its blindness
to the offering of light seems ultimately to be a proven fact. Only
for this reason does it become theologically dependent on *charis*,

grace. Whoever abides in it is lost in it to such a degree that she can be pardoned only from *outside* it. This is the salvific–juridical sense of redemption from evil. Redemption occurs as a result of insight into the grace [*Gnade*] of no longer having to belong to the unredeemable totality of injustice called the world. The cross – says Simone Petrement – separates God from the world; here it is at least as correct to say that the cross is the visible symbol of the obstinate fury with which the world powers insist on their realisms. Already the first theologian of the cross, Paul, is also the genius of casting accusations against the world. As the prototype of all converts, he is more skilled than anyone when it comes to the psychology of guilt and debt – and to that of redemptive refinancing. Had he not himself gone from being a persecutor to being a disciple – from zealous accomplice in the murder of God to global missionary, from capital criminal against the spirit to reprieved apostle of the first class? It was he who founded the universal religion of bad conscience – the exportation of guilt and the wholesale of its forgiveness.

From now on, the lords of the world have indeed been figured out as marionettes of evil powers. When the Christian philosopher Justin Martyr directed his apologetic missive to his Stoic colleague Marcus Aurelius, in order to protest against the empire's murderous policies toward Christians, he already had his theological dagger under the cloak: in an unparalleled exegetical stroke that would behoove pirates, he derived the entire race of Roman Caesars from the fallen angels in chapter 6 of the Jewish book of Genesis. There the perverse, demonic structure of Roman imperiality was laid down on paper in a genealogical argument. If the Caesars are themselves descendants of a race of toppled, counterdivine powers, then their domain of rule – the inhabited Mediterranean world, the entire globe – must represent the epitome of unjust worldliness. Justin's argument was irrefutable when it came to his own person: an executioner beheaded him twenty years later, in accordance with the rules of the game in this world. As a martyr, Justin fully became what he had been as a theologian: a witness for the prosecution in the metaphysical trial against "this world."

The violent climate of Roman politics toward Christians, which had been simmering for centuries, triggered one of the ambient preconditions for the Gnostic readiness to give short shrift to "this world." In this sense, Gnosticism offered an internalized replacement of the imminent end of the world that had been promised by apocalypticism – with no less fervor than futility. It was probably Jacob Taubes, the Jewish philosopher of religion, who, following Scholem's suggestions, provided the most intimate view into the regularity with which heretical extremism escalates, be it ancient or modern: when propheticism fails, apocalypticism emerges; if apocalypticism fails too, then Gnosticism emerges. This tendency changed course only when the first "courtly theologian," Eusebius of Caesarea, was compelled to invent a principal witness regulation for the Roman Caesars. After Constantine had changed to the Christian side, a reinterpretation of the office of world ruler became necessary; overnight, a descendant of the demons became the thirteenth apostle. Shortly afterwards one could see the imago of Christ the "Lord" enthroned, in the posture of the Pantocrator, in church cupolas of the East and West. From then on the voices of Gnostic critique of world power drop out of the historical record – and for a long time.

The formation of the political–ontological partial object called the "evil world" has its parallel in the theological realm. There a shadow grows among the attributes of God. All of a sudden, this shadow makes the world's attribution to God unbearably problematic. The agonized world – thought of as creation – towers up like a protrusion of irrationalism into the sea of divine wisdom. This diagnosis leads to a contradiction in theology – and the emergence of the question of the origin of evil has rightly been interpreted as the symptom of a severe crisis of monotheism. Either the creator god bears responsibility for the state of "this world," in which case irrationality flares up in his very being and obliterates his unity and goodness; or his wisdom and supreme goodness should remain intact, in which case he must be released from direct responsibility for "this world." He is not permitted to have intended and created "the existent" to be as it now appears. After God has been released from the world, however, the latter as a whole must fall completely; only as a result of God's separation from it can the world plummet so low that it can be proved to be, and negated as, an abundance of badness, a creation of fools. Now it is the work of a confused partial god, a mistake of subaltern eons, an object of a degraded "love" gone astray. The fact that Valentinus, a contemporary of Justin Martyr, calls the world-creating power, of all things, Sophia betrays a new sort of devastating irony against the "wisdom" of the biblical God and his theological ministrants. Almost two thousand years will pass before an equally deeply ironic term will be coined for the inevitable self-deceptions of the human mind: the Freudian expression "rationalization."

Tertullian was right: heretics cut their teeth in the school of the *unde malum* [whence comes evil?] question. From an orthodox point of view, whoever looks for the origin of evil is already on the best path toward defecting to the camp of malice; an affront to God's majesty looms in contemplating whence, or rather from whom, evil comes. It is obvious that the Gnostic temperament comes into play here. Whoever would be clever rather than pious with questions about truth has a predisposition toward Gnosticism. The ability to be evil to an evil creator is part of the damned cleverness of Gnosticism; whoever has a Gnostic disposition is skilled at countering the works of a confused demiurge with the blessed cold-bloodedness of one who sees through the cosmic concoction, after being only temporarily taken in by it; hence the heretical sympathy for clever snakes, rebellious angels, and Luciferian paradoxes. When life, ill-treated in the wayward cosmos, is not afflicted at the source of its pride – its birthright to success – it will rebel against the wretchedness of being dependent on salvation. The Gnostic soul may know nothing of *charis*, which is offered as if it were a reprieve for a crime. What lends it wings is the charismatic recollection of a pre-original right to perfection. "Everything that gets called 'grace' has its 'sufficient reason' in the failure of the world."[7]

The distinction between "in the world" and "of the world" marks a revolution in the power of negation. This gives rise to a sort of theological splitting of the atom. It becomes impossible for the creator of "this world" to remain the same as the one who redeems people from it. The possibility of remoteness from the world becomes metaphysically attached to a redemptive alien god. He is the authentic guarantee of unworldliness. His logical "localization" had to set in motion a process that led to negative theologies. In the course of this process God himself becomes unbound; he becomes the god of autonomous negation, a divinized nothingness, an abyss of predicatelessness, a fullness of having no determinacy and actualization. The god of Gnosticism is largely spared from condescending to existence; he is exempted from creating the world directly. This, obviously, will have exciting existential consequences. The thoughtful remembrance of such a god must incite a pneumatic turn in the serious thinker – so long as she does not remain stuck in neophyte confusions and see mirages. As soon as the thought of negation flares up, those capable of aligning themselves with this de-creating, supra-existing, predicateless, and acosmic supergod in their own thinking will reckon that they are awakening from a life-distorting nightmare of baser realism; the naughted god becomes a partner in the soul's effort to unbind itself from the compulsion of the world. The soul's alignment with such a "father" gives rise to a world's downfall with eyes wide open. Here too, *imitatio Dei* [the imitation of God] makes the human being what he ultimately can be: a being of the limit.

This disempowering of faith in the world is what brings élan to the early Gnostic–early Christian success story. News about such possibilities of "redemption" spreads like a happy-go-lucky psychosis; worldlessness becomes infectious, too, and not just to those who have nothing left to lose "here" anyhow. The early Gnostic–early Christian trend was hardly *just* a religion of the sick, as Nietzsche wished to present the movement of the new deserters of the world. Remarkably affected, adults listen up when they hear that they are no longer under an absolute obligation to pay tribute to the demons of reality. This most incredible piece of news quakes through the possessed and resigned world. The aura surrounding such evangelism is not limited to the myth of the Christian redeemer; it penetrates every form of thought that leans toward liberation from the spellbinding character of the world – even Neoplatonism and Jewish apocalyptic literature have a certain evangelical appeal.[8] For the first time, something new "is given" above and under the sun. Whoever can grasp it experiences the world as falling away from her eyes. The good news entices the sensitive people around the Mediterranean and puts them on the path to a multifarious shimmering "beyond the cosmos principle." "The gospel of truth is joy for people who have received grace from the Father of truth, that they might know him through the power of the Word. The Word has come from the fullness."[9] Thus begins the "Evangelium veritatis" ["Gospel of Truth"], as it is transmitted in Codices I and XII from Nag Hammadi. It intones most purely the mild deliriums of the white Gnostic knowledge of resurrection. The word "joy" signals what's new. Ever since everything that stems from the world became capable of negation, a new tone has resounded in the world: jubilant dissidence.

3.3   A short history of authentic time

Whoever has comprehended himself fully despairs of himself fully [...] Whoever despairs of himself begins to know him who is.

> Philo of Alexandria, *On Dreams*, 1.36[10]

According to a *bon mot* of Adolf von Harnack, Gnosticism signifies the acute Hellenization of Christianity. This *bon mot* would itself remain a profound remark only if one were successful in confirming the hypotheses about the non-Christian origin of Gnosticism. For, wherever Gnosticism may have arisen – in heretical and apocalyptic Judaism, in irrational dualism, in an orientalizing Platonism, in Hermeticism, or somewhere else – we would have to characterize its inner dynamic, in each case, as the collision between an eastern, religious aspect and a Hellenistic, logical one. The conflict between theoretical insight and holy excitement, between jovial discussion and panicked striving for redemption pertains to the restless nature of Gnostic system creation. The chief contradiction of the West – the duality of Athens and Jerusalem – makes its first productive appearance within the space of early Gnostic and early Christian thought. It is the frequently invoked opposition between seeing and hearing, between self-conscious knowledge and faithful obedience. It finds expression in the interreligious quarrel between theologism and fideism. It is potent at the psycho-dynamic level, in the mutual rejection between the charismatic holders of pneumatic credentials and the proudly contrite hearts that down the chalice of first-degree masochism and devote themselves to the edifying thought that we are always in the wrong vis-à-vis God.

The "acute Hellenization of Christianity" also involves a remythologizing of Greek culture. It will be necessary to show that this amounts to more than a colorful regression below the level of Hellenistic theory. Surging from the East is a redeemer myth, which tells of events in time that have essential implications for the truth. This myth effects nothing less than a demolition of the Greek doctrine of timeless beings. The eastern tales of collapse and redemption, of errancy and illumination pressure the Hellenistic spirit to open its static ontology to drama. To this extent, Gnosticism, whether Christian or not, launches an intellectual revolution of unforeseeable consequences. Gnosticism is the first philosophy of the event. It compels Hellenizing ontotheologians to become metaphysical theorists of catastrophe. Philosophers have now to deal with a set of problems that previously was completely unknown to them. It is time for a new sort of self-apprehension of the spirit, as something that has come into the world and exists. It now becomes necessary to assume and theoretically elucidate at least three principal points of catastrophe; these are three fundamental events endowed with such a force as to change the meaning of the world. They are the first catastrophe of creation, the second catastrophe of falling into sin, and the third catastrophe or epistrophē [reversal] of redemption. Creation, fall, and redemption are the three great discontinuities within the continuum of beings. Dealing with them now befalls theological–theoretical thought. Gnosticism and Catholicism part ways on the disputed question of the Fall. For Christianity, Adam was the first one to fall. For Gnosticism, by contrast, the fall of Adam is only a reflex or an implication of the occurrence of a pre-fall [Vor-Fall] "in Heaven." The great heresy teaches that the first two catastrophes, the creation and the Fall, are basically identical. Insight into this identity *is* the quintessence of Gnosticism. The world is everything that is in the fall.[11] Adam is thereby relieved of his burden, and Eve with him. All significant theologies of the next two thousand years will, however, slave away trying to make the doctrine of being into something compatible with the doctrine of the fundamental events. Seen from a broad perspective, the result of these efforts is ironic: the event-theoretical bursting of Hellenistic ontology remains an effect that outweighs the Hellenization of Christianity, which was acute in Gnosticism and took place gradually in the age of scholasticism. It was no longer possible to still the motion of the world under the eyes of a Greek theory. All such attempts had to fail when faced with the Gnostic provocation to think events that have ontological implications. If the world itself is the primary locus for catastrophic events of obfuscation and illumination, then ultimately its dramatic structure will drag theory itself, too, into the flood of time. Heidegger spent his whole life trying to show that his great rival Hegel had not gone far enough in letting himself be taken along by the self-temporalizing of truth. Hegel remained too jovial, too Hellenistic, too theoretical – incapable of considering the trembling of being in existence. Yet the task of thinking of being as time had already been issued, from the moment in late antiquity when the Gnostic impulse began to agitate the souls of humans with questions about "who we were, and what we have become, where we were or where we were placed, whither we hasten, from what we are redeemed, what birth is and what rebirth."[12] Under the influence of these Valentinian baptismal formulae, quoted by Clemens of Alexandria in his *Excerpta ex Theodoto* [*Extracts from the Works of Theodotus*], philosophical Hellenism would eventually have to surrender. The end of philosophy that Heidegger talks about began nearly two thousand years ago, in the cathartic existentialism of the Gnostic traversal of the world. Already from that point on, being and beings "in the truth" were no longer to be grasped as correlates of a vision tasked with thinking the whole. Rather they were to be seen only as a task and a path for an interiority that was weary of the world and was seeking to pass through and hasten across all beings. Hence one of the first results of the collision between Greek theory and eastern myths of the soul was the elevation of philosophy into a discipline of self-transformation. At any rate, we can say that postmetaphysical philosophy lived on as a method of conversion. What it is able to accomplish is ministering a path of sorts for the benefit of beginners in worldly detachment – or a recess music for the contemplative moments of the children of the world.

Gnosticism inaugurates a transposition of psychological life from nature into history. The manifold myths of the soul's fall and ascent introduce something new into the psychological time of the world, with all its natural cycles, and the contingent rise and fall of empires. What they introduce is authentically human historicity. The concept of the path [*Weg*] – *hodos* – is the great result of this essentialization of time. The Gnostic understanding of the human arrival "in the world" gives rise to a radicalized, path-like way of thinking, in various senses of the word. The human being is a creation that has arrived. On her outward path [*Hinweg*] that leads "to the world," she is, to this extent, a soul "in the fall." Getting caught up in, being born, taking up residence – these are just forms of the soul's increasing self-forgetfulness in the here below. On the outward path that leads to falling prey, the soul becomes qualified to sojourn in the world by surrendering to what it discovers: the world as a congealed unconsciousness and as habituated oblivion. Giving oneself up for the sake of the massive whole in the world belongs to the structure of the outward path, be it a *kathodos* [descent] or *prohodos* [way forward, procession]. The soul is at first compelled to develop its ego by drawing on the preponderance of what is given in the world. It is in just this way that it conforms to what is different from it. The kinetic metaphor of the "plunge" makes evident the violence of the primal alienation of the downward movement. "The human being is the *away* [*das* Weg]."[13] The "plunge" – as the unity of a fate that has been suffered and a self-will that has not been illuminated – gives rise to the inner world syndrome of reality fitness, character armor, will to power, and to the entire misunderstanding about the self-preservation experienced by the world self. Gnosticism calls *psuchē* [soul] this world self that is not even worthy of preserving. The soul willfully inclines toward handing itself over to the prevailing character of the world, as it is in itself, and toward becoming like it and like everything in it. This constitutes the necessary tragedy of human existence along the outward path. But, insofar as it is a path, the outward path – the path of wandering off into the world and of becoming like it – is also distinguished as an occurrence within authentic time. As a phase of self-forgetting – which recently has also been called "involution" – it prepares the possibility for a turn, a path back, an evolution. When the turn takes place, the reignited pneumatic self is suffused with the light of authentic historicity. This light retrospectively illuminates the time of errancy and transfigures the "remainder of time" into the path of (redemptive) resolution. From the point of the turn onward, to exist means to turn back, to unbind oneself, to take oneself back. On the path back [*Rückweg*], on the *anodos* [way up], the self gradually gives its own *psuchē* – the inner sediment of life in the trash of the world – back to the cosmos. This gradual return of properties is most beautifully depicted in the treatise *Poimandres* from the *Corpus hermeticum*. The self effectively works itself back out of the prison of having become. In doing so it must choose between two extremely different styles of redemption: "to undergo everything" or "no longer to have contact with anything." The amoral style leads to a homeopathic askesis: this weakens the evil by perpetrating it thoughtfully, ironically as it were, like a task to be accomplished. The Gnostic embraces sin and, in going through it, experiences his body decay in a critical manner. When he is spent, he can then at last climb out of the gutter – the world is a pornographic purgatory from which spotless *pneumata* [spirits] are filtered out. By contrast, the abstinent style deploys allopathic devices against the sickness of the world. It administers an immediate flight from the world as antidote to the poison of the cosmos. Civil disobedience against the belly, general strike against the astral factory, baths in tears, fasting of the heart – these are the mêlée weapons of Gnostic sapience. This dissociative askesis dreams of refuting reality by being constantly other than it. But, when the soul has shaken off the dust of its acquired properties, it grasps itself in its original freedom from properties, as though for the first time and yet once again – as something perfect, something that has not come to be, something hovering. The complete measure of de-worlding is able to fall to the soul in its rapture; from then on the soul lets its own production of "time" fall away like a final crutch. We would admittedly be hard pressed to express this "experience" in language – other than that of a complete displacement. In the fulfilled moment, "being in the world" has come to be, again, a "being in God." The extreme fascination with this return includes the representation of a happy end[14] in the lap of the Father. A faint fever of death may accompany the fantasies of cessation in God. If great resignation is at play here, it would be marked more by the phantasm of retuning to the pleromatic, logico-paternal seed than by the urge toward demise in the dark lap of the mother.

It is easy to recognize that the discovery of authentic time in the Gnostic's awareness of passing through the world prepared a pattern of thinking we are familiar with from the so-called philosophies of history. Authentic time – the event order of outward path, U turn, return path, which is generative of truth – is, first and foremost, a matter for individuals alone. There is an acute individual–eschato-logical feeling at the core of Gnosticism. Only for souls is there a total movement from the first through the middle to the last – and souls "exist" per se as living singulars. If the great loop of going away and turning back describes the structure of the path of the individual "in the world," it follows that to exist as a human in authentic time – that is, to exist in light of the essential historicity of self-knowledge – can take place only for those individuals who have resolved to be themselves and have converted to the process of de-worlding. All "authentic" temporality is thus the historicality of the path to salvation and the historicality of the soul's self-comprehension. There are no other subjects of "authentic history" than individuals.

There is a certain steadfastness to defending this knowledge against the temptation to get involved in the affairs of external history. Whoever gives in to this temptation gets sucked into the undertow of the philosophy of history, where there is a proliferation of speculation about the salvation of what cannot be saved. Then the idea of saving the whole world begins to flourish. Here we always find false answers to the inherently right question of what must happen in the history of the world for it to be more than a calamitous evil, sometimes well masked and sometimes not. Yet it is only by means of an illegitimate projection that authentic, salvational–historical time can be transferred to collective magnitudes in the world. As a rule, the result of such projections is fatal. They typically end up idolizing the masses in "decisive" movements – whether these be churches or parties, peoples or states, moral orders or cognitive elites. To appreciate just how powerful this undertow is, one need only look at Heidegger, who lapsed into belief in the possibility of an ethnic–nationalistic [*völkisch*] authenticity, a German "turn." The philosophy of history emerges from the misleading transference of Gnostic logics of the path to the developmental course of world powers. Hegel demonstrated this in exemplary fashion, albeit with the help of a world spirit that took precedence over world powers. The betrayal of the movement *of* the world itself by the schema of a redemption *from* the world is not immediately evident. Only at a second glance does one notice with what lack of concern, indeed in what grobian spirit the pseudo-Gnostic in the Prussian civil service has sacrificed the soul of the individual in need of redemption to the learning Moloch of world spirit. Since Kierkegaard, individuals have demanded their soul back from the philosophers of history. "The crowd is untruth."

Owing to the irreducible multiplicity of *pneumata*, the Gnostic novel of self-knowledge will be written in many different ways. Because every individual narrative is projected from one's own position on a path, there cannot be a universally acceptable or valid image of "the" path itself. "My path" [*Weg*] is, fundamentally and uniquely, a movement [*Bewegung*] on the beam of my coming into the world. In the vulgar versions of Gnosticism, however, the spirit of individuals does not reach a point beyond mythical external perspectives on being on the way. Then the interested party reads soul stories as if they were metaphysical dime novels in which God and *pneuma* always end up fighting. Plotinus's polemic against the ones he calls Gnostics, who continually move about "as though in a dream," with "horror stories in the heavens" before their eyes, is a case in point. When greater logical forces come into play, it is understood that the mythologists' soul stories[15] can be used only as a propaedeutic; one must leave them behind as beginners' material and replace them with instructions for one's "own" elevation to unworldliness. The flights of fancy through the externalized heavens must give way to a nonobjective, internalizing recollection [*Er-Innerung*]. In the very mature and clear Gnosis – and we may, with Hans Jonas, place in it the thought of Origen, and even that of Plotinus, at least in certain respects – the task is to train the soul, ethically and noetically, so as to make it able, as it were, "to join in the process of thinking" the emanation of the supra-existent One right up to the world and to the ego. The clearer the Gnostic temperament, the more serene its understanding of the *kathodos-* or *prohodos*-related stretches of the path; it empathizes with the gods' universally divine embarrassment about having to sully their name by creating or allowing an actual world. With speculative mirth, the greatest thinkers of late antiquity have understood how to reenact God's abasement into the world and the dissemination of individual souls into the field of becoming. For them, the catastrophe index of the world's events is at a low point; they let beings "flow down" from God at many soft levels of emanation.

Here we come to the modern philosophical form of thought called "system." It emerges from the logical reworking of God's unfolding into the world of appearances. Thinking "systematically" is a paradoxical result of the Gnostic subordination of theoretical vision to the consciousness of the path: whoever thinks of "paths" will in some way also form the notion of the "total path"; this is the kernel of the idea of "system." Although working on one seems to be theoretical and atemporal, existentially it already tumbles onto the path back. ("If you wish to know what I was: Through the Logos I have joked in everything, and have not thereby become a joke. / I hopped; / But you grasp the whole." *The Dance Song of Jesus from the Acts of John.*[16]) In its upward, *anodos*-related movement, the soul tends to its *apotheiōsis*, divinization through insight. As soon as it knows that it is close to it, it looks back on its own period of obscurity almost in gratitude, one could say; after the reversal, it feels, for the rest of its life, the sweetness of an error overcome. To think greatly means to have erred greatly. Happy theory lives on the promise of overcoming the ontological precedence of anxiety.

Not so with the dark temperaments. For them, the downward, *kathodos*-related branch of the curve into the world remains a highly catastrophic plunge – a hellish journey into the unforgivable. The concern of such catastrophists must be entirely for redemption from the world's spell. They run against the cosmic wall, the fence of doom. As impatient seekers of the path out or as athletes of universal suffering, they work out only the upward branch of their existential curve; if they are thorough, this is only about going back. As witnesses for the prosecution against totality, pregnant as it is with death, they give it their best. They gleefully polemicize against the infamous equanimity of their white Gnostic colleagues, who take their time to paint the picture of the outward path. For them, the theorization of the path is the errant path par excellence – just as they think that the theorization of evil delivers you into the hands of evil itself. Gershom Scholem went so far as to lament it as a calamity that the Kabbalah depicted the path from God to the world in Plotinizing style, as a mild outpouring, rather than holding fast to the pure dark doctrine of the primal catastrophe in God. But even catastrophists are receptive to the dialectical appeal of being propped up. "I do not forgive myself for being born. It is as if, creeping into this world, I had profaned a mystery, betrayed some momentous pledge, committed a fault of nameless gravity. Yet in a less assured mood, birth seems a calamity I would be miserable not having known."[17] What would the way back be, if the world did not exist as something whose darkness one must flee, where the flight alone is what gives meaning to the rest of time? Even dark Gnosticism needs the scandalous world in order to flee from it.

3.4   Gnosticism as negative psychology

Now, the idealist sages of the world will have no truck with the word "births."

Oettinger, as cited by Koslowski

In Gnosticism metaphysics is transformed into psychopathology and pneumato-pathology. It deems the arrival of the soul in the world to be a catastrophe of alienation; all life in the dazzling direction of the outward path is, in a fundamental sense, "grieving" – which is the effect of separating from the self. As a critique of the hypnotic power of the world, Gnosticism implies the first great psychotherapy. Hence the Gnostic messengers act rightly as world healers, bearing the authority to coax souls with a dosage of words that is capable of forcing recollection. They take themselves to be saying what individuals need to hear in order to be dehypnotized. As logicians, they are psychagogues; as psychagogues, they are therapists; as therapists, they are theosophs. For them, psychotherapy is theotherapy from the get go – insofar as it can help the divine "in us," the pneumatic spark. However, because the god of Gnosticism is remote from the world and only a negative theology could suit him, the soul's theotherapeutic guidance toward this god leads straight into a negative determination of the soul. To this day, whenever there is any noteworthy gesture towards a philosophical psychology, it always stays in the realm of possibilities of negative psychology opened by Gnosticism. From that point on, talk of a lucid self-ignorance has stood at the center of the pneumatic doctrines of the self-comprehension of the "soul."

In order to grasp the therapeutic valences of the Gnostic approach, it is advisable to bring to mind the situation of the black Gnostic psychics. They are the world's diseased in the full sense of the world, the misfits[18] of the cosmos who taste to the bitter end the disadvantages of being born. In particular, we often find among them an effect that could be described as a contraction of Gnosticism into dark existentialism. There is a wanton spark to the diseased melancholy of these psychics – one might say a pride in incurability, which manifests itself in the refractory derision of all trends toward illumination. Thus Hans Jonas is incorrect when he all too quickly brings modern dark existentialism into parallel with the ancient Gnosticisms. In name and substance, the latter are oriented to the connection between knowledge and redemption. The modern dark "Gnosticisms," in contrast, develop only a halfway consciousness. Their representatives grant that we have fallen into the cosmos; however, by dogmatizing the outward path into darkness, they cut off all regard for upward experiences. They are incapable of forgetting the world and themselves; they live as memories of fury. They are pathetic paradigms of remaining stuck, truculent victims of being forced against one's will into having to be – the spark of their self-consciousness gleams in their insistence that they have the right to remain aggrieved.

Psychological research of the past half-century has gone extraordinarily deep into the dynamics of complex fundamental disturbances of this variety. These depths are not without epistemological pitfalls: for reasons that lie in the nature of the subject matter itself, the results of analytic research into psychoses, of prenatal psychology, and of psychological perinatalistics cannot be popularized – according to the rules of "representational thinking," they can only be copied and communicated in the form of external vantage points or stories.[19] What Gustav Hans Graber propounded about primal ambivalence, the awareness that Stanislav Grof generated about the subjective catastrophe of birth, what Béla Grunberger was able to say about aggression in Anubis baboons – all this has the structure of self-contained primary knowledge that cannot be transmitted. Only a primary, process-like performance can open it up on its own terms; it is precisely this that touches on the Gnostic type of knowledge. *Gnōsis hodou* means knowledge of the path – which designated, initially, the Gnostic consciousness of the "path back" and, later, the mystical consciousness of it. However, an integral part of *hodos* understanding is the recollection of plunging into the world. Modern primary psychologies draw consequences from this for the earliest and potentially most fruitful transitions of the coming into the world of human beings.

In view of such problems, the Gnostic double determination of the soul as *psuchē* [soul] and *pneuma* [breath] can turn out to be extraordinarily fruitful. In general, it gives rise to the imperative that the realm of *psuchē* be pneumatically sublated; where *psuchē* was, there *pneuma* should come to be. This holds in particular for the catastrophic levels of the most starkly occluded realm of the psychological. Pneumatic therapy leads the subject back to pre-psychic enstasies, in which even the tendencies of the failed life to annihilate the world and the self are brought to naught. Another memory is thereby constructed – a memory whose content allows one to live again: it stores recollections of a "sufficiently good" world. The logical side of these transformations includes work on personal pronouns, in particular "I" and "it," and on spatial prepositions, above all "in" and "vis-à-vis." Psychics as defined in Gnosticism and psychotics as defined in modern pathologies suffer from a disturbance in their capacity to use the words "I" and "in" correctly at a deep structural level. They do not know what it means to say "I" and "in" well. The pronoun "I" threatens them with a problem of explosion, while dangers of asphyxiation slumber in the preposition "in." For the dark psychics, the inner space of the world is mined by the "I" and the outer space of the world is walled up by the "in." They are therefore incapable of being serene either in themselves or in the world. This positional inability to "exist" corresponds precisely to the darkest versions of Gnostic "kathodology" [science of the downward path]: the outward path into human existence is a plunge into a prison-world. Older Gnosticism, however, ties a great promise to this interpretation of the outward path; it teaches that a turn and a path back "are given," if only the soul recollects "itself" and its "provenance" correctly. In this recollection, the resurrection of the dead, which you already are, is supposed to occur.

But *is* a turn really "given," *is* an upward process really "given"? Who or what is the subject that could give the turn? Pneumatic therapy really gets going when it tries to answer this question. The only possible agent of the turn in me is, naturally, an event "in" my very self. "I," however, am already the path away from myself, which corresponds to my self-experience in the hell that really exists. If the turn is only able to take place "in" me, it is initially impossible for me, because I cannot be the place of the turn or be at the place of the turn. "I" and "in" are incompatible with each other. In this sense, it would be correct to say that the turn can only occur "of itself." I would therefore have to reach the point at which, "of itself," I am able to be myself and to be in myself – other than in my current state, where I am the one who carries on as usual with my desperate "being the path away from myself." If the turn to the good is to take place "in me," it can only occur in such a way that, "of itself" – and thus not through "myself" – I reach the point at which I can be in myself. I can, however, be in myself only when I withstand myself – when I no longer shrink back, when my injury from occurrences in the world is put in the past. Yet how do I reach an authentic past? I "settle" the injury by transforming my explosion into language. Here we find the possible upward significance of excessive negativity. The path back for the black psychics can begin with eventful eruptions of hatred. Gnosticism of the injured life emerges when this hatred goes all the way to the core, amid its pain. From now on this life knows what it absolutely no longer wants: all *that*. Its one-sided hatred erupts as the unrestrained affirmation of frenzied negation. With its eruption and mine, I am finally in myself. The daring explosion brings movement to the soul – while the cowardice of psychopaths gladly makes ends meet in the cunning deadlock of a black kitsch.

The wounded *psuchē*, the composed I, passes over into an unwounded and uncomposed self-being whose goodness is essentially conditioned by its negativity. Because it *is* not, it is good. Thought of in terms of Gnosticism, its partner in this goodness is the negative, the superexisting non-god. Even this god would be good only to the extent that he were different from everything that is. If he were something, he would be simply the unwounded that does not inflict wounds; at the same time he would remain the one who cannot be prosecuted for what has actually wounded you. Thus he would be the absolute accomplice in your right to neutralize what has confined and annihilated you. News from him has the same effect on suitable recipients as do psychotropic drugs – they are *logoi*, opening words that speak directly, as though from within, to the unbecoming self. When I listen to the news from this worldless source of the "self," a turn takes place in me of itself.

Thus Gnosticism becomes primary cognitive therapy – it opens up another memory. The subject can say *metagennōmai*, "I am reborn," I understand myself *anew*, indeed I am new, since now I know that I am the other understanding. Pneumatic therapy leads to the "liberation of the imposed continuity of being a self that is concerned about its relation to the world."[20]

When this turnabout is successful, the subject finds the space in which it can be *there* [*"da" sein*]. With this it also has, "in the world," the free space that befits it. It can now become the inhabitant of a reality, because it can let the world be in itself. When the soul's being in *God* is grasped, the world's being in the soul also becomes possible. Gnostic therapy heals by means of the integrity of the nothing. Yet the nothing is the anonymity of the human being. I can be in the world when I am capable of being in myself; "in myself" means in nothing; "in nothing" means in "God"; "in God" means in you. "In you" means, curiously enough, toward you, vis-à-vis you, in a world henceforth open, within earshot of calling, within the scope of love. Minutes become precious on this Gnostic reinterpretation of the meaning of being. Ascension to heaven passes over into everyday life. Through its concomitant knowledge about the paths of others, this form of everyday life creates human community anew.

3.5 Demiurgical humanism: On the Gnosticism of modern art

Krankheit ist wohl der letzte Grund
Des ganzen Schöpferdrangs gewesen;
Erschaffend konnte ich genesen,
Erschaffend wurde ich gesund.

Illness was the especial ground
Of my creative inclination;
I might recover by creation,
Creation made me once more sound.

Heinrich Heine, Songs of Creation[21]

A re-creation of the world corresponds to the rebirth of the individual. Just as modern psychotherapeutics led, whether covertly or overtly, to a great retrieval of Gnostic motifs, so did modern aesthetics have to intervene in the controversy over the meaning of creation in a new way. Ever since the Renaissance, western culture has moved about on a terrain that is neo-Gnostic in the broadest sense. For the most part, western culture has done so without being clearly aware of its situation.

Seen from a psycho-historical perspective, this is connected to a change of phase in Trinitarian theology: from Augustine to Thomas à Kempis, orthodox Christianity was above all a religion of obedience that tried to interpret itself lawfully, as an *imitatio Christi* [emulation of Christ]. After the mystical eruptions in the fourteenth and fifteenth centuries, it is the two other "persons" that take the psychodynamic upper hand within the force field of the Trinity. The mediating religions turn into a religion of immediacy; from Ficino to Emerson, the Christian spark is transposed into a doctrine of enthusiastic self-reliance. The imitation of Christ recedes into the background, in favor of an imitation of the Father and of the Spirit. *Imitatio Patris* [the emulation of the Father] unleashes a new, creative connection between knowledge, will, and power. Here the theological mold of human work skills is made ready for serial production. *Imitatio Spiritus* [the emulation of the Spirit], in contrast, enables post-Christian forms of enthusiasm, which become epoch-making under the Roman concept of "genius." Geniuses and engineers rise to an elite class of a new type: they stand for the group of epoch-making people. Now one lives before or after them – before or after Columbus, before or after Titian, before or after Kant, before or after Siemens. Discovering, inventing, producing, elaborating, accomplishing, surpassing: the human *vita activa* [active life] organizes itself as a demiurgical project. *Imitatio Patris et Spiritus* changes the meaning of human work in a radical way. Work is no longer the mere trace of our expulsion from paradise; it is not just the curse that followed the break with the oldest orders. In the modern age, to work means to keep open the process of creation. Expulsion from paradise now looks like a cunning of reason; it is the prelude to the enthronement of the human as creator of her "own world." From the very moment humans set to "work" in a typically western way, creation has entered its second week. Only a fallen and expulsed humanity could make good on the idea of achieving *more* than the God of Genesis. So far as Catholicism is concerned, human work can be nothing more than the fulfillment of epigenetic tasks – conservation of holdings, laboring in the vineyard of the Lord, stewardship[22] on Spaceship Earth. The nuclear modern age, however – the Protestant–humanist–neopagan complex – has pledged itself to the motto of creativity and interpreted the meaning of human work to be hypergenesis. This means nothing less than to surpass the old creation through the contribution of ingenuity, to increase the old nature through additional technological–aesthetic creation. The Fall of Man morphs into productivity, the metaphysical catastrophe of humans launches the hypergenetic process. The human is the god of the second week of creation. "Modern history" records the successes of our interventions.

Meanwhile there was evening and there was morning, an eighth day. The question arises whether God still has the courage to see (and to say) once more that it was good. In 1929 Sigmund Freud noted that the human has "almost become a god himself," "a kind of prosthetic god" – yet one that "does not feel happy in his Godlike character."[23] Meanwhile, we know that the civilized human being's discontent with his situation is more than a consequence of the inevitable self-aggressions of the superego; in this discontent we can see the immediate truth of demiurgical humanism. As the construct of a post-paradisiacal creativity, modern human works are, from the ground up, ambivalent symptoms of an ontological catastrophe: curse and cure in one, sickness and therapy together. The American ecologist Bill McKibben brought to a head the postmodern discontent with creativity in his book *The End of Nature*: "When changing nature means changing everything, then we have a crisis. We are in charge now, like it or not. As a species we are as gods – our reach global [...] How are we to be humble in any way if we have taken over as creators?"[24]

The spirit of a post-demiurgical aesthetics lights up in such questions. If already the god of Genesis was not safe from Valentinus's ironic remarks about the wisdom of his creation, how are we, the ones responsible for technological hypergenesis, supposed to protect ourselves from posterity's critique of our feral creativity? The post-demiurgical critique of the world targets the works of the eighth day – that is, the man-made New World, including its most virtuosic artistic productions – as sharply as the Gnosticism of late antiquity did Elohim's six days' work. A new form of dissidence emerges necessarily from this: the non-consent of the human being to the works she has made. This is more than discontent with civilization; it is discontent with the demiurgical authority of the human being, an ailment from the pressure toward power and toward making. Great artworks, as defined by Gnostic aesthetics, would therefore be more than another monument to the aesthetic will to power; they would bring something other than additional memories of human perversity into the archive of time. In such works, we would be able to hear something of the creature's protest against the catastrophe of creation. Within the interiority of the work, the spirit of world-lessness returns as the breath of worklessness. The Gnostic work, as a sublime breach with one's own power, is the trace of a nostalgia for that which surpasses works.

References for Chapter 3

Baur, Ferdinand Christian. 1835. *Die christliche Gnosis oder die christliche Religionsphilosophie in ihrer historischen Entwicklung*. Tübingen: Osiander.

Bloom, Harold. 1982. *Agon: Towards a Theory of Revisionism*. New York: Oxford University Press.

Graber, Gustav Hans. 1924. *Die Ambivalenz des Kindes*. Bern: C. Fromme.

Grof, Stanislav. 1979. *Realms of the Human Unconscious: Observations from LSD Research*. London: Souvenir Press.

Grunberger, Béla. 1988. *Narziß und Anubis: Die Psychoanalyse jenseits der Triebtheorie*, 2 vols. Munich: Verlag Internationale Psychoanalyse.

Heidegger, Martin. 2012. *Contributions to Philosophy (Of the Event)*, translated by Richard Rojcewicz and Daniela Vallega–Neu. Bloomington: Indiana University Press.

Jonas, Hans. 1934, 1954. *Gnosis und spätantiker Geist*, vol. 1: *Die mythologische Gnosis*; vol. 2: *Von der Mythologie zur mystischen Philosophie*. Göttingen: Vandenhoeck & Ruprecht. [An abridged and revised English 1958 version is available as *The Gnostic Religion: The Message of the Alien God and the Beginnings of Christianity*, Boston: Beacon Press.]

Kierkegaard, Søren. 1998. "The Single Individual": Two "Notes" Concerning My Work as an Author. In *Kierkegaard's Writings*, vol. 22: *The Point of View*, edited and translated by Howard V. Hong and Edna H. Hong, Princeton, NJ: Princeton University Press, pp. 103–26.

Koslowski, Peter. 1989. *Die Prüfungen der Neuzeit: Über Postmodernität, Philosophie, Gnosis*. Vienna: Passagen Verlag.

Pagels, Elaine, 1989. *Adam, Eve, and the Serpent*. New York: Vintage Books.

Pétrement, Simone. 1993. *A Separate God: The Origins and Teachings of Gnosticism*. San Francisco: HarperSanFrancisco.

Quispel, Gilles. 1951. *Gnosis als Weltreligion: Vier Vorträge: Allgemeine Einführung in die Thematik der Gnosis*. Zurich: Leiden.

4

CLOSER TO ME THAN I AM MYSELF

A Theological Preparation for the Theory of the Shared Inside[*]

We must set forth the ontological Constitution of inhood [*Inheit*] itself. [...] What is meant by "*Being-in*"? [...] Being-in [...] is a state of Dasein's Being.[1]

"What is this 'in'?" Agathe asked emphatically. Ulrich shrugged his shoulders and then gave a few indications. [...] "Perhaps the *psychoanalytic legend* that the human soul strives to get back to the tender protection of the intrauterine condition before birth is a misunderstanding of the 'in,' perhaps not. Perhaps 'in' is the presumed descent of all life from God. But perhaps the explanation is also simply to be found in psychology; for every affect bears within it the claim of totality to rule alone and, as it were, form the 'in' in which everything else is immersed."[2]

So where are we when we are in a small inside? In what way can a world, despite its opening towards the immeasurable, be an intimately divided round world? Where are those who come into the world when they are in bipolar intimate spheres or bubbles? On our path through some of the folds and turns in the human-forming microcosms of interlocked interiority, seven layers of an answer to this question have so far taken shape. We are in a microsphere whenever we are

---

* *TRANSLATOR'S NOTE* This chapter was first translated by Wieland Hoban in *Spheres*. I have modified it in accordance with certain changes that Sloterdijk made for its appearance in *After God*, as well as in order to make it cohere stylistically and linguistically with the translation of the book as a whole.

- first, in the intercordial space;
- second, in the interfacial sphere;
- third, in the field of "magical" binding forces and hypnotic effects of closeness;
- fourth, in immanence, that is, inside the absolute mother and its postnatal metaphorizations;
- fifth, in the co-dyad, the placental doubling and its successors;
- sixth, in the care of the irremovable companion and its metamorphoses;
- seventh, in the resonant space of the welcoming maternal voice and its messianic–evangelistic–artistic simulacra.

It will be noted that the inter-genital relationship and the inter-manual connection are absent from this list, as if to suggest that coitus and handshakes are excluded from the intimately spheric field. In truth, the two gestures are fairly peripheral from the perspective of microspheric analysis, even if they – especially the sexual one – represent intimate relationships that are prototypical for everyday consciousness. Sexuality in particular, even though it occasionally releases suggestive intimate experiences, has no intimate light of its own, any more than the encounter between fighters inside a ring creates spherically intimate and relevant contacts in and of itself. If de facto intimacy comes into play here, it is only through the transference of closeness relationships from real intimate scenes of the kind listed above to genital or athletic confrontations and pairings. Such transferences distinguish human sexuality from that of animals. While animals can content themselves with slotting their reproductive organs together for intercourse, that same quandary motivates humans to produce an increase in intimacy. This can be drawn only from the reservoir of memories of closeness transferable from elsewhere – down to the Tristan embrace, in which the lovers enact for each other the return to the original womb. Nothing shows more clearly that humans are condemned to intimate surrealism than the fact that most of the time even their genital interactions have to be arranged on a virtual inner-world stage.

*

At first glance, the variants of intimacy relationships treated here share only one formal quality: they never separate the subject from its environment or place it in confrontation with something that is present in concrete form or faces it as a state of affairs; rather they integrate it into an encompassing situation and take it up into a space of relationships with two or more locations, where the ego side represents only one pole. Hence the common thread in this sevenfoldness [*Siebenfaltigkeit*], if the term were permitted and current, would be its "structuring" through *inhood*. This neologism, which surfaced like an apparition in Heidegger's early work,[3] expresses, oddly enough, the fact that the subject or the Dasein can be *there* only if it is contained, surrounded, encompassed, disclosed, breathed-upon, resounded-through, attuned, and addressed. Before a Dasein assumes the character of being in the world, it already has the constitution of being in. Having admitted this, it seems justified to demand that heterogeneous statements about intimately spheric enclosedness and openness be brought together in an overarching pattern. The aim is thus a theory of existential spaciousness – or, differently put, a theory of interintelligence or of presence in spheres of ensoulment. This principle of a space for intimate relationships should make it clear why a life is always a life in the midst of lives.[4] Being in, then, should be conceived of as the togetherness of something with something in something. We are therefore – we shall repeat the thesis – inquiring about what is known in current terminology as a "media theory." What are media theories but suggestions of ways to explain the how and the whereby of the connection between different existents in a shared ether?

Looking around in search for models for such an undertaking, one is pulled *nolens volens* into the broad field of old European theological traditions. It is above all the authors from the period of the Greek – and also Latin – church fathers and apostles who, in their treatises on the Trinity, in their mystical theologies, and in their doctrines of the two interlocking natures of God and the human being, occupied themselves with the question of how to think the containedness of conceived and created natures *in* the one God, as well as God's relationship with himself. It was inevitable that these branches of dogmatics would become a school of reflection on the *being* of intimate relationships. While it is characteristic of modern thought that it begins with Dasein's being in the world or the system's being in its environment, it is the specific feature of Christian monotheism, and also of philosophical monotheism, that it must begin with the being in God of all things and souls.[5] As the all-pervading God, who is beyond all finite localizations, cannot be anywhere other than everywhere *in himself*,[6] there seems to be, for theonomic thought, no alternative to being in. God is in himself and the world is in God, so where could we locate the slightest remainder of that which is, if not in the circle of influence of this absolute *in*? One cannot seriously speak of externality in a world that is God's work and extension. Nonetheless, the totalized inside of God is provoked by a disruptive outside, whose theologically correct name is "creation after the fall." For where are the people who live in sin, in willfulness, or in freedom, if not outside, so to speak – albeit in a licensed externality that, because bound to creatureliness, should never be able to deny the connection to the originator entirely? And where if not out there below should a savior look for the fallen souls that are to be led home?

So, for the theological question of the *in*, the emergency is triggered by two logically disturbing relationships: first the problematic one between God and the human soul, of which it is initially far from clear how it could continue to be *in God* or with him after the Fall; and, secondly, God's excentrically intimate relationships with himself, which, in the light of his self-exit in the guise of the savior, encouraged the most pensive of investigations. So how and in what sense could one say that humans – or the human soul – are still contained in God, even in their fallen state? And how and in what sense should we henceforth think of God, after his incarnation and Pentecostal outpouring, as seamlessly contained in himself?

These two questions triggered two mighty waves of theological reflection on the conditions of being one and being in: the Christian era identifies itself by the urge to reflect on God and space in a fundamentally theoretical way; it is the golden age of subtle topologies dealing with places in the non-where [*im Nicht-Wo*]. For, if God were the absolute vessel, how thick would its walls be? How was it possible to go forth to the outside from within him? Why did he not want to take everything he had created back into himself, unconditionally? And by what possible mediation might lost things return home? While the question of the relationship between God and the soul is mostly answered in the mode of biunity theories, the question of the nature of God's self-inhabitation finds its answer primarily through Trinitarian doctrines.

For a spherology, these discourses are not interesting on account of their religious claims or dogmatic willfulness; we are not visiting them as attractions of intellectual history. They are of legitimate concern to us only to the extent that until recently they had a virtually unchallenged monopoly on the basic principles of thinking about the logic of intimacy. Only Platonic erotology had been able, in contemporary adaptations, to break the predominance of Christian theology in the field of the theory of intimate connections. Anyone wanting to learn more closely about the spirit of closeness and more intimately about the spirit of intimacy before the advent of modern depth psychologies in the eighteenth century inevitably had to turn to the most withdrawn regions of the theological tradition. In this tradition, as far as the more esoteric aspects of the relationships between God and soul were concerned, mystical transmission was almost the sole authority; anyone interested in the inner workings of God's life, so richly and enigmatically self-referential, had to tackle the daunting mountain massif of Trinitarian speculation. It is in these still rather inaccessible areas that the patinated treasures of a premodern knowledge of primary relationships are stored. Much of what preoccupies modern psychologists and sociologists concerning the concepts of intersubjectivity and inter-intelligence is prefigured in the theological discourses that, in millennial serenity, deal with the intertwined co-subjectivity of the dyad God–soul and with the co-intelligence, cooperation, and mutual love of the Trinity within God. Thus, if the concern is to deal with participatory phenomena and structures of constitutive being in each other and being with each other at a fundamental conceptual level, parts of the theological tradition can become a surprisingly informative source for the free spirit. It is in theological surrealism, as will be shown, that the first realism of spheres lies hidden. Only through its reconstruction can we sufficiently clarify what immanence actually means.

This applies first and foremost to the field of God–soul relationships. Whoever attempts to comprehend the language games of mystical theology about the soul's reentry into the divine sphere is immediately faced with a subtle web of statements about de-objectified interconnections. For, if one asks about the reason for the possible orientation of God and the soul toward each other, one stares at the abyss of a disposition for relationships that go deeper than any inclinations of kinship or sympathy one can normally assume between people or beings. The nature of the bond between the two cannot in any way be explained by a posteriori affections or halfway meetings. It may be true of human love, in a certain sense, that it does not exist at all until it occurs. What precedes human love is – viewed from the perspective of individualistic modernity – two lonelinesses that are uprooted through encounter. So one could apply Alain Badiou's statement about the late Beckett's meditation on love: "The encounter is founding of the Two as such."[7] As far as God and the soul are concerned, they do not face each other like parties or business people who see a common benefit in occasional coalitions; nor do they merely form an amorous couple occasionally consumed by passion, depending on the coincidence of encounter. If an intimate response occurs between them, this is by no means a simple result of what psychoanalysis – with a phrase of limited wisdom – calls a "choice of object." If God and the soul are connected, this is due to an interpersonal element older than any search for a partner or any secondary acquaintanceship. And if their relationship seems passionate at times, this is only because there is, under certain circumstances, a resonance between them so radical that it cannot possibly be attributed merely to the empirical contact they have with each other. The fundamental resonance, however, if it were to be recognized as an initial, constitutive one – how should we conceive of it, when it is initially and usually "in the world," and consequently located in a place that, to put it mildly, is characterized by a certain distance from the transcendental pole? How should one interpret God's and the soul's ability to belong together and be affected by each other, when there is no doubt that they cannot be connected without problems regarding their status quo, let alone be identical? Did the incident in paradise not open up a primordially painful chasm of estrangement between them? Sure, religious sermons have always insisted, tirelessly, that a re-encounter is still possible between the two estranged poles, that this is indeed the epitome of all that is worth seeking and finding for the soul, and that God is only waiting to lead the alienated soul back to himself. But such an immersion of the soul in a renewed familiarity with its lost great other can never develop from a chance acquaintanceship. Nor will the soul take God back "to itself" any more than it could simply be taken by him; for then where would each one be at home outside their encounter? If they become acquainted, it is through the soul's realization that it has long known the thing it is getting to know again. Implicit in such knowing is the fact that, long ago, each one took the other along with itself, in a sense, or was taken along by the other. Hence they have, in a very unclear fashion, already been inserted into each other, as they could not have made each other's reacquaintance if they had not previously become estranged, yet could not have been estranged if they had not known each other from time immemorial. ("I certainly have seen his face somewhere," Dostoyevsky has his heroine Nastasya Fillippovna say of Prince Myshkin, the idiot, after their *first* meeting.)[8] Their fitting together encompasses the oldest openness towards each other, as well as the primordial rift. However, because the rift makes the relationship possible and recognizable for what it is in the first place, the truth about the overall situation can come to light only retrospectively – retrospectively from the outset. The always already must appear in retrospect, while that which has always been valid asserts itself, with delayed force, in the coincidental. The epitome of these postponements is salvation history, insofar as it deals with God's economy – his attempts to rectify soul losses after the fact. God and the soul get to know each other because they already know each other, but their knowing is molded from early on – or even from the start? – by a tendency toward misjudgment that manifests itself as resistance, jealousy, estrangement, and indifference.

It is Saint Augustine who, in his *Confessions*, developed the dialectics of recognition from misjudgment, in exemplary escalations.[9] Although church historians do not place Augustine within the mystical tradition in the strict sense,[10] he can certainly be considered the great logician of intimacy in western theology. This is outstandingly demonstrated in Books 1 and 10 of the *Confessions*, as well as in those books of his cryptic magnum opus *On the Trinity* (*De trinitate*) that deal with the accessibility of God through traces of him left in the soul – especially Books 8–14. The *Confessions* in particular, in the way it was written, constitutes a fabulous document of intimist discourse. Through its form – a monumental narrative prayer with inserted dissertations – it produces a paradoxically intimate situation *coram publico*, openly: what Augustine tells his God during a form of auricular confession, in a tone of agonized self-renunciation, is at the same time a literary and a psychagogic act before an ecclesiastical public. The author relies on the established genres of prayer and confession, which have played a part in structuring the theo-psychological space since the days of early Christianity. The glorifying prayer seeks to replace the subaltern praise of the Lord with jubilation, while the confession seeks to outdo the forced admission by facilitating an escape into the utterance of truth; both genres are thus destined to form a sort of "unshakable foundation" for truthful discourse of the Christian type. Christian language analysis is guided by the assumption that the unveiling force of confessional discourse reaches deeper than the compelling disclosure of the truth through slave torture at trials in ancient times.[11] In the matter of bringing the truth to light, the religious confession seems more productive than the forced juridical confession, as it can already be uttered in the hope of forthcoming mercy; under torture, however, the motive for concealing or distorting one's own deeds or those of others can never be eliminated for good and with the inner agreement of the confessed offender. Whoever can withstand the pain of torture can exercise denial to the very end and seal his lips permanently, in an act of resistance against the cruel interrogators. In the religious confession, on the other hand, lying would be nonsensical, as the very idea of the *confessio* hinges on realizing the advantage of telling the truth. The reward for confession is that whoever speaks the truth comes "into the truth": this is precisely what begins the drama of the logic of intimacy that gives Augustinian thought its vibrant tone. For after the switch to the "true religion" truth can no longer be considered just a property of statements and speech; truth should form the "in" into which all speaking and life seeks to be immersed.[12] The benchmark of whether a confessing sinner is "truly opening" herself is the pain of confession, which moves, authenticates, and purifies her and separates her from her past. Confession traces the escape route to blatancy, as it were: it gives the Greek notion of truth – *alētheia* or lack of concealment – a Christian turn, and thus a dialogic one; now the true word appears on the human side as admission, and on God's side as revelation. What revelation and admission have in common is that each in its own way effects the retroactive (in Christian language, gracious) conciliatory reopening of a lost entrance to the inside of the other part. This leads to the repetition of tragic catharsis with Christian resources; it need hardly be said that a prototype of old European psychotherapeutics entered the historical stage with the game of truth brought by the religious confession.

In his *Confessions*, Augustine drew the most radical conclusions from the equally suggestive and demanding paradigm according to which whoever ventures to speak the truth about himself must already "be in the truth." That an individual *wants* to declare the truth about her turning toward the truth gives a first indication of her "being in" with respect to the truth; and the fact that the declarer *can* say what he is required to say amounts to an irrefutable proof, or to a divine judgment via the quill. According to the paradigm, the declaration of guilt before God and the congregation would be doomed to failure had God himself not foreseen it, approved of it, inspired it, and caused it. Hence the impossibility of telling the untruth is already ordained in exemplary confessional speech. Just as a prophet could not lie in the moment of inspiration, an author who accuses himself of sinning in the same way as Augustine does cannot fall short of the truth. Presenting himself as sub-author in God's management of language, Augustine effectively states that his confessions have been put into his mouth by the highest authority: through his illuminated bishop, the creator of all things confines to the written page salvifically important additions to his own previous declarations. "Sub-author" is an analytical term for what is usually meant by "apostle"; for an apostle is someone who speaks or writes as a representative of the absolute author.[13] Consistently with this, Augustine speaks as a therapeutic apostle in the account of his resistance to God. The *Confessions* can be read, convincingly, as an *ex cathedra* medical history; they deal with the curability of unbelief in God – through God. In this manner the bishop of Hippo Regius manages discreetly to subvert the difference between human confession of sins and divine revelation; his admissions provoke a continuation of revelation by other means. Whoever tells in such a fashion of their own unsaved life, meanwhile overcome through grace, is writing evangelistic apocrypha – supplementary good news

about the possibility of converting those who resist the early good
news; in this way, too, the Holy Scripture writes itself as the success
story of its own dissemination.

Being in denotes here a situation in the stream of true language:
whoever speaks in it includes her own speech in the divine main text,
in such a way that (as far as possible) no external remainder is left.
In *vita christiana* [the Christian life], however, the concern is not
simply to fit one's own words into the spreading of the Lord's word;
one's entire existence is meant to be remolded from a willful one
into one that is contained *in God*. Certainly, with a willful person of
Augustine's rank, the victim of willfulness is significant: as discreetly
and clearly as possible, the *Confessions* make it known that, on
this one occasion, the reduction of genius to apostle succeeded
with God's help. For Augustine, his own conversion is therefore an
example of epoch-making value. He himself is the ancient world
that converted to Christianity; he is the ancient world in his capacity
as unholy genius and agent of a spiritless society, which has disintegrated into atoms of ambition and greed. In addition, however,
as co-inventor of a new sphere of God that promises the infinite to
countless people, he is already the Christian era. As a witness to this
difference, Augustine puts on record in his *Confessions* that heathen
egotistical externality has been overcome through a spheric wonder
– through the organized inner world of salvation manifested in God
the human being and organized by his apostolic successors, which
manifests itself in a new way in the midst of this externalized reality
of power [*Gewaltwirklichkeit*].

According to Augustine, once drawn back to God, the formerly
rebellious soul must account retrospectively for the fact that it
had been seen through from the very outset and incorporated
into a divine economy at every moment of its seemingly idiosyncratic development. Now it admits to finding happiness under the
all-pervading, constant observation of its great other.

> And even if I would not confess to You, what could be hidden
> in me, O Lord, from you to whose eyes the deepest depth of
> man's conscience [*abyssus humanae conscientiae*] lies bare? I
> should only be hiding You from myself, not myself from You.
> But now that my groaning is witness that I am displeasing
> to myself, You shine unto me and I delight in You and love
> You and yearn for You, so that I am ashamed of what I am
> and renounce myself and choose You and please neither You
> nor myself save in you [*et nec mihi nec tibi placeam nisi de te*].
> To You then, O Lord, I am laid bare for what I am. [...] For
> whatever good I utter to men, You have heard from me before

I utter it; and whatever good You hear from me, You have first spoken to me.[14]

Just as here Augustine provides a classic articulation of his own transparency toward the absolute intelligence and of his role as a medium for the transmission of the great other's truth, elsewhere he expresses his existential interconnection with the all-encompassing in formulations that present the relationship with God as a being there[15] in an encompassing and pervasive entity:

> But how can I call unto my God, my God and Lord? For in calling unto Him, I am calling Him to me: and what room is there in me for my God [*et quis locus est in me, in quo veniat in me deus meus?*], the God who made heaven and earth? Is there anything in me, O God, that can contain You [*capiat te*]? All heaven and earth cannot contain You, for You made them, and me in them. Yet, since nothing that is could exist without You, You must in some way be in all that is: [therefore also in me, since I am]. And if You are already in me, since otherwise I should not be, why do I cry to You to enter into me? [...] Thus, O God, I should be nothing, utterly nothing, unless You were in me – or rather unless I were in You, *of whom and by whom and in whom are all things* (Romans 11:36). So it is, Lord; so it is. Where do I call You to come to, since I am in You? Or where else are You that You can come to me? Where shall I go, beyond the bounds of heaven and earth, that God may come to me, since He has said: *Heaven and earth do I fill* (Jeremiah 23:24).[16]

This thought movement betrays a finite consciousness in the tendency to surrender for the sake of the infinite. Here Augustine follows the paths of Greek metaphysics, which suggests to ephemeral life a demise in eternal substance. If God is truth and truth is substance, then the unstable subjectivity of individuals – if they are serious about the truth – must break away from itself and escape from its inessential and illusory state into the essential and real. Who can deny that a large number of Christian theologies were always in more or less explicit agreement with this basic principle of substance metaphysics? Where metaphysical concepts dominate, the search for truth is understood as a run-up to the conversion from nothing to being – or, in Christian terms, as a striving away from a sham death toward a life in the truth. The Latin tradition refers to this self-salvaging into substance as transcending – a word too little mentioned, if one considers that it made history in the thought and feeling of old Europe. Thought about transcendence [*Transzendenzdenken*], just like Christian metaphysics, organizes the flight of an inane existence to the good reason, as it were. It characterizes the ingenuity of Augustinian theology, which began by balancing out the inescapable metaphysical emancipation from oneself with God's accommodation of the seemingly null self. Augustine forces the illuminated soul to immerse itself in its own complexity in order to uncover within it the traces of the God who is three times folded onto himself. The null subject's exit from itself and its overstepping into substance are requited, or rewarded, with an entry of the substance into the subject, which is henceforth essentially used to become acquainted with God through the creature and to hold on to this acquaintanceship. In this manner, subjectivity or the "inner human," as Augustine calls it – now elevated to being a carrier of God's trace – is afforded uncommonly great dignity. The human spirit may roam through the universe of created things in all their instantiations, but it will never find outside what it is searching for. If God is to be found, it is only after the searcher has turned inwards. It is in his own mental faculties that the successful searcher experiences a reflection of what he is looking for.

See now how great a space I have covered in my memory, in search of Thee, O Lord; and I have not found Thee outside it.[17] For I find nothing concerning Thee but what I have remembered from the time I first learned of Thee. From that time, I have never forgotten Thee. For where I found truth, there I found my God, who is Truth itself, and this I have not forgotten from the time I first learned it. Thus from the time I learned of Thee, Thou hast remained in my memory [*manes in memoria mea*], and there do I find Thee, when I turn my mind to thee and find delight in Thee [*in te*].[18]

But where in my memory do you abide, Lord, where in my memory do You abide? What resting-place [*cubile*] have You claimed as Your own, what sanctuary built for Yourself? You have paid this honor to my memory, that You deign to abide in it; but I now come to consider in what part of it You abide.[19]

And indeed why do I seek in *what place of my memory You dwell* [habites] as though there were places in my memory? Certain I am that You dwell in it, because I remember You since the time I first learned of You [*ex quo te didici*], and because I find You in it when I remember You.[20]

Where then *did I find You to learn of You*, save in Yourself, above myself [*in te, supra me*]? Place there is none, we go this way and that, and place there is none.[21]

Late have I loved thee, O Beauty so ancient and so new; late have I loved thee! For behold Thou wert within me, and I outside [...] Thou wert with me and I was not with Thee.[22]

Now it becomes clear why the soul that seeks to clarify its relationship with God inherently requires time to do so. Though God's connection to the soul is transhistorical, the soul's connection to God is temporal or historical insofar as history, from a Christian perspective, is the affair between the finite and the infinite.[23] In this affair the decisive event always comes late on. The soul is fortunate if it is fortunate late on; being fortunate late on means learning to love the right thing properly, just in time. At the center of genuinely historical events thus understood stands the precarious rescuing of souls from their self-inflicted externality. In Augustine, the affair aspect of the relationship between the soul and God is marked by the reference to *learning of* him.[24] This, as shown above, refers to a knowledge that cannot be entirely posterior. If the soul gets to know God again, this is a coincidence with nothing coincidental about it; its progress uncovers the a priori interconnection between the two. The gathering of knowledge – which initially means Augustine's conversion and study of the Bible – necessarily deepens the insight into an original self-knowledge that extends back to a time before the affair, that is, before the estrangement and its reversal. In his interpretation of this primordial acquaintance, Augustine lays his catholic cards on the table: if the soul returns to its outermost limit, it does not achieve its complete self-negation in substance, as demanded in metaphysical transcendence; rather it climbs only up to that mysterious place where, despite being held in the most intimate containedness, it began to set itself apart from God, in non-violent difference. I am referring to the moment of creation and the breath of life that turned the clay creature into a human. Augustine always treated the soft primordial differentiation of the soul from God's totality with the greatest discretion, never allowing himself to be seduced into statements that would have inevitably put him in an awkward position. He gave a wide berth to the mystery of the soul's pregnancy in God, and he barely ever spoke affirmatively of a *unio*. The only certainty for him was that the soul's differentiation from God was a process of creation in which identity and difference both receive their due; the biblical catchword for this balance is the image of God. In both "orthodox" and "catholic" manner, Augustine clings to the doctrine of the soul's creatureliness. For him there is no longer any question of sharing that Neoplatonic and Gnostic exuberance that seeks to give the spirit soul the same age and value as God. In relation to the epitome of the spirit that is God, the individual soul is indisputably its junior, to put it in Christian language, though its juniority does not impair the intimate bond of kinship; even as created and younger, the soul is still spirit from spirit. Before the start of the alienating affair – that is, before the egotistical revolt and its miserogenic trace of violence – there is no sufficient a priori reason why the younger should have become estranged from the older. In his interpretations of Genesis, Augustine therefore places great value on the successful primary coexistence in paradise – for it is meant to prove that the creation of humans is something that was not doomed to failure from the start. After all, without the honeymoon of the morning of creation, the exclusion of the individual soul from God would itself have been a disaster of the creator's own making, and the creation itself would have proven an inescapable trap for the soul. That would compromise the creator, however, and a savior could come into play only as the non-identical one; only he, the completely other, would know what the soul requires for its salvation. Orthodoxy must turn away in horror from such Gnosticizing atrocities. If all is to be well in a catholic sense, one must insist on a joyful primordial acquaintance between the created soul and its creator. Only then does the fatal affair explain the rest – Adam's wanton fall into hubris, along with his era, also known as world history (which is balanced out by countertime, namely salvation-historical time). If this primitive acquaintance is renewed, the soul can sink back to its place beyond all physical places, in the certainty that the great other inheres in it more deeply than it does itself: *interior intimo meo*.[25]

*

One can see that, in the theo-psychology and theo-eroticism from the time of the Latin fathers, an analytics of being in was formulated that showed no lack of complexity or explicitness. If there was a way to develop the Augustinian logic of intimacy further, that would be only by radicalizing its already fully crystallized structures. This concerns especially that hot spot[26] in the Augustinian field of intimacy, the relation between God and the soul – which is a latent but real relation of primordial acquaintanceship. It is easy to understand why the interpretation of this relation held a latent heterodox potential, and equally why this had to be released, once genuinely mystical temperaments undertook attempts to radicalize the God–soul relation to the point of pre-relative unions. This ascetic–theoretical spectacle unfolded – usually in discreet forms – behind the dense curtain of Christian metaphysics, of which Martin Buber (among others) showed at the start of the twentieth century that it is mirrored in the mystical testimonies of the other monotheistic traditions, as well as in the ecstatic disciplines of world cultures.[27] Only occasionally, especially at the trials of heretics, was this curtain lifted, to give the audience a glimpse of battles in the non-sensory realm. In mystical literature, the analytics of "being in" developed into an exercise in biunity that brought forth virtuosos of its own. It was under mystical–theological patronage that thinking through reciprocal interconnections first grew into that highly explicit form that still lends such documents an enthralling nimbus of relevance today, even if one cannot say to what they are relevant. If countless modern readers found the body of mystical literature not just vaguely fascinating, but really meaningful, it was probably because, in its dark clarity, the mystical text emits a conceptual and visual potential for which no comparable substitute has been found so far: I mean a theory of that strong relationship that can be understood only as bi- or co-subjectivity – in my terminology, a microspheric dual or elliptical bubble.

That the connection to the congenial [*das Gleichartiges*] is not something produced afterwards or by the side, between monadic substances or lonely individuals, but for some beings is the very mode of being – this is a thought that especially the minds conditioned by philosophy could not initially understand. It had to be worked out from the forbidding material of fundamental concepts in Greek and old European thought, through a laborious and hazardous exercise. If it were still possible to invoke a cunning of reason in intellectual history, one could say that it was at work when the aim was to assert, with the aid of mystical and Trinitarian theologies, the idea of a strong relationship against the prevailing grammar of the western culture of rationality – and hence against the fixation on substances and essences that had driven the European process of reasoning since the ancient Greeks. Even today, despite dialectical, functionalist, cybernetic, and media philosophy revolutions in our way of thinking, the case of the strong relationship has by no means been won; in the human sciences as they are now, the idea of constitutive resonance is still as much in need of explanation as the affair between God and the soul in mystical theology.

It is precisely in modernity, not least where it seeks to be profound or radical, that the dogma of a primary human loneliness is propagated more triumphantly than ever. It is no mere coincidence that what one calls a relationship in today's parlance is something that takes place between individuals who have met by chance and who, while still frequenting each other, are already practicing how to do without each other some day. The mystical task, on the other hand, was to understand the relationship not as posterior and fortuitous, but rather as fundamental and immemorial. If religious mysticism had had an anthropological mandate, the latter would have been to explain in general terms why individuals are not primarily defined by inaccessibility to others. If mysticism were to speak in a moral voice, its demand would be: warm up your individual life past its melting point – and do what you wish. If the soul thaws, who could doubt its inclination and aptitude to celebrate and work with others?

To grasp the meaning of this insight, it will be advantageous for the free spirit to free itself from the anti-Christian affect of recent centuries as if from a tenseness that is no longer necessary. Anyone seeking to reconstruct basic communion and community experiences needs to be free of anti-religious reflexes. Did early Christianity not find its strength precisely in basic collective experiences? Their self-interpretation urged a new theory of the spirit, one that would articulate why humans are able to be together in animated communes. The principle of a power of association that creates solidarity [*solidarisierenden Vereinigungsmacht*] is given classical formulation in Paul's doctrine of the spirit, especially in his statement that God's love is poured out into our hearts through the Holy Spirit, which is given to us (Romans 5:5). Admittedly, it primarily concerns the access of souls to their own kind; there is a long way from the pneumatic enthusiasm of early Christian communal experiences to the pretension of some medieval mystics to break through the barrier between God and the individual soul entirely.

As far as the mystical dual in the stricter sense is concerned, there is an immeasurable body of literature in which, with a wealth of impoverished words, the soul's intimate advances to God are developed to the point of a complete dissolution of boundaries and unification. If one encounters almost without exception, in the language of linguistic criticism, stereotypes and variations in this field, it is because in the Christian and old European space – as in the Islamic – the final stages of the affair between God and the soul are under Neoplatonic monopoly, however occult the connection to this source might be. Whatever documents one opens, among the most diverse authors' names and the most colorful classifications of direction and origin, there is a single model that succeeds in reaching the mystical finale; the Neoplatonic mode of reading becomes inevitable, even where authors miss their own dependence on the Plotinic model and readers are deceived through the anonymity of the source. The thoughts expressed in countless documents, by innumerable authors, in a tone of passionate declaration endlessly reproduce the same sequence of primordial scenes and final scenes that the soul must go through on its way back into the One. Looking at the mystical movements of medieval Europe, one has to note that the most arousing among our own thoughts are foreign thoughts that use our heads. So, even if medieval theology faculties had the true doctrine firmly under their control, the most talented still studied – it is hard to say how – at a Plotinic tele-academy[28] that, under Christian pseudonyms, disseminated late Greek knowledge about salvation and the ascent of the soul.

As one witness among countless others, I shall quote a passage from *The Mirror of Simple Souls*, a work written shortly before 1285 and condemned as heretical. Its author, the Beguine Marguerite Porete, was born around 1255 near the northern French town of Valenciennes and burnt at the stake as a heretic on June 1, 1310, in the Place de Grève in Paris. In a markedly anti-ecclesiastical tone, her book shows the search for an unmediated consummation of the biune conjunction of the soul and God.

> This Soul, says Love, has six wings like the Seraphim. She no longer wants anything which comes by a mediary. This is the proper being of the Seraphim: there is no mediary between their love and the divine Love. They always possess newness without a mediary, and so also for this soul: for it does not seek divine knowledge among the masters of this age, but in truly despising the world and herself. Great God, how great a difference there is between a gift from a lover to a beloved through a mediary and a gift that is between the lovers without a mediary![29]

It is clear that the rejection of an intermediary between the communion partners must ultimately eliminate any third entity. Thus the gift can neither have a bearer nor remain a material offering; it is absorbed into the self-gift of the giver. Marguerite Porete speaks at length about the need for the soul on the way to simplicity to annihilate itself to the point where its particularity no longer obstructs the gift of the divine self-giver. Her aim is that, through this great change of subject, the will of God will will for her and through her in the future:

> And thus the Soul removes herself from this will, and the will is separated from the Soul and dissolves itself, and [the will] gives and renders itself to God, whence it was first taken, without retaining anything of its own in order to fulfill the perfect Divine Will, which cannot be fulfilled in the Soul without such a gift, so that the Soul might not have warfare of deficiency. [...] Now she is All, and so she is Nothing, for her Beloved makes her One.[30]

It is conspicuous how the theo-erotic, bipolar figures of resonance
in Marguerite's text are increasingly surpassed by the metaphysical
urge to become one. This urge is so powerful in the self-willed
Beguine that it wastes little time with the usual degrees and steps of
ascent; Marguerite Porete has no interest in the drawn-out stages of
the itineraries, where the soul's path to God is detailed in a whole-
somely roundabout form. She is, in a sense, already at her goal from
the start, and if the mystical exercise could normally be carried out
correctly only as patient elaboration of an impatient haste, speed
itself becomes an agent of illumination in the case of this illuminated author. The impossible task has scarcely been uttered before
its completion is announced. What unleashes mystical individualism
is the end of the speed limit for self-enjoyment in God; thus the dual
structure of the affair between God and the soul is also infringed
upon, and subsequently bypassed. If it became the standard,
the Neoplatonic ambition to exit twoness entirely in order to be
subsumed under the One would ultimately suffocate the love play
of the interwoven partners, were it not for the fact that the mystic's
unfettered verbal élan ensures, through an antagonistic effect, that
the affair still continues expressively and loquaciously, even at the
apex of its completion. At the climax of the relationship, the soul
declares its peculiar unrelatedness; it now claims to have ascended
to a space of immanence that precedes all difference:

> *All things are one for her*, without a why, and she is nothing in
> a One of this sort. *Thus the Soul has nothing more to do for God*
> than God does for her. Why? *Because He is, and she is not.* She
> retains nothing more of herself in nothingness, because He is
> sufficient of Himself, that is, *because He is and she is not.* Thus
> she is stripped of all things because she is without existence,
> where she was before she was. She has from God what He
> has, and she is what God is through the transformation of
> love, in that point in which she was before she flowed from the
> Goodness of God.[31]

Like countless related documents, Marguerite Porete's resolutely
Neoplatonic account demonstrates the high price of conquering the
language of unconditional love or the primordial relationship. The
soul's absolute belonging to God, and that of both to each other,
could only be stated at a price, namely if the soul's pole of relation
made room, through self-annihilation, for the great other to enter
it. With this, the very thing that was meant to make the relationship
a radical one destroys it. Where there were two, one of them must
now leave; where there was a soul, God is to become everything.

The idea of mutual inhabitation, of which Augustine was able to speak in a rich instrumentation, sinks into the background when confronted with the overheated Neoplatonic model of union. In exchange for this loss of reciprocity, an opportunity is given to push back the intimacy between God and the soul to pre-creation areas. Consequently, at least on the semantic surface of mystical confession, the pull toward the subject's self-sacrifice in favor of substance inevitably becomes dominant. What was supposed to be a mystical wedding seemingly becomes the subject's self-burial in substance. But are our ears deceiving us? Does the ear-pricking opening of a great speech on the strong relationship end with this pitifully paradoxical revocation: "In God I am nothing, and God can have no relationship with nothing"? Indeed, when it comes to the wording alone, the schema of transcendence defrauds the concern for resonance, stealing the word from the tip of the tongue – just as well-rehearsed language routines lend false tongues to the unsaid as it wells up. Under the dominance of the metaphysical code, the new words for the strong relationship sprout only hesitantly, like some foreign language unheard of. What must be expressed semantically using the figure of self-annihilation, however – the radical participation in the great other and the stimulated interweaving with its being – permits the most impetuous self-release of the new speech event in the poetics of the mystical text and its performative unfolding: uttering formulae of abdication, Porete progresses to a state of the most penetrating intensity. She turns herself into a privileged resonant body of her radiant other. Naturally God is the One in all everywhere, but here he irrupts into an individual voice, formulating himself through its vibrations. At least that is what this voice is presently claiming. Who could distinguish between the voices now? Who is something, who is nothing?

The reader of the mystical text can say this much: instead of reaching the inside of God through a silent withdrawal, the de-selfed subject plunges into the most daring of performances, as if the unutterable one somehow needed to be uttered through it, assisted by the martial law of movedness. We know of Marguerite Porete that she sometimes traveled through the country like a show woman, reciting from her *Mirror of Simple Souls* in front of highly diverse audiences. The Neoplatonic diva managed to prove to her contemporaries that the enjoyment of God – which was simultaneously the first legitimized form of self-enjoyment – can liberate itself from church walls and churchmen; Marguerite Porete is one of the mystical mothers of liberality. Would this make mysticism be the matrix for performance art? Would performance be, then, the impulse that releases the subject? Would the subject be the manifest

side of biune emotion? Would emotion be an emergence from the
shared? And God, through woman, an expressionist?

*

Suggestions of this kind can be relativized and inspected through
a side glance at an example from the mystical theology of medieval
Iran. Even in the dogmatic environment of Islam, Neoplatonic
impulses had manifold offshoots, both orthodox and subversive,
and brought forth a rich world of forms of biune mystical asceti-
cisms and language games. In this context, too, one question
became especially pressing for the mystical protagonists: how can
the word of God be staged in a presentist fashion? And here also,
the executioner pushed his way into the foreground as the most
important critic of the theater of God. Among the most impressive
actors in the Islamic theodrama is the poet-theologian Shahab
al-Din Yahya Suhrawardi, also known as Suhrawardi Maqtul,
"the Murdered," born in 1155 in the northwest Iranian province
of Zanjan. At the instigation of Orthodox legal scholars, who
accused him of questioning the privileged prophetological status of
Mohammed, he was executed on Saladin's orders on July 29, 1191 in
Aleppo. In the Iranian tradition, the memory of Suhrawardi, whose
followers also call him Sohrevardi Shahid, "the Martyr," is preserved
under the description *shaikh al-ishraq*, which is conventionally
translated "master of illumination"; as Henry Corbin has shown,
however, a more accurate description of the "philosophy of illumination" would be the "doctrine of the rising of light in the East."
In Suhrawardi's teachings one finds a confluence of principles from
Koranic theology and Neoplatonic arguments, as well as traces of
the ancient Persian theosophy of light. I shall cite the ninth chapter
from "The Language of the Ants" ["Lughat-i-Muran"], a twelve-
part sequence of short symbolic tales:

All the stars and constellations spoke to Idris[32] – peace be
upon him. He asked the moon: "Why does your light decrease
sometimes and increase at others?" She replied: "Know you!
that my body is black, but polished and clear and I have no
light. But when I am opposite to the sun, in proportion to the
opposition an amount of his light appears in the mirror of my
body; as the figures of the other bodies appear in the mirror.
When I come to the utmost encountering I progress from the
nadir of the new moon to the zenith of the full moon." Idris
inquired of her: "How much is his friendship with you?" She
replied: "To such an extent that whenever I look at myself at

the time of encountering I see the sun, because the image of the sunlight is manifest in me, since all the smoothness of my surface and the polish of my face is fixed for accepting his light. So every time when I look at myself, I see the sun. Do you not see that if a mirror is placed before the sun, the figure of the sun appears in it? If by Divine decree the mirror had eyes and looked at itself when it is before the sun, it would not have seen but the sun, in spite of its being iron. It would have said 'I am the sun,' because it would not have seen in itself anything except the sun. If it says 'I am the Truth' or 'Glory be to me! How great is my glory' its excuse must be accepted; even the blasphemy 'wherefrom I came near, verily, you are me.'"[33]

Using conventional poetic images, Suhrawardi's didactic tale presents the well-known thought patterns of Neoplatonic speculation on biunity, muted in typical Islamic fashion by references to the unequivocal distance between God and all other beings. This tendency toward subordination comes to light clearly enough in the images of the sun and the moon, in what initially looks like irreversible gradations; not without reason is Islam – in keeping with its name – a religion of subjugation in ancient ontological style. In its exuberance, however, the moon is subversively granted the license to think itself to be the sun, as long as it simply respects the original relationship that gives the first light primacy over its reflections. Thus the second element is not only connected to the first by participation in reflection; it also has an original right to exuberant communication with the origin itself. Through its pictorial character, Arab mystical poetry seems more deeply infused with the dual erotic understanding of resonance than any other – the only work in the Judeo-Christian tradition that is comparable to Arab theo-poetics in this respect would be the Song of Songs; but this poetic speech is also controlled by the unrelenting monarchy of substance, which is overdetermined by the monarchy of Allah. Islamic theology is constrained even more strictly than Christian theology to reject the soul's pretensions to being of equal worth with the Highest; nevertheless, by pushing the one God and the one substance further away in subservient superelevations, the Islamic language of devotion stirs the theo-erotic embers. Blissful yearning takes care of the rest; and, last of all, the inflamed souls, desiring light, know how to go about forcing their dissolution in the fiery substance. What the moon cannot do through its discrete position in relation to the sun, the butterfly will achieve in the flame. The death-seeking moth represents the spirit of exaggeration that brings literature and emergency close together. Suhrawardi's flight around the fire becomes audible in the two quotations from the sayings of the Sufi martyr al-Hallaj (858–922), who is said to have beaten the "drum of unity." With the notorious proclamation *ana'l-haqq* – "I am the truth" – and the final statement of our parable, Suhrawardi adopts two of the most successful and incendiary theo-erotic phrases. In his doctrine of angels – which I shall not examine here – Suhrawardi found a way to bring the relationship between the soul and God into equilibrium, in an intermediate region: human souls are not simply in immediate proximity to God, even if they strive back to their origin in his direction; they possessed preexistence in the angelic world; they split, for whatever reasons, into two parts, of which one remains close to God on high while the other descends into the "fortress of the body."[34] The worldly part, unhappy with its lot, searches for its other half and must seek to unite with it again to regain completeness. With these mythical figures, which transfer Plato's tale of the first humans to the angelic sphere, Suhrawardi cancels the fatal suction of substance monism, making space for images that are suitable for the never-ending task of developing the original supplement by creating permanently new forms and symbols. The sublime idea of *henōsis* or *unio* [unification, union, making one] may have established and spread the philosophical prestige of mystical Neoplatonism; but its angelology is far more fruitful from a psychological point of view, because, without making concessions to the ambiguous unionistic references to annihilation, it formulated in images, if not in words, the original – creative and forward-looking – supplementability of the soul. It testifies to the power of productive separateness to elicit signs, a power that manifests itself as a primordial duality. Its traces show up not only in the Islamic but also in the Christian hemisphere. Angelology is one of the historically indispensable means of access to the theory of mediatic things.[35] Media theory, for its part, opens up perspectives on an anthropology beyond individualistic semblance.

As far as mystical theology in the Latin West is concerned, it reached its culmination in the work of Nicholas of Cusa (1401–64). In his work we find penetrating analyses along the question of how to envisage the being in of finite intelligences in the infinite intelligence of God – a turn in which one justifiably sees a didactic transformation of the question of the soul's relationship with God. We are essentially prepared, broadly at least, for any adequate elucidation of this relationship through the Platonizing discourse, animated by Augustine, of awareness of God within those who recognize him and of the sublation of the knower in the known; nonetheless, Nicholas of Cusa enriched this basic outline with nuances that can be seen as explicit gains for the theory of the strong relationship. It is especially in his 1453 treatise *On the Vision of God* (*De visione Dei*) that Nicholas adds a number of unforgettable pictorial and argumentative features to the known repertoire of statements about the intertwinement of God and the soul. This applies not least to the splendid analogy with painting that opens the treatise. Nicholas brings up recent cases from portraiture that give the observer the feeling that, wherever she might place herself in the room, they watch her in a very particular way. If one can believe the text, the author enclosed one such painting as an object of devotional exercise when he sent his dissertation to the monks at the Abbey of Tegernsee in Bavaria.

I am sending, to your charity, a painting that I was able to acquire containing an all-seeing image, which I call an icon of God.

Hang this up some place, perhaps on a north wall. And you brothers stand around it, equally distant from it, and gaze at it. And each of you will experience that from whatever place one observes it the face will seem to regard him alone. [...] Next, let the brother who was in the east place himself in the west, and he will experience the gaze as fastened on him there just as it was before in the east. Since he knows that the icon is fixed and unchanged, he will marvel at the changing [*mutatio*] of its unchangeable gaze. [...] He will marvel at how its gaze was moved, although it remains motionless [*immobilius movebatur*], and his imagination will not be able to grasp how it is moved in the same manner with someone coming forth to meet him from the opposite direction. [...] He will experience that the immobile face is moved toward the east in such a way that it is also moved simultaneously toward the west, that it is moved toward the north in such a way that it is also moved to the south, that it is moved toward a single place in such a way that it is also moved simultaneously toward all places, and that it beholds a single movement in such a way that it beholds all movements simultaneously.

And while the brother observes how this gaze deserts no one, he will see that it takes diligent care of each, just as if it cared only for the one on whom its gaze seems to rest and for no other, and to such an extent that the one whom it regards cannot conceive that it should care for another [*quod curam alterius agat*]. He will also see that it has the same very diligent concern for the smallest creature [*minimae creaturae*] as for the greatest [*quasi maximae*], and for the whole universe.[36]

What is notable about the analogy is that it transports us to an interfacial or, more precisely, an interocular scene. One can admire the artful daring with which Nicholas bridges the chasm between universalist and individualist theological motifs. How could a cursory and unspecific God for all be at the same time an intimate God for each and every person? Only a logically and existentially convincing answer to this question could provide the theological foundation for a religion that inspires both imperiality and intimacy. The painted portrait, with its living, wandering eyes, gives an excellent representation of a God who, even as he oversees all humanity, in pantocratic manner, nevertheless turns only to one person at a time. Here we see a God of intensity, whose outpouring of power is as present at its minimum as it is at its maximum. God cannot love the whole of mankind any more than a single human being (just as, according to a similarly constructed proposition by Wittgenstein, the whole earth cannot be in greater distress than *one* soul).[37] The reference to the presence of the maximum in the minimum gives a sharper logical profile to the familiar idea that God distinguishes the individual soul through "being in" inside it. Certainly the metaphor of the portrait with static yet wandering eyes cannot be developed beyond the external encounter between the subject and its circumspect observer. As it presents an external object, the picture on the wall remains at an unbridgeable distance from the believer. Nicholas is concerned only with placing God's eye into the individual, in a twofold sense: as my internalized, constant being monitored by the great other; and as the fluctuating inner guard of my own intelligence. The eye of God, equipped with absolute vision, is implanted in my own eye – in such a way, admittedly, that I am not blinded by its all-seeing nature but can continue to see from my local and corporeal perspectives in the way I am able. Nicholas draws the doctrine of the portrait metaphor – the constant following of my movements by the eyes on the wall – into the soul itself: it must now envisage itself locked inside the field of view, with an absolute eyesight that calls everything into existence through its gaze, constantly encompassing and seeing through the objects of that gaze. He thus creates a wonderful plausibility for the idea that, even in my inner life, I am intended and contained in the calmly following gaze of a total intelligence. In my thoughts and feelings I may wander from east to west any way I please: the eyes of the great other within me still follow me into every position of my thinking life and emotional life. In seeing, I am always seen – to such a degree that I can believe myself destined to exhaust God's entire eyesight on myself. This calling gives me a direct sense of the reason for my similarity to God, for

I am factually gifted (or, in medieval terms, enfeoffed) with eyesight of my own and see an open world around me; thus I imitate God's worldview or world espial in absolute world immanence. From a psychological perspective, the maximum-in-minimum idea sets me apart as the only child of the absolute. Nicholas of Cusa is level-headed enough to emphasize that every single case, especially my own, is like that of an only child – for the God of intensity, who lacks nothing in the smallest, is with himself equally elsewhere and everywhere, in my neighbor as much as in the universe. His being in me does not restrict him to my perspective, because his intensity, capable of infinite expansion as it must by its nature be, cannot be diminished even by not being in me. Nonetheless, I have a valid entitlement to my own world-opening view, as if it were the only one – assuming that I bear in mind that eyesight is not private property, but that my seeing is something like a branch office of God's actually infinite vision; to continue the metaphor, the view of a preferred only child of heaven. Nicholas finds a precise term for this branch connection that pinpoints the contraction of universal eyesight into my own: *contractio*. If I have functioning eyes and see a world, it is only through the contraction of sight itself to my seeing.[38]

Every contraction of sight exists in the absolute, because absolute sight is the *contraction of contractions* [*contractio contractionum*]. [...] The most simple contraction, therefore, coincides with the absolute. Indeed, without contraction nothing is contracted. Thus, absolute vision exists in all sight because every contracted vision exists through absolute vision and is utterly unable to exist without it.[39]

God, then, the actual infinite viewer or the maximum view, contracts himself into me, a minimum; now he is – and, in this specific sense, acts – *in me*. God's indwelling me should therefore not be imagined like Saint Jerome's indwelling his study or the genie indwelling the bottle; its logic resembles that of a handing over of office or inves-titure, whereby official authority is transferred from the master to the incumbent – albeit with the nuance that the latter is at the same time the creation of the former. The nub of this enfeoffment is that my being me itself takes on official character and my subjectivity is conceived of and approved of as a post in God's household. Thus God's unextended extension determines the sense of immanence or being in in every respect. My containedness in God's magnitude can be compared to a point on an all-encompassing ball whereby the point mirrors and contains the ball in its own way.

Thus God acts as a lender of eyesight to humans – or, more
generally, as a lender of subjectivity. Here the word "lend" can be
understood in both its feudal and its financial capitalist sense, for
both fief and credit are authentic modes of giving being or awarding
strength – self-contraction, in Cusan terms – which reminds us of
the precondition that no one is eligible for being the feudal lord
or the lender – save the actual infinite itself. These circumstances
provide the last reason for the basic figure of modernity, which is the
replacement of the all-causing God by all-sweeping capital. Cusa's
reflections show how the most inspiring minds of the early modern
age were opening up to the adventurous and serious idea that the
subject, by becoming involved through knowledge and action,
works with the credit of the absolute. This is where the change of
meaning from guilt to debt begins.[40] We are touching here on the
formative process of the recent history of European mentality: the
birth of entrepreneurial subjectivity from the spirit of the mystical
duty to repay.[41]

That Nicholas of Cusa articulates being in not only as an
optician (a theo-optician, to be precise), but also as an eroticist (a
theo-eroticist, to be precise) is proved by the further course of his
tract on *visio dei* [God's sight], which – like some later addition
to the *Confessions* – displays Augustine's spirit and approach on
every page. While metaphysical optics speaks of contracted vision,
theological eroticism speaks of contracted loves. If I am a branch
eye of God's in contracted vision, then I am a relay of divine love
in contracted loves.[42] Divine love also contracts into a beam that
penetrates me, pours over me and privileges me, as if it were a
fountain that expresses itself in each individual jet as intensely as in
its entire overflowing. In powerful formulations, Nicholas of Cusa
expands on the thought that I see because the absolute vision sees in
me and through me, up to the idea that I exist and have enjoyment
as a loving being because I am held into the world as a vessel and
outlet for divine attentions and emanations.

> And what, Lord, is my life, except that embrace in which the
> sweetness of your love so lovingly holds me! [...] Your seeing
> is nothing other than your bringing to life, nothing other than
> your continuously imparting your sweetest love. And through
> this imparting of love, your seeing inflames me to the love of
> you, and through inflaming feeds me, and through feeding
> kindles my desires, and through kindling gives me to drink
> the dew of gladness, and through drinking infuses a fountain
> of life within me, and by infusing causes to increase and to
> endure.[43]

This passage can be read as a poem that argues in the spirit of the strong relationship; using images of a liquid communion, it articulates the existential situation of participation in a circulation of superfluity. It is a piece of sanguine literature in the literal sense of the world – formulated from intuition into the reality of the blood, which provides the first communion. Being in amounts now to allowing oneself to be embraced, flowed through, nourished and cheered by the divine medium of blood; and gratefully considering this embrace, flowing-through, and cheering as a primordial scene and singing its praises. One could, by way of transposition, say that "consciousness in" includes perceiving that I am surrounded, carried, and reached through by a force that anticipates me and flows toward me in every sense. This understanding of being in remains integrated into a basic attitude, which is religious and feudal as long as the subject aligns itself with this anticipation and this interwovenness without deviating into outraged or claustrophobic reactions. The Satanism of disgust and its small change[44] – unease – would thwart an understanding of the matter itself. In truth, the subject finds herself in a position of revolt if she ceases to view herself as a mere vassal of being; whoever invokes capital of his own and refuses to define his actions as work with the credit of the absolute becomes a rebel. But, from a Catholic perspective, have not humans always striven toward a certain independent power and felt irked by the unreasonable demand of having to be grateful for everything? Was the modern age not founded on the axiom that those who begin with themselves have shaken off the burden of compulsory gratitude once and for all? How would one even envisage a non-rebellious anthropology under the banner of monotheism, when the race of Adam exists on the whole – *toto genere* – under the sign of Satan and has a part in his initial ingratitude? Has not the human being, from a Christian perspective, always been the creature that wants to reserve a part for itself? Can there be such a thing as a human being in non-revolt?

The answer to this, insofar as it is affirmative, articulates itself in the Christianized idea of service, which states that reintegration into the One converges with the ability to serve. In examining the question of how the independent power of humans can be placed *in* and under the power of God, Nicholas arrived at a mystical politics or a doctrine of interwoven power. It gives being in or unconditional immanence the meaning of empowerment to isolated moments of power through the actual infinite power itself. In the first book of the dialogue *De ludo globi* [*The Game of Spheres*] (1462), the learned cardinal converses with John, duke of Bavaria, in formulations of surreal clarity, about a game invented by Nicholas in which the aim is to position a non-circular ball at the center of a target drawn on the floor. Here comes the passage on the general kingship of the human being.

> THE CARDINAL: *By all means man* is the small world in such a way that he also is part of the large world. [...]

> JOHN: If I grasp you correctly, then it follows that the universe is one great kingdom and so also man is a kingdom, but a small one within *a great kingdom* as the kingdom of Bohemia is a small kingdom within the great kingdom of the Romans, or the universal empire.

> THE CARDINAL: Excellent. A *man* is a kingdom similar to the kingdom of the universe, established in part of that universe. As long as the *embryo* is in the mother's *womb* it is not yet its own kingdom, but when the intellectual soul, which is put in the *embryo* in the process of creation, is created, the embryo becomes a kingdom, having its own king, and is called a man. *But when the soul departs*, the man and the kingdom cease to be. However, as the body was part of the universal kingdom of the large world before the advent of the soul, so also, it returns to it. Just as Bohemia was part of the Empire before it had its own king, so also it will remain if its own king is taken away. Therefore man is directly subject to his own king who rules in him, then he is subject to the kingdom of the world in an indirect way. But, when he has not yet a king or when he ceases to be, he is directly subject to the kingdom of the world. This is why nature or the world soul exercises vegetative power in the embryo as in other things having vegetative life. And this exercise of the vegetative power actually continues in certain dead men in whom the hair and nails continue to grow.[45]

So the world of power, as an exercise of abilities to rule as well as to produce, is constituted through interweaving or contraction. Any human gifted with a mind is king through the contraction of the emperor (God) into an individual dominion. As a human being among others, each individual is self-governing under the emperor, having power in her own small world through the relationship of enfeoffment or credit with the highest bestower of power. In the mode of contraction, the imperial (divine) maximum is present in the kingly (human) minimum. If the minimum is already a kingdom, however, each individual, as the ruler of the kingdom, can be socialized only in a group of royal colleagues – or in a gathering of self-governing free classes. This is the prototype of a *democrazia christiana*. With shimmering arguments, the papist cardinal paves the way for the egalitarianism of the citizen-kings; it would barely take a century for civil individuals and laypersons to understand how one can claim one's earthly sovereignty as a kingly minimum under the divine maximum. From Nicholas of Cusa to Rousseau, one can follow the progress of that way of thinking, which sees competent service and active subservience, in any given context, as the factors that enable people to be lords and legislators in their respective domains. Cusa was the first to give the thought its precise form; Ignatius of Loyola had the ingenuity to implant it in monastic politics and propagate it psychotechnically: service is the royal road to power; active subservience and independent power are one and the same; if you want to rule, you must serve. Serving means developing under a lord as energetically as if there were no lord. This is the first philosophy of the subject. The modern age and the late Middle Ages join their hands over the idea that all forms of exercising power constitute vassalage in a homogeneously divine empire that is equally intense in all its parts; thus every subject that reaches around itself in its area of the world is allowed to develop as a minimal power *sui generis*, in immediate proximity to empire and God. Each minimum is a minister, and each competent subjectivity is a civil servant of the absolute. This opens up the path on which businessmen, public servants, petits bourgeois, and artists will be able – as only clerics and nobles were before them – to view themselves as functionaries of God; it is a path that will lead to the Reformation, democratism, and entrepreneurial freedom. In democracy, admittedly, individuals will no longer claim their right and duty to power as servants of God but as owners of human rights: now humans envisage themselves as the animal entitled by nature to stake claims. The people of the modern age can formulate the principle of human rights explicitly only after withdrawing from the world of God and moving to the realm of nature – where, according to the Cusan, humans are subordinate solely as embryos and corpses. Incidentally, one can see very clearly, in this argument, where the paths of the modern age will separate from those of the Middle Ages: while modern people – provided they think broadly enough – view especially the embryo's or the fetus's stay in the womb as part of the archaic matrix of animation, Nicholas teaches that the child has only a vegetative status there and does not yet belong to the realm of spirit souls. That would make the embryo's being in the mother a passive prelude to life animated by spirit – and only after the allocation of spirit, in other words after baptism, would the individual be socialized not only in nature, but also in the kingdom of God. *Mutatis mutandis*, Hegel essentially still taught the same.

*

In moving from the microspheric to the macrospheric interpretation of the meaning of being in, a few remarks – however cursory – on *Trinitarian theology* are indispensable. For this discipline, in its logical structure and extension of meaning, belongs to both dimensions: to microspherology, insofar as it articulates a three-part intimate relation – Father, Son, Holy Spirit – and to macrospherology, insofar as it identifies the "persons" of this triad as actors in a world-crossing and world-pervading theodrama. Thus Trinitarian discourses cover both the smallest bubble and the largest orb, the densest and the widest inner space. I will give an inkling of why, from the start, Trinitarian theology could advance only as a theory of the strong relationship and, *eo ipso*, as the doctrine of a living orb.

At an early stage in this problem process, the Greek fathers, especially from the Cappadocians onwards, invented a new form of meditation on surreal interpersonality. Their purpose was initially to reformulate the statements in the New Testament, especially those by John, about the singular relationship between Jesus and God in the spirit of Greek onto-theology. This task amounted to squaring the circle, or rather circling the ellipse; for basic Greek terminology was not ready to express equal communions of multiplicities [*Mehreren*] in the one substance. At this point, however, early Christianity, which had begun to consolidate itself theologically and in its political mission, could not withdraw even one step: When John wrote "anyone who has seen me has seen the Father" (14:9), "believe me when I say that I am in the Father and the Father is in me" (14:11), or "the Holy Spirit, whom the Father will send in my name, will teach you all things" (14:26), this was the announcement of a program that grew into a thought task both inevitable and explosive for Greek theologians and their heirs. It involved the unreasonable imperative to think up, at the level of the One, strong relationships between three. That this could somehow succeed without a relapse into tritheism may have seemed plausible to the conventional and simple minds of late antiquity, if one assured them often enough, and with authority, that one was three and three was one. The theologians, however, who stepped into the arena of theory, standing face to face with advanced pagan philosophers to defend the intellectual honor of their religion, realized that an abyss had opened up for orthodoxy, one that threatened to swallow the entire conception of right and wrong. One of the most powerful discursive vortexes of old European culture formed at the interface between ancient Greek and New Testament language games. Its rotation began when the biblical talk of relationships made the Greek ontology of essences dance. Here, strangely enough, the learned patriarchs of the Byzantine world acted as the dance teachers; it was they who taught the static One the steps by which it learned to differentiate itself into eternal triplets. This revolution in rhythms took no less than a millennium to develop into a mature, lucid concept; it extends from the Cappadocian theologians to Thomas Aquinas, in whose doctrine of "subsistent relations" the inconceivable finally seemed to have become conceivable after all. Through carefully considered risks, Trinitarian speculation felt its way forward, into the field of relational logic, as if its mission had been to unmask a God who, philosophically, could be imagined only as a light reactor and as a smooth-stone eternity, to reveal him as a bottomless well of friendliness, and to imitate him as the true icon of a loving relationship. In this sense, Adolf von Harnack was not entirely right with his sharp-edged hypothesis that older Christian theology amounted to a gradual Hellenization of the Gospel. It was at the same time – and not just by accident – a Jewish-inspired intersubjectification of Hellenism.

*

How the many can exist undivided in one: this basic question in the theory of life spheres initially occupied the early theologians less in its numerical and quantitative dimension than from the angle of the spatial disposition of the three in one. Here theology came under pressure from itself to explain itself topologically. This first access to the intra-godly sphere initially displayed unmistakable under-tones of a philosophy of nature, even if it had been transferred to the intertwined dwelling of spiritual entities a long time ago. This can be observed particularly clearly in the famous lamp analogy from the treatise *On Divine Names*, by the late fifth-century Syrian monk-philosopher known as Pseudo-Dionysius the Areopagite. His explanations are instructive in that they show the starting point of the later development; for they still interpret the possibility of the three divine persons being together entirely within the framework of the Neoplatonic debate on how the many can be anchored and integrated in the one. Neoplatonism already knew a pathos of the differing of the different within the One, a pathos from which later references to the "mutual validation of the person-principles of the Trinity" would still profit.

In a house the light from all the lamps is completely interpene-
trating, yet each is clearly distinct. There is distinction in unity
and there is unity in distinction. When there are many lamps
in a house there is nevertheless a single undifferentiated light
and from all of them comes the one undivided brightness. I do
not think that anyone would mark off the light of one lamp
from another in the atmosphere which contains them all, nor
could one light be seen separately from the others since all of
them are completely mingled while being at the same time quite
distinctive. Indeed if somebody were to carry one of the lamps
out of the house its own particular light would leave without
diminishing the light of the other lamps or supplementing their
brightness. As I have already explained, the total union of light,
this light that is in the air and that emerges from the material
substance of fire, involved no confusion and no jumbling of
any parts. [...]

Theology, in dealing with what is beyond being, resorts also to
differentiation. I am not referring solely to the fact that within a
unity, each of the indivisible persons is grounded in an unconfused
and unmixed way. I mean also that the attributes of the transcen-
dentally divine generation are not interchangeable. The Father is
the only source of that Godhead which in fact is beyond being and
the Father is not a Son nor is the Son a Father. Each of the divine
persons continues to possess his own praiseworthy characteristics.[46]
    The images of Pseudo-Dionysius clearly present an intimist
version of Plato's sun analogy. Here Plato's sun shines in miniature,
in a strangely touching fashion, as if trifurcating via a three-armed
chandelier, withdrawn from the open world into the house. Because
the sun – a heroic symbol of the monarchy of principles ever since
Akhenaten and Plato – is not suitable as an image of internal
communion, or even of separation of powers in the absolute, the
mystical theologian had to resort to the lamp analogy. This at least
shares with the sun paradigm the fact that it represents the central
power of light, and thus designates the original function, but
can also render plausible the transition to the idea of Trinitarian
differentiation. Certainly the Pseudo-Dionysian lamps offer only a
precarious analogy to intra-godly communication, for they illustrate
how one should imagine the interpenetration between light able to
propagate and other, similar light; but they contribute nothing to
an understanding of the interactions between the lighting partners.
Their ability to interweave is envisaged more in line with Stoic
philosophies of bodily mixture than in interpersonal terms – which
is also evident in the inevitable analogies of closeness and mixture

among Greek and Latin fathers: the mutual being in of divine persons – just like the merging of divine and human natures in Christ – is tirelessly represented as the mixing of wine and water, or compared to the propagation of aroma and sound. One finds everywhere the image of glowing iron, which is presented as an interpenetration between the substance of metal and the substance of fire; it also returns several times in variants, for instance in images of glowing gold or coal embers. All this is meant to express a repression-free, non-hierarchical interweaving of substances in the same section of space – which can be understood quite naturally as a primitive attempt on the part of theological speculation to approach the problem of spatial formation in the autogenous container of the intimate sphere. The physiological images of mixture reach their natural conclusion in the Platonizing similies of light in light, which lead almost automatically into subtler metaphysical associations between mind and space. These visual figures can certainly be nothing more than preparatory exercises to approach the interpersonal dimension of the strong relationship. If one takes Pseudo-Dionysius's lamp analogy further, however, one can at least develop the idea that the triune chandelier not only emits light outwards but also holds the inner life of the parties on the side of light. This is most clearly suggested in the text through the negative statements, which certainly make a great deal out of the fact that the Father is not the Son and the Son is not the Father. These "not in God" bring life or personal difference into the gleaming gray of the primordial unity. The three (or six) "nots" in the Trinity (Father *not* Son or Spirit; Son *not* Spirit or Father; Spirit *not* Father or Son) light the fire of relationship in the divine space. All definition is negation, Spinoza would later say; and all negation is relationship, the ancient theologians already taught.

The task, then, is to conceive of a difference that does not lead to separation, that is, to becoming external to one another; for, if there is one thing in ancient theology that is even more pronounced than the pathos of non-mixture or non-coalescence between the divine persons, that is the pathos of their a priori connectedness. But how can unity still be envisaged, if the tripersonal model mobilizes a maximum of centrifugal forces within it? This problem is solved through the supposition of an expressive or discharging act in God in which genuine differences appear without any cut surfaces or gaping seams. A perceptible gap, after all, would indicate that the separating externality had gained the upper hand over the continuum of belonging together.

The Greek fathers already managed to overcome this difficulty by ascribing to the Father two gestures of self-exit that posit difference without endangering continuity: conception and breath. The third of God's expressive acts, that of making, is passed over, as it leads not to co-divine figures but to sub-divine creatures – that is, to the sensual world and its inhabitants. Begetting and breathing life are viewed as productions or settlements whose products remain intrinsic to the producer – a circumstance for which fourth-century theological subtlety established as canonical the admirable term "procession," *ekporeusis* in Greek and *processio* in Latin. Thus God "himself" proceeds from himself and into the Son and the Spirit, but does not leave the shared inside being in these; there is here no dialectic of the self and of externalization that spans processes of estrangement yet – only the seamlessly shared enjoyment of a common wealth. The intra-godly communards do not sustain any onsets of agonal ailments of externalization and reappropriation as a result of the processions; such phenomena come into play only in the dimension of a history of salvation, where the Son has to share the agony of the world down to the end.[47] Begetting and breath, then, are expressive acts with no separable result: the begetter retains in himself the begotten (the Son), just as the breathers (the Father *and* the Son) keep the breathed (the Spirit) in and with themselves; and, even if the origin also goes outside itself in a sense, it by no means enters a state of externality in relation to itself. God's inner space produces itself as a relationships workshop, or as an apartment in which every inhabitant is the room of another. The intra-godly spatial demands transform the Platonic ball of light into a communal sphere. Its "inhabitants" find themselves in the logically and topologically unusual situation that their inter-twinement permits an equality of extension without spatial rivalry, as well as a sharing of functions without competition for primacy – even if the original, patrocentric rage of the older Trinitarian discourses, especially the Byzantine ones, tends to conceal this "egalitarian" trait. It is precisely this unbroken sharing that is prefigured through the ancient images of contraction and mixture in natural philosophy. Trinity is more than a perfectly shaken emulsion of three different liquids, however: it is meant to be no less than an a priori love life and an original inter-intelligence, superior to the world. The inside of the living orb can be described with this formula: three times one equals three times everything.

The doctrine of unitrinitas, then, provided the first coherent articulation of the idea of the strong relationship, and it emerged in unparalleled radicalism from its very first appearance. If the idea of an a priori "intersubjectivity" was ever taken into consid-eration, it was in this intertwinement of the Trinitarian persons. Now the idea of an absolute inside was established: through it, physical space is sublated in relational space – the surrealism of the persons' coinherence [*Ineinandersein*] had found its classical model. In this space, the persons no longer stand close to one another, each shining by itself, like Pseudo-Dionysius's lamps in the room; rather, by forming the primordial residential community, they put together a pure spatial connectivity, or throw a first love sphere around themselves. Here the rules are: First the inner world of love, then physics; first the union of three, then their historical household. Only in this order can the relationship between the absolute trio and its outside environment be grasped. That is why theologians place such value on conceiving of the coinherence of the tri-une [*Drei-Einen*] without any separating in-betweenness.

The learned monk John of Damascus (ca 676–749) made a number of decisive points in his well reputed treatise *An Exact Exposition of the Orthodox Faith*, which became a reference work for the Latin scholastics from the late twelfth century onwards. Here he defended the absolute synchronicity – or syn-achronicity – of the hypostases or persons: "Accordingly, *it is impious to say* that time intervened in the begetting of the Son and that the Son came into existence after the Father."[48] Any interval of time would indicate a triumph of the external over the primary being inside with themselves of the divine persons. At the same time, their radically relational intertwinement creates the possibility of doing away with the objectionable numerical paradox of the one that is supposed to be three:

> Thus, when I think of one of the Persons [*hupostasis*], I know that He is perfect God, a perfect substance [*ousia*], but when I put them together and combine them, I know one perfect God. For the Godhead is not compounded, but is one perfect, indivisible, and uncompounded being in three perfect beings.[49]

This argument, which had already been rehearsed by the Cappadocian fathers in the fourth century, would remain current until Cusa. It still returns in his text *On Learned Ignorance*, in the formula *maximum est unum*. It looks as if the perfection argument was the early form of a naïve attempt to bridge the gap between theology and the mathematics of infinite magnitudes, for three times one is certainly not one, but three; viewed in this way, the Trinitarian dogma would be mathematically absurd. But three times infinity is infinity; now the dogma makes mathematical sense.[50] The infinite is imagined in the figure of the all-encompassing orb, in which externality simply cannot appear. This model now simultaneously guarantees the absolute intimacy and reciprocal immanence of the divine persons. A letter written by Basil of Caesarea (329–379) to his brother Gregory of Nyssa gives the classic formulation of the rejection of external differences in the divine inner sphere:

> And through whatever processes of thought you reach a conception of the majesty of any one of the three persons of the Blessed Trinity [...] you will arrive invariably at the Father and Son and Holy Spirit, and gaze upon their glory, since there is no interval between Father and Son and Holy Spirit in which the intellect will walk in a void. The reason is that there is nothing which intrudes itself between these persons, and that beyond the divine nature there is nothing which subsists that could really divide it from itself by the interposition of some outside thing, and that there is no void, in the form of an interspace in which there is no subsistence, between the three Persons, which could cause the inner harmony of the divine essence to gape open by breaking the continuity through the insertion of this void.[51]

It should not be surprising that the internal coherence of the unified three could only be imagined with the aid of explicit or implicit circular and spherical models. Gregory of Nyssa, at any rate, knew that the unbroken nature of the intra-godly relationships could not be envisaged without a rotational concept: "Do you see the circulation of glory through the same cyclical movements? The Son is glorified by the Spirit; the Father is glorified by the Son. And reciprocally, the Son receives His glory from the Father and the Only Begotten becomes the glory of the Spirit."[52]

With arguments of this type, the ancient theologians achieved something that even modern sociologists have not yet been able to repeat, even when they tried: they arrived at a completely de-physicalized concept of the space of [the trinitarian] persons. With this, the meaning of "in" was freed from all forms of container-oriented thought once and for all.[53] If Father, Son, and Spirit could still be localized, it was only in the housing they provide for one another. Thus the topological surrealism of religion entered its learned phase.

John of Damascus reintroduced the word *perichōrēsis* [rotation, circling] to describe the strangely placeless yet self-locating coexistence of the divine persons. Its meaning in ancient Greek was probably something like "dancing around something" or "being whirled around in a circle."[54] By elevating this ancient word for movement into a technical term – one that denotes coinherence, intertwinement, interpenetration – he came up with one of the most brilliant terminological inventions in the western history of ideas. One senses in this word something scarcely thinkable or impossible to think about – which is evident, not least, in the fact that even theologians – let alone philosophers – are only rarely aware of it and, when they are, their understanding is usually inadequate. Whoever imagines *perichōrēsis* as the coinherence of inseparably connected elements is not wrong, yet is still far from grasping its essence. This strange term represents no less than the challenging idea that the persons cannot be localized in external spaces borrowed from physics, but that the place in which they are located is itself created through their interrelationship. By housing one another, the divine relational beings, the hypostases or persons, open up a space that they inhabit together and in which they call one another into existence, pervade and acknowledge one another. God's privilege, then, is to be in a place for which room is made only through relationships between inhabitants and co-inhabitants within himself. This is so difficult for trivial spatial thought to grasp that one would have to be entirely entangled in love stories – but under no circumstances a modern subject – to get an intimation of its meaning.

> three persons [...] united without confusion and distinct without separation, which is beyond understanding.[55]

> The abiding and resting of the Persons in one another [*perichōrēsis*] is not in such a manner that they coalesce or become confused.[56]

In the case of such a residential community, in the absolute, the question is where it sets itself up and how it apportions the different household duties to itself. John of Damascus has the answer to this question too; in Chapter 13 of *An Exact Exposition of the Orthodox Faith* he writes:

> Place is physical, being the limits of the thing containing within which the thing contained is contained. The air, for example, contains and the body is contained, but not all of the containing air is the place of the contained body, but only those limits of the containing air which are adjacent to the contained body. And this is necessarily so, because the thing containing is not in the thing contained.
>   However, there is also an intellectual place where the intellectual and incorporeal nature is thought of as being and where it actually is. There it is present and acts; and it is not physically contained, but spiritually, because it has no form to permit it

to be physically contained. Now, God [...] is not in a place.
For He, who fills all things and is over all things and Himself
encompasses all things, is His own place. However, God is also
said to be in a place; and this place where God is said to be
is there where His operation is plainly visible. Now, He does
pervade all things without becoming mixed with them, and to
all things He communicates His operation in accordance with
the fitness and receptivity of each in accordance with their
purity of nature and will, I mean to say. For the immaterial
things are purer than the material and the virtuous more pure
than such as are partisan to evil. Thus, the place where God is
said to be is that which experiences His operation and grace to
a greater extent. For this reason, heaven is His Throne [...] The
Church, too, is called the place of God, because we have set it
apart for His glorification [...] In the same way, those places in
which His operation is plainly visible to us, whether it is realized
in the flesh or out of the flesh, are called places of God.[57]

Therefore places of God – in non-theological terms, places of
co-subjectivity or coexistence or solidarity – are not things that
simply exist in external space. They only come about as sites of
activity of persons living together a priori, or *in a strong relationship*.
Hence the answer to the question "Where?" is, in this case, in one
another. *Perichōrēsis* means that the environment of the persons is
entirely the relationship itself. The persons contained in one another
in the shared space locate themselves in such a way that they
illuminate and pervade and surround one another, without being
harmed by the clarity of their difference. One could say that they are
as invisible to one another as air – but an air in which they lie for
one another; each one inhales and exhales what the others are – the
perfect conspiration; each breaks forth from itself into the others –
the perfect protuberance. They give one another neighborhood – the
perfect being surrounded. Thus the Christian God – together with
the Platonic universe – would be the only being with magnitude
but no surroundings, because he himself supplies the "around" in
which he self-referentially acts out his multirelational nature. So
this God would perhaps not be worldless, but he would certainly be
environmentless.[58]

Whoever began to exist like this God does would not have to
start with being in the world; for pure relationships would already
constitute a world before the world. External conditions would never
be the first data, and even the world as a whole would not be given
any earlier than the complicity between those initially united. No
thing could be given separately for itself; every gift would be, always

already and always only, an addition to the relationship. That the totality of conditions known as the "world" can exist at all is itself only a consequence of the primordial gift of belonging to one another. Theologians called this – with reference to the third person, who acts a priori as *copula* [connection], or as the spirit of community – *donum dei*, God's gift. The gift that gives the relationship is – to use an ominous modern term – immanence. Someone lives immanently if he knows how to be "remaining" (*manens*) in the inside (*in*) for which the strong relationship makes room. It would be a misconstrual of this inhabitation and remaining in one another, however, if one simply took it as a calm state – as the later Latin translation of *perichōrēsis* as *circuminsessio*, a sort of mutual sitting in, suggests. The earlier Latin version of this artificial word, *circumincessio*, emphasizes the dynamic character of the interpersonal relations, and was sometimes also equated with a mutual pushing forward or storming into one another.[59] This word highlights with greater psychological realism – assuming that psychology is not out of place among divine persons – the invasive sense of the influx of each into the others.

*

The characteristic of living together or in one another in the strong sense or a priori does not belong only to the intra-godly persons but manifests itself, in a sense, in human associations of persons as well. Families and peoples in their historical reproductions create and inaugurate the place in which their kin can learn to be themselves by distinguishing themselves from their ancestors and descendants. It is therefore significant that the emergence of the Son from the Father, a process theologically termed begetting, is the sensitive point in the intra-godly game. For what is Trinitarian theology other than the most sublime form of a generational theory? Richard of Saint Victor – whom medievalists consider to be one of the subtlest thinkers of the twelfth century – stated this in an explicit analogy:

> For a (human) person proceeds from another person, in some cases only directly, in some cases only indirectly and in some cases directly and indirectly at once. Jacob, like Isaac, proceeded from the substance of Abraham; but the procession of the one occurred only indirectly, while that of the other occurred only directly. For only through Isaac's mediation did Jacob spring from Abraham's loins [...] Consequently, in human nature the procession of the persons encompasses three distinct modes. – And even if this nature seems very far from the unique and most excellent nature of God, there is nonetheless a certain resemblance.[60]

The cohabitation of younger and older persons causes a constant regeneration of the place in which the different parties practice being in, and proceeding from, one another. Because tribes and peoples can be devastated by traumatizing magic and political pestilence, however – and in such ways that their distant descendants will still stumble over the ills of their ancestors – monitoring or adjusting the procession from the Father to the Son through the Spirit is at the same time an indispensable critical theory of the generational process. The Spirit – that is, the life-giving knowledge and mutual love between the older and the younger – is the norm of mental transference from one generation to the next. Aside from that, the Spirit – in the view of theologians – must not be identified simply as the grandson of the Father; then the Son would move up to the paternal position and the grandson, as a second-degree son, would be back-to-back with his grandfather. Then great-grandchildren would also come into view, creating a leak in the triad and breaking it up into an inexorable sequence of further begettings. In intra-Trinitarian fashion, the Spirit is meant to complete the liaison between Father and Son – and its being breathed by the Father *and* the Son seals the absolute conclusion of the internal processions. A transition to a fourth party would be impossible in this immanence.[61] The number four would be the start of a chain reaction of processions from God: It would send the generational reactor out of control, and the first cause could no longer repeat itself identically, or at least with sufficient similarity, in the effects it would have on more distant degrees. This would, potentially and actually, cause a degeneration of intra-godly events; externality would triumph over the vigorously self-differentiating inside; God's process would become monstrous and his capacity to communicate with himself in forms of strong relation could no longer curb the tendency toward processions into the dissimilar. In the central Trinitarian process, consequently, the breathed person, who guarantees unity and similarity between the first, the second, and itself, must form the final part. The Spirit, understood as *amor* [love], *condilectio* [shared affection], *copula*, and *connexio* [link], ensures that begetting causes a beneficial difference that remains in the continuum and does not lead to estrangement or degeneration.

*

In the generational processes of peoples, however, this rule is chronically violated; here offspring very often means a degenerative continuation of the chain of life – the failed generation is an unpleasant begetting. It breaks open fatal gaps between the age groups; the earlier and the later generations genuinely become alien or monstrous to one another. With reference to the actual procreations, distorting and de-animating, the old church was entirely right to break away from the peoples and their forced union in the Roman Empire through a pneumatic secession, establishing a new, regenerative generational process in a pneumatic or baptismatic people. The generations of the church members are spiritual generations that set themselves apart from the biological–cultural generations. Idealistically put, the children of the Christian people would be the descendants of a spiritual stream of love that seeks to act as a corrective for an inadequate empirical form of parental love. This is simultaneously the critical purpose of early Christian chastity: better to produce no offspring than failed offspring. While the history of actual generations over the last millennia is largely a history of unwelcome humans, the history of spiritual generations keeps itself on the right track, as the strength to welcome to being, in the name of a superhuman authority, individuals who are ill-greeted by humans. Christianity would never have survived forty generations or two millennia without performing its latent function – that of a sewage treatment plant for generativity – with some degree of success. But this function has increasingly slipped out of its grasp since the birth of modern civil societies; and the nation-state society, with its educational system and its therapeutic subcultures, has largely emancipated itself from the inspiratory services of Christian churches. The generative processes in modern social systems have become too complex for religious authorities to play more than a marginal role in them. The institutional churches themselves, both the reformed and the Roman, have meanwhile taken on more of a subcultural character; they have primarily become filtering systems for their own offspring and have forfeited their task of moderating the amorous processions in natural societies. To most people today, their welcomes seem more like disinvitations, and the general crisis of fatherhood has deprived the "fathers" of most of the authority their office once held. Modern political mothering agencies have long had far better material and media resources than the churches; the rest is self-referentiality. On a subsidized stage, it is not easy for a pantomime of childlessness and contempt for daughters to stay on the program. Even the fall of Rome occurs twice, it seems, and here – as elsewhere – the first time is a tragedy, the second a farce.[62]

*

At its medieval zenith, Trinitarian theology had led – as we have attempted to show through perspectival abbreviations – to the

discovery of a language for the *strong relationship*. The partners of
the immanent Trinity produce, harbor, and surround themselves in
such close reciprocity that their intertwinement exceeds all external
conditions. Here one can see the reward for absurdity: for the
first time, being in relation can be addressed as an absolute place.
Whoever lives in such total relationships as do the Father, the Son,
and the Spirit – according to a depiction carried out in Trinitarian
logic – is, in a newly clarified sense, unconditionally inside. Being
in means *existing* – or, as medieval authors strangely yet under-
standably say, with the same intention, *inexisting* – that is, in a sphere
that is originally opened by internal relationships.[63] In spherological
terms, speculation on the Trinity is informative primarily because it
developed to its ultimate conclusion the phantasm of never being
able to fall out of the inside position. It is inspired by a fanaticism
of immanence for which there is simply not meant to be any outside.
In this respect, Trinitarian theology acts as a logical application
form for membership in an absolute inner world, on the model of
the exemplary three: by declaring my allegiance to *deus unitrius*, the
"unitrine" God, I apply for admission into a community that rests
on indestructible immanence. And yet this intimate community,
too, is constituted like a group that owes most of its cohesion to
external compulsion. Perhaps the curia's teacherly statements on
the Trinity sound increasingly mechanical because, with the establishment of the great theological sums, the intellectual tension
began to disappear from the Trinitarian motif and the hour of the
confessional administrators had come. At the Council of Florence
in 1442, in the papal bull on the union of the Catholic Church with
the Copts and the Ethiopians, the coinherence of the divine persons
was only referred to in conceptually empty officialese:

> Because of this unity the Father is entire in the Son, entire in
> the Holy Spirit; the Son is entire in the Father, entire in the
> Holy Spirit, the Holy Spirit is entire in the Father, entire in
> the Son. No one either excels another in eternity, or exceeds in
> magnitude, or is superior in power.[64]

Whoever declares this adheres to a creed that places at its center a
communal fantasy of inseparability. The price of formulating this
fantasy is that whoever does not profess the same is ejected from
fellowship [*Communio*]; it is no coincidence that the passage quoted
is followed by pages of lists detailing heretical teachings whose
originators and followers are anathematized and cursed.[65]
It is clear from this how all attempts to elevate microspheric
intimate structures – of which the Christian Trinity may be the

most sublime formulation – to the norm or the central icon for large communities involve a high psycho-political risk: if inclusion fails, the ones who cannot be integrated face the threat of elimination. The primordial ecclesiogenic fantasy of stretching an intimate bubble to the size of the world may give the faithful hope that one day everything they now encounter as a hostile and self-centered outside will be disarmed and incorporated into their own circle of life; experiences of communal enthusiasm and solidarity also have a natural tendency to overflow, and the passing on of spiritual and charitable advantages need not always result in harmful expansionism.

Nonetheless, the Christian politics of communities of love displays a paradox that can be illuminated only through fundamental spherological research. The attempt to draw the outside world comprehensively into the bubble leads to errors of format. What Ernst Bloch called the "spirit of utopia" gives the greatest possible format error its official title. For nothing misjudges the autonomous laws of both micro- and macrospheres as much as the attempt to turn the whole dark, overpopulated world into a transparent and homogeneous home for all, without any further ado.

5

GOD'S BASTARD
The Caesura of Jesus*

"Christ was a bastard and his mother dishonest."
Christopher Marlowe
[attributed by his accuser, Richard Baines]

The most consequential attack on the patriarchal order of things did not emanate from the enlightenment produced in Greek cities of the fourth and fifth centuries BC by the sophistic movement and the theater, but from a Jewish sect, initially almost unnoticed, that was active in Jerusalem and Damascus and invoked the authority of a miracle healer and prophet of the kingdom of God by the name of Yeshua ben Yosef, executed by the Romans – most likely in AD 30. Whether this man had been a resistance fighter hostile to Rome, or whether he had been content to proclaim a spiritual revolution, he clearly had attained the status of a troublemaker. After his demise, this exceptional preacher was given the title of Messiah, which in its Hellenized form gave rise to the designation Christos, "the anointed one" [christos]. This is the origin of the name of the religious movement that, up until today, at approximately 2.2 billion nominally "faithful" members of all denominations, has a spiritual influence on a little more than a quarter of the current population of the earth.

Given that, already during the composition of the oldest documents regarding the existence and the teachings of said Christos

---

* *TRANSLATOR'S NOTE This chapter has been translated by Oliver Berghof and is forthcoming in his translation of Sloterdijk's Die schrecklichen Kinder der Neuzeit: Über das anti-genealogische Experiment der Moderne. I have modified the translation in accordance with changes Sloterdijk made to it for After God and so as to ensure consistency of style across the book.*

(the Epistles of St. Paul, the Gospels of the New Testament, and the Acts of the Apostles), an interest in sacred deception and pious stylization was dictating what was written, it will be forever impossible to arrive at a realistic image of the Jesuanic[1] "original" appearance – regardless of the fact that, to this day, the academic subdiscipline of New Testament studies would want to derive its right to exist from the surmounting of what is philologically impossible, to say nothing of the theologian-pontiff Benedict's most recent wanderings, in three volumes, through the realm of pure maybe.[2]

Faced with the fact that posterity does not – and never will – have an authentic image of the origin, appearance, presence, and ministry of the *christos*, but only some overpainting on top of an older layer of "data," then some more overpainting on top of that overpainting, the only way to reconstruct the primary material is to point carefully to those few passages in the canonical documents where some of the pigment of the initial fabric shows through the edifyingly tendentious cover images.[3]

Foremost among the latter are the evangelists' indications of the child Yeshua's unexplained familial descent. Apparently already during his lifetime, ever since he began to draw attention to himself with miracle cures and scandalous sermons, the genealogical irregularities that accompanied his appearance surfaced all over the country in the form of rumors. Decades later they formed such a fixed element in the imago of the anointed one – the *christos* – that they had to be incorporated into the unbridled invention of myths that overgrew the man's memory after his death – in local conversations carried out among the first congregations no less than in later accretions of written material and missionary embellishments. The anomalous descent can be traced through the mythopoetic work of generations of believers and aspiring believers, from Golgotha to Nicaea, from the ominous greeting of the angel who indicated an alternative method of conception through the mocking question of contemporaries – "From Nazareth? Can anything good come from that place?" (John 1:46)[4] – to the pronouncements of the Apostles' Creed, charged as they are with the theology of mystery: *et ex patre natum ante omnia saecula* – born from the father before all time. Indeed, one can claim that early Christianity in its entirety, from its Jesuanic center to its philosophical and dogmatic periphery, represents nothing but work on the vexatious element of genealogical anomaly that was attached to the key figure – starting with the transformation of the real absence of a father into a sense of mission stimulated by an imaginary closeness to the father, and culminating in the logical and ontological audacities of Trinitarian theology, from the Cappadocian Fathers to Saint Augustine, Saint

Thomas, G. W. F. Hegel, and Karl Barth. It is through this work
that the idea of a seamless descent from God was sublimated into
an enigmatic three-person household.[5]

In all likelihood, those passages that betray the anti-familial
affect demonstrated by the preacher Jesus from the beginning of his
appearance in public can be counted among the authentic pigments
in the image of Jesus painted by the Gospels, from the devastating
pronouncement "Woman, what do you want from me?" (John
2:4), with which he dismissed his mother at the wedding at Cana,
to the guarded silence that the prophet upheld all throughout his
life regarding his corporal father – a silence where the trite phrase
"telling silence" is for once appropriate.

A man called Joseph, who is supposed to have begotten the savior
in the darkness of a Jewish night, cannot be part of how Jesus
represents himself – even though, for almost two thousand years,
the later Christian imagination spared no effort in its attempt to fill
this omission with images from the life of the Holy Family.[6] Three
quarters of a century later, the synoptic evangelists write fantastic
supplements into the initial gap – most unscrupulously Matthew,
who pretends to know that the angel of the Lord appeared in
Joseph's dream to explain to him the delicate state of affairs: that
his wife Mary is pregnant, but that he should not worry about
it, "because she has conceived what is in her by the Holy Spirit"
(Matthew 1:20) – whereupon Joseph turns into the first believer by
demonstrating how one asks no further questions.

By contrast, scattered circumstantial evidence suggests that Jesus
– growing up as a mother's recalcitrant boy and, like a Jewish
Parsifal, meditating on his own questions about existence – devoted
himself from relatively early on in his life to an idiosyncratic form
of patro-poetry. This is highlighted in the bizarre scene in which, as
a twelve-year-old, he is said to have called the temple of Jerusalem
his "father's house," in front of his worried parents who were
looking for him. This story, too, probably harbors an anecdotal core
that, despite all the unmistakably edifying exaggeration, contains
a real memory trace. This would mean that young Jesus lived
rather like a foster child with his birth mother and her later
companion – the ominous "carpenter" who was properly speaking
a construction worker (*tekton*) – and saw no reason to enter into a
closer relationship with these unpresentable parents. During that
time he would have conjured up for himself an adequate father – a
representative, even though invisible father, who had the advantage
of being above all slander. Later on, almost as a supplement to
the glamorous otherworldly progenitor, he would have created for
himself a system of relations composed of brothers and sisters who

were caught up in the same dream and would assist him in his efforts to end the embarrassment of the real obscurity of his descent once and for all.

*

The theopoetic synthesis of the young Jesus would have been as plausible, in terms of the story of his life, as it was coherent in terms of the dynamic of ideas. Where the contours of the real father are becoming blurry or are missing altogether, a process can start in the son that fills the unoccupied position in psychic space with figments of his own patro-poetic energy. What Pierre Legendre claimed about the paternal function of the classic old European state might already be true of Jesus: thanks to his unauthorized absorption of the holy books, he had become a "child of the text."[7] One could say that he designed for himself the life of a self-taught son.

Numerous commentators, philologists as well as the pious,[8] tarried over the detail recorded in the Gospels, according to which Jesus is said to have addressed the "father in heaven" using a children's idiom in Aramaic, *abba* [daddy], particularly in the prayer at Gethsemane, as described at Mark 14:36 – generally to conclude that the young prophet believed himself to have been in a "close relationship" with God. Since it is hard to make up an idiosyncratic trait like this, it is plausible to accept a trace of authentic observation in this instance as well. The infantilism of the form of addressing God would testify to the fact that, to a large extent, Jesus avoided entering into the sphere of majesty that is part of the Jewish concept of God, only to put himself into a quasi Benjaminian or Josephinian position of intimacy in relation to the father in heaven. Thanks to this maneuver, he would have been placed in the position of the favored youngest son – indeed, in the position of an only son, who could profit excessively from a paternal benevolence that was tantamount to a weakness. The sovereign and terrifying attributes of the supreme being probably remained blanked out in the internal dialogue between an eccentric son and his father; they appeared only later in the apocalyptic threatening speeches of the prophet, but then in the guise of an outwardly directed violence that shook the world to its foundations.

Analogous reflections can be tied to phrases recounting the legend of baptism according to Mark 1:11. In that account, a voice sounded above Jesus, who had just been baptized and emerged from the waters of the river Jordan: "You are my Son, the Beloved; my favor rests on you." Later narrators' concern for Jesus's edginess about his father that emerges from this scene has already reached such proportions that God is personally called upon to engage in the gesture of "adopting" the young man; for how else should one interpret the salutation "my Son, the Beloved"?

In fact, from the vantage point of contemporaries as well as from that of the immediately following generations, the phenomenon of Jesus could not be made comprehensible without resorting to the pattern of adoption, otherwise hardly known in ancient Judaism. This pattern seemed most readily suited to capture the hybridity of the father–son relationship in this case. The further development of the irritating motif allows for the conclusion that the initial, genealogic anomaly could never be put to rest. It manifested itself in the "realistic" legends, in circulation since the second century among "interested circles" in Judaism, according to which a Roman soldier by the name of Panthera, stationed in Israel, was the one who had begotten Jesus – a supposition that made the mother into a collaborator, indeed, into a soldier's whore. On the theological side, they escalate into the monstrosities of the Trinitarian relationship between God the Father, the Son of God, and their jointly aspirated emanation, the Holy Ghost. The primitive acts of colportage as well as the subtle constructs are distilled from the initial embarrassment, – in part born of animosity, in part aiming at exaltation – caused by Jesus's ancestry. While the rumor about Panthera satisfies the urge for disparagement, the exalting élan reaches unknown heights in the doctrine of the Trinity. Indeed, thanks to a new kind of metaphysics of relations, the son can be elevated to the status of a co-substantial pole of divine internal life in Trinitarian Christology – which seems to be remotely compatible with the quite a-theoretical statements of Jesus himself at the height of his prophetic belief in his unlimited power, regardless of the philosophical distortion of the primary message.

From the point of view of the history of ideas, the insertion of a motif of adoption into Jesus's father complex in the scene at the river Jordan is not implausible. One can assume that, after a century of Roman presence in Judaea, Mark, like the other Gospel authors, had a certain familiarity with Rome's adoption practices.[9] In addition, one can take it for granted that they were all familiar with the second psalm, where one reads, in the seventh verse, "You are my son, today I have fathered you."[10] Once this sentence was put into Yahweh's mouth, the thought of having a second birth gained a firm place in Jewish ritual; and if the sentence was recited by the high priest at Jewish royal coronations in order to mark Yahweh himself as a father and as the ruler's adopting father, as experts in Jewish studies conjecture, then it could have been used also during a baptizing initiation into the imminent kingdom of God, transposed into the desert. This would confirm the observation that heaven, if it opens itself at all, likes most of all to quote itself.

*

Whoever goes looking for evidence of the mode and scope of Jesuanic anti-familism will find something without having to go to great lengths, despite the repeated overpainting of memories pertaining to the anointed one in the Gospels. It is above all bizarre, practically forgery-proof passages in Jesus's speeches that indicate sufficiently the thrust of the original messages. First among them is the symptomatic remark Jesus is said to have made in the course of his great scolding of the Pharisees, according to Matthew 23: "You must call no one on earth your father, since you have only one Father, and he is in heaven." Since this injunction to cease and desist using "father" as a form of address occurs in close proximity to the banning of the titles "rabbi" and "master," it seems evident that these objections betray an anti-authoritarian attitude. These traditional forms of address shall henceforth be forbidden – as emphasized especially by the evangelist John – because from now on only one, the anointed himself, will be deserving of these appellations. Here of course the falsifying intention becomes again noticeable, in the form of a post hoc prophecy: the evangelist, who has never seen his master, insinuates that the prophet Jesus already during his lifetime bore the title Christos, which became associated with his name only later.

The punchline of Matthew's and John's statements is hard to miss: the greeting "father" had to be banished from earthly use after Jesus had extended his concept of the supernatural father to the circle of his followers. All names indicative of authority – father, rabbi, master – are off limits from then on, because the formerly paternal prerogatives of educating, teaching, and interpreting scripture have been transferred completely to the authorized son, the father's confidant. The Gospel of John, which is theologically the most offensive, sharpens the transfer of authority to the point of using the phrase "the Father and I are one" (10:30); it makes Jesus's criticism of the Pharisees escalate into open anti-Jewish polemics. Indeed, one reads in John that indignant Jews were picking up rocks to stone Jesus on account of the sacrilegious expression. The point of the "report" is easily understood: whoever wants to kill the "word" that speaks itself is a victim of the most fatal delusion.

From what has been said it becomes clear why the new preacher's ancestry complex, patro-poetically overcompensated as it was, had to entail an anarchic subversion of the language games then current in Jewish rite. If up to that point Judaism had always been based on maintaining a discretionary distance between God and the human being, now all of a sudden the question of the proper distance was to be negotiated anew – in the spirit of a reduction of distance that has a new kind of interiority and culminates in fusion between the high and the human poles. To be sure, the psycho-political and theological institution of prophecy, at home in consolidated diversity in the Jewish scriptural tradition from Moses to Isaiah and from Jeremiah to Malachi, had admitted a penetration of the speaking human medium by the divine assignment to speak. However, this form of using human beings as conveyors of trans-cendent messages always included awareness of an abyssal distance that ought to separate the human medium from the sender. So far one had shrunk from the temptation to allow the medium to engage in traffic in the opposite direction, toward the divine.

It seems that, in the history of maturing monotheism, the Jesuanic Abba God introduces for the first time the option of psycho-theological two-way traffic. The word "son" turns into a cipher for the envoy's permission to gain unlimited access to the sender – even further, it develops into an indication of the real presence of the sender in the messenger, and in his message. Accordingly, the messenger filled with God has the right to interpret the scriptures according to the spirit, not according to the letter – which results in a cascade of interventions that break the law. But, from the perspective of the inspired, what else is the old law, if not a collection of rules that generate misery and whose true sense slipped away long ago? They offer the practitioners of the Jewish form of irony, the Pharisees, an opportunity to engage endlessly in their equivocal talk: they let one pretend to treat what has long ago become incomprehensible and unlivable as a directive one could follow in the here and now – until finally the pretense of meaning becomes the meaning itself.

Even if the New Testament did not prove anything else, it proved this one thing, unambiguously: already in antiquity, religion was not available without the self-governing of the absurd. But in later generations not every person was willing to enter into the tired games without revision proposals of her own. What later came to be known as Christianity was in the beginning a revolt against the irony of scriptural learning.

In psycho-historical perspective the appearance of the fatherless Jesus of Nazareth, world history's most terrible child, is connected to a new form of personalization, which proceeds from the assumption that the patro-poetically created father dwells directly in the inspired son. The Christian pattern of mediated personhood has as its goal the real presence of the dominant father figure in the dominant figure of the son. Whatever the son says and does, the father says and does, according to the son's own conviction, in the present, in actuality, through him. John captures the issue in the formula according to which the word has become flesh and has dwelt among us.[11]

*

Among the protagonists of the next generation, no one had understood the change of personalization through Jesuanic patro-poetry and its forward-looking potential better than the erstwhile anti-Christian zealot Paul in his letters to the new Christian communities in the Mediterranean and Asia Minor, as he applied there, without further ado, the emerging idea of indwelling, which subsumed older forms of personal mediation, to the relationship between the *christos* and himself, his privileged apostle. The culminating formulation of the changed pattern of personhood shines forth in the suggestive sentence of the Letter to the Galatians: "and yet I am alive; yet it is no longer I, but Christ living in me."[12] With a daring leap into free imitation, the resurrected superson [*Übersohn*] is being called upon to dwell in the superapostle. The structural change of aspects of the soul that accompanies the turn toward the Christian *modus vivendi* manifests itself in this *locus classicus* of Christian mediumism [*Mediumismus*] more clearly than anywhere else.

Afterwards, whoever claims participation in a life aimed at the truth shall gain access to it by way of a complete transfer of the soul. This change is being guaranteed sacramentally, through the act of baptism. Wherever this is insufficient to seal the transfer of the soul, the faithful have the option, particularly since the appearance of the Egyptian desert fathers, to enter into the anachoretic or monastic *modus vivendi* that, in the parlance of early western Christianity, was called *religio* – in an act whereby a technical term of correct Roman cult observance was being repurposed in favor of Christian interests in superior theological self-expression. In every case the transfer of souls *more christiano* implies a complete change of the subject, in which the worldly subject exchanges its "I," which had been formed under immanent psychological laws, for a transcendent self; it exchanges an earthly state of being possessed for a metaphysical passion.

From the point of view of the history of civilization, the process of generations in the West detaches itself for the first time from physical reproduction[13] and from the classic series of legitimate transmissions between father and son, and changes into a purely spiritual order of succession, in which sons follow upon sons, without the possibility or permission for a real father to intervene. A new series of traditions is being initiated with this spiritual- izing gesture. However, it is obvious that here, to begin with, the concept of "tradition" is used in a way that doesn't make sense, since, with the apostolic succession, tradition will be much more a matter of iterative connections than of transmission on the basis of a generative tie. Under the influence of the Jesuanic pattern, physical procreation and its psycho-juridical supplement, the formal recognition of the son by the father, lose, with the inventor of Christianity, their past authority – indeed, they are completely robbed of their power to constitute a people. According to the Pauline vision, a new people consisting of those who are baptized is to emerge, and its members are at least virtually freed from the spell of their past affiliations.[14] No more can one's actions and the law alone bring about salvation from now on than can one be redeemed by entering into the time-honored chain of tradition passed down from father to son.

All of Paul's writings can be read as if he had constantly circled around the sentence that he could not bring himself to pronounce: "Where there was generation, there shall be imitative succession." We no longer procreate, we baptize and call forth. We don't propagate, we teach and convert. We no longer believe in a future that lies in the power of our children; we prepare for a completely different world, which will open itself to us at the imminent end of the current age.

In the dim transition from the Jesuanic to the Pauline model a fundamentally changed logic of succession becomes apparent, according to which physical sons no longer follow upon physical fathers and grandfathers. From now on spiritual sons are supposed to succeed metaphorical "fathers," who in turn can act only from the position of being one of the successors of an authorized son. From an anthropological point of view, the logic of unilineality, typical of the old kinship system, finds its perfection in the apostolic order of succession. This logic was subsequently displaced by the kind of bilineality we take for granted nowadays: the counting of descendants' descendants in the paternal *and* the maternal line alike. By addressing the recipients of his letters, on occasion, as if he were their father, Paul puts the new pattern of succession into effect both for himself and for his readers. In this pattern – when correctly understood – sons follow sons only, and a siring father in the old style must not come in-between. Classic patriarchy is being dissolved through the intervention of the incommensurable son and his apostle, who is ready to pounce, so as to transition into a new, unprecedented genealogic order. What emerges from this catastrophic turn is no less than the western spiritual filiarchy – better known under the name of Ekklesia, alias the Christian and Catholic Church.

To start with, the Pauline–Petrine community is indeed nothing but a paradoxical new social formation, which grew out of the anti-familial rage of the fatherless, father-besotted preacher Jesus and its moderation by the later ecclesiastic apparatus. The prohibition to address any earthly human as "father" was, obviously, only the momentary manifestation of a comprehensive anti-authoritarian affect, which one would have characterized, in twentieth-century jargon, as a "great refusal" or as a turning away from the order of "things as they are." More recent attempts to interpret Jesus's performances as provocations of an anti-imperial zealot shed light on some features of his physiognomy; but on the whole they are misleading, since the thrust of Jesuanic speeches, even if they sound "zealous," is apocalyptic and anti-Pharisaic, not anti-Roman or critical of established power.

Undoubtedly, in the eyes of someone inflamed with his own power of salvation and oratorical force, the everyday jobs of his followers counted among the circumstances that had to be overcome; how else would he have dared to ask them to cast aside everything they were used to in order to join his anarchic itinerant commune? Hegel summarizes the imposition laconically: "Thus subsistence labor is repudiated."[15]

The remaining family ties of his listeners also fell victim to the prophetic verdict on existing "conditions." Otherwise one could not imagine with what justification Jesus was allowed to say this to his faithful followers – and here, too, the original pigment of a disturbing aggression shines through the later overpainting:

Do you suppose that I am here to bring peace on earth? No, I tell you, but rather division [*diamerismon*] [...] From now on [...] father [will be] opposed to son, son to father, mother to daughter, daughter to mother. (Luke 12:51)

In none of Jesus's statements can one hear the pitch of *counter-culture* ecstasy[16] more clearly than in the following phrase recorded by Luke; owing to its excessiveness and moral abnormality, this phrase probably belongs among the few authentic fragments that emerged at least half-way undistorted from the workshop of tendentious Gospel literature: "Anyone who comes to me without hating father, mother, wife, children, brothers, sisters, yes and his own life too, cannot be my disciple" (Luke 14:26). This corresponds to the statement circulated by Matthew: "No one who prefers father or mother to me is worthy of me. No one who prefers son or daughter to me is worthy of me" (Matthew 10:37).[17]

With such statements of inspired violence, all familial and genea-logically informed "traditions" are being unhinged. It is their function to create space for a new reason to form associations, a reason that consists exclusively in the participation of the followers in the Jesuanic ecstasy in the here and now. Even if collective entities such as kin, people, and empire continue to exist, they will do so only as trivialities in the background, which affect from afar the ever present movement to gather followers – no matter how much their reactions will shape the course of later ecclesiastical history.

Those with whom Jesus surrounded himself during the short period of his public appearances, intending to take them with him into his "kingdom," were for the most part a hastily gathered motley of characters; they were prepared to share with their master the fundamental apocalyptic sentiment of this vitalist itinerary sect and were motivated by a drug-like mixture of desperation over their old lives and a fascination with perspectives seen never before. The fever of eschatological excitement could infect this unstable group of followers without being filtered in any way. Like its leader, this lively group had abandoned the superfluous sense of what was real, to abandon itself to the radically other, in a strengthened here and now and in an intoxicating then and soon.

If one looks at the first cohort of fellow enthusiasts, fellow uprooted existences, and fellow inspired ones, Jesus's anti-familial, anti-authoritarian, and anti-realistic utterance finally becomes fully comprehensible: "Anyone who does the will of my Father in heaven is my brother and sister and mother" (Matthew 12:50) – an utterance delivered in a situation where his real mother along with his biological brothers is said to have stood in front of the door without so much as being looked at by the prophet – this, too, a detail so inhuman and strange that one can hardly assume that it was invented retroactively. It belongs in the small stock of remnants of reality in the stream of a work of fiction dedicated to the Gospels that point to the existence of a severe disturbance about the sense of family in the young candidate for the title of Messiah. If, among his followers, this disturbance was translated into an analogous loosening of feelings of attachment, then that is completely in keeping with normal psychological plausibility.

The adherents of the prophet must soon have felt more attached to their new community of brothers than to the families they had had so far. They were the most resolute proponents of imitating a model that had emerged almost at the same time – and in this regard they counted among the first of the moderns. With them starts the incursion of current events into the immemorial traditions of several generations. Not a few among them must have been convinced that the liberating end would come during their lifetime – which is why they espoused the idea that they would neither die nor rise from the dead, but instead be transferred to the impending kingdom of God *in vivo*.

By contrast, the formation of the new commune under its singular fundamental pneumatic law happened completely beyond all normal psychology. For the time being the community of disciples was deeply hurt, mentally, by the event at Golgotha. Some time had to pass before it dared to advance in a post-traumatic counteroffensive, which spurred it on to grandiose new interpretations of the events in Jerusalem. The gradual transformation of the forlorn troop into a lasting institution inevitably led into unknown psychosocial territory.

The formation of a spiritual community after Jesus Christ's crucifixion not only required the reformulation of the shock of Golgotha into a premeditated act of redemption; it also made it necessary to create an innovative type of apostolic subjectivity, of which we have just noted, with reference to Paul, that it was based upon a newly coined personalization. The apostle, or the priestly subject, sees himself as presently re-souled, first in a personal vision, later by way of being anointed. From then on he thinks of himself as the medium of a divine power to speak and act, in which the son who has risen to heaven remains present. As a result of re-souling, an alternative type of positional subjectivity is created that the church subsumes under the concept of "succession."

One of the problems consists in the fact that the representative apostle for foreign affairs, Paul, did not know the "Lord" personally and attained the position of someone called upon only through a unilateral tie, which was stylized into a privileged and unobservable vision of conversion. By contrast, after the evening at Gethsemane, the leading apostle for interior affairs, Peter, was tainted with the stigma of denial – this, too, a particle of reality that, thanks to its distribution within the first commune, could not be made to disappear, even in the synoptic evangelists' redactions that were willing to engage in any pious lie.

From the point of view of the dynamics of culture, what is important in these stories is the circumstance that the impulse to transmit the message of Jesus could not be assimilated in any form to the cultural norm of a genealogical succession. Peter, who was approximately the same age as Jesus, might have been all kinds of things, but certainly not a legitimate son of his recently departed master. Finally Paul, who was half a generation younger, represented the prototype of a stray who had become a follower and who nevertheless recognized the chance to engage his son-like predecessor as "father" in new and indirect role-playing games. Initially, owing to these circumstances, apostolic "filiation" could happen only as a sending forth in close temporal proximity, without real father–son relationships coming into play. Later, with the passing of time and in the absence of a return of the Lord in glory, it had to devolve into a succession of messenger-sons.

At the same time, what triggered the foundation of a hitherto unknown form of temporality lay concealed in the construction of a subject out of the position of "succession" after the crucifixion of Jesus Christ. The matrix of what would be known in Europe, one day, as "history" could take shape only through the development of a chain of succession in a non-genealogic and post-apocalyptic situation: according to the Christian logic of succession, all "history" had to be, for the time being, Acts of the Apostles.[18] Its content was made up of reports on the difficulties encountered by messengers in the course of spreading the gospel in the inhabited world. This pattern remained in force even when the history of the apostles settled into a seemingly neutral cultural history, which arose from a combination of church history and imperial history.

The temporal structure of essential "history" is fundamentally determined by the command to preach the truth of the "good news." With the help of the latter, the former gains its tension toward the future. What later is called "history" develops as a result of the cooling down of the apocalyptic movement during the time of waiting – whereby all time turns into a limited time in-between. This pattern will be suspended at the beginning of the early modern period through the transformation of a time of waiting into an unlimited time of progress. But, no matter how thoroughly "proper" history wanted to hide in the incognito of imperial histories, the histories of peoples and states, revolutionary histories, and histories of civilization, for the historian of salvation or the historian of truth the cunning of apostolic reason remains transparent.[19] She knows that the theme is always the same: God and time.

The transition to existence in Christian time came with a price: with the invention of history as the time span "after Christ," the endeavor to reverse the Jesuanic ecstasy's annihilation of patriarchy urges itself upon the leaders of the community in the second, third, and later "generations." This intention directs the process of committing the gospel to writing. Even if, in the case of the enthusiastic prophet, traces of the anomalous family background cannot be suppressed any more than the numerous reports of his present-oriented, anti-traditional, and anti-genealogical furor, the leading intention of the evangelists, who were probably active between AD 75 and 110, was nevertheless to suspend the state of emergency in which the original community lived and to convert the rash illegitimacy of Jesus's appearances into a form of hyperlegitimacy instituted before the beginning of time.

For this reason the authors of the Gospels invested their energy for pious fictionalizing in the task of embedding retroactively the Jesus event that caused the caesura, so as to give it the greatest possible continuity. Doomed by the circumstances to have hindsight *post eventum*, they obeyed the injunction to reconstruct the narrative arc of the fatherless prophet's life and its catastrophic end as a history of fulfillment, thoroughly determined according to salvation history and prefigured in the prophets' foreknowledge, beginning with the transfiguration of the unplanned crucifixion into a voluntarily suffered passion – one could speak here of the mother of all re-interpretations – and ending with the triumphant reintroduction, into a neo-patriarchal order, of the son who invents stories about his father.

The most massive interventions of the evangelists in the Jesuanic biography can be found in Matthew and Luke, who both obviously felt the need to fill in the initial gap in the older evangelical document, that of Mark: Mark started his narrative in medias res, with Jesus's baptism in the river Jordan and his subsequent public activities, which shows that he felt no need to create genealogical derivation and legitimation. Matthew and Luke answered with a mass mobilization of confabulations. All of a sudden, they knew everything about the conception and the birth of the child and could recite who his ancestors had been and the earliest part of his lineage, as if they professed this maxim: the bigger the distance from the events, the better one recognizes the little details.

Both Matthew and Luke prefixed their stories about the deeds and the words of the master with genealogical lists, the so-called "genealogical trees" of Jesus, with whose help the one elevated to the status of Messiah was to be proven a descendant of David. This could have been important only for the Jewish–Christian communities of Jerusalem and Damascus. Only they were familiar with the prophecy of Isaiah, according to which the savior of Israel was to come from the house of David. Accordingly, in Matthew, Jesus's line of descent is traced, in brave monotony, down to David, and from there to Abraham – perhaps Matthew used Jewish genealogical tables that, admittedly, have not been transmitted anywhere else. This lineage comprises forty-two generations composed of three times fourteen "members," of whom the first fourteen cover the period from Abraham to David, the second fourteen the time span from David to the Babylonian captivity, and the third fourteen the period from the Babylonian captivity to Christ. Particularly remarkable in this series is the last member, of whom it is said: "Jacob fathered Joseph the husband of Mary; / of her was born Jesus who is called Christ" (Matthew 1:16).

Only three verses later, the evangelist inserts the story of how the Holy Spirit fathered Jesus. With Matthew, the left hand doesn't seem to know what the right hand is doing: the Annunciation renders the long-winded derivation of Jesus from Abraham and David pointless, since it suspends the patriarchal chain of begetting and introduces a supranatural factor into the events. After all, the last son in the series is born as scion of the spirit "from on high," and not as a child in a series of past acts of procreation – regardless of how seamlessly these followed one another, in unflinching legitimacy. Thus the enumeration of the intermediate members, from Abraham to Joseph, misses its declared objective: to prove the legitimacy of Jesus through his position in the most venerable Jewish chain of transmission. It has to miss its target, since Joseph is excluded *expressis verbis* as physical progenitor of this son.

At this point the implacable ancestral Jesuanic anomaly flourishes most garishly for more than a half century after the death of the preacher: there shall be no doubt that the Messiah emerged as the son of God from asexual conception and a supranatural cause of embodiment. At the same time Jesus is supposed to descend from Abraham and David in a straight genealogical line – even though the last railway carriage had been disconnected before arrival.

This obvious misconstruction speaks not so much of pious fraud as of the overzealousness of proselyte writers. In his panic-stricken quest to restore Jesuanic legitimacy through internal Jewish resources, that is, resources that are based upon the fulfillment of prophecy, the evangelist Matthew trips over his own feet. Of course one can't get around the embarrassing situation by prolonging – like Luke – Jesus's "genealogical tree" beyond Abraham and all the way to Adam: the contradiction between the doctrine of the immaculate birth of the Messiah and his inclusion among the oldest lines of descent remains irreconcilable. The only reason why this was not called into question by believers from the very start is that the injunction not to ask questions – an injunction one had acquired along with the pious attitude – made it invisible to the pious for a long time. It seems that Eusebius of Caesarea was the first one to articulate the problem in his *Ecclesiastical History* and to try to subdue it with a pseudo-logical answer.[20]

At least the Greek evangelist John, the last of the canonical authors to pick up the quill, expresses his contempt for the Judaizing bricolages of his fellow evangelists by letting his report about the actions and the sufferings of the Messiah begin with a steep metaphysical myth, according to which at the true beginning there was the Word: "the Word was with God / and the Word was God." One cannot reject in a more determined manner the patriarchal fictions of legitimacy of the inventors of the genealogical trees. Whoever emerges from the absolute needs no bearded ancestors from the tents of the patriarchs. For the rest, John picks up the thread from Mark and his sudden beginning with the appearance of John the Baptist in the desert – in this, too, he proves his distance from the fabulating canonical genealogists.

The later fortunes of Christianity announce themselves in the redactions of the evangelists Matthew and Luke: one can best encompass them with the formula "re-genealogizing the anti-genealogical revolt." That this manoeuver carries with it reintroducing the idea of the family into the original doctrine of the prophet, which was harshly inimical to the family, needs no further explanation. The son of all sons, who had broken out of the patriarchal system of ancestry, is caught again in the gravity of genealogic relationships, albeit in a manner that will entail an unforeseeably consequential modification of the hitherto valid models of family and succession.

*

The first of these concerns the already mentioned transformation of the usual series of generations into a line of apostolic successions. In this line, as noted, only sons can follow sons, through omission of the intermediate station of real fatherhood, in conformity with the wayward character of the new psycho-genealogical relationships. Nevertheless Christian conventions of speech soon pick up the banished term "father," in order to produce mystification by passing the unfamiliar filiarchal structures off as a neopatriarchal order. It is not a coincidence that the established Christian church distinguishes itself through the extensive use of hybrid father titles – from the desert fathers to the church fathers and the father confessors, to say nothing of other names for para-fatherly figures such as the pater, the pope, the abbot, the abbé, and similar psychosemantic neologisms that run the gamut of patrological vocabulary.[21]

The transformation of Christianity into a religion of sons who, by exercising pastoral power, push themselves back into the father role, which had been forbidden by Jesus, mirrors the unrecognized spiritual main event of late antiquity: one could call it "the bishops' counter-revolution" or "the clericocratic restoration." It was mainly driven by the internal imperatives of a growing large-scale organization that could not help but seize upon the distinction one came across in practice, between Christian laity and professional religious members, as a leading distinction. Without the gradation into sheep, shepherds, and über-shepherds, the Catholic apparatus would have been unthinkable and ungovernable. The turnabout by the church of bishops – beyond the reintroduction of genealogy and family into the message that the evangelists already strove for – triggered the extreme repaternalizing of Christian communal life without which one could not picture the physiognomy of Christianity between AD 300 and 1800 either in everyday life or in church doctrine.

In the sphere of influence of Roman Catholicism as well as in the Greek and Russian orthodox churches, this patrocentric image prevails to this day, no matter how much it has been tarnished recently through the revelation of chronic – rather than occasional – pederastic activities among the Catholic clergy; these, too, are indicative not so much of fatherly competencies among the spiritual personnel as of a heritage of sexual neurosis shaped in advance by Paul and Augustine – to say nothing of the virtually immortal undercurrent of church-related pathologic eccentricities amid spiritual corporations.

Since the clericocracy of the European Middle Ages consistently took the form of a political "patristic" class, in other words of a para-patriarchal ecclesiastic aristocracy, it is easy to understand why the paternalist clerics of those centuries shuddered at the very thought of laity reading the Bible. What answer would a pater, an abbot, or a pope have been able to give a lay person who, in reading the Gospel according to Matthew, had come across the following passage: "You must call no one on earth your father, since you have only one Father, and he is in heaven"?[22] At that time the only ones entitled to give something other than a hypocritical answer to this question would have been at most the simple brothers and sisters, *fratres* and *sorores*, who, through their membership of institutions distanced from the world – such as monasteries, hermitages, mendicant orders, and orders dedicated to the care of the sick – had remained more or less faithful to the anti-familial and anti-genealogical impulse of Jesus's itinerant community more than a thousand years later. The significance of the Protestant Reformation consisted, not least, in restoring to its rightful place the anarchy of a community of brothers against the political patristic class of the Catholic Church – which Carl Schmitt defended as power of the Roman "form" – and in doing so in the life of each individual believer, outside of the walls of the monasteries, between noisy workshops and congregations that sang choral music.

The second, even more consequential modification of existing models of the generational process and of succession concerned the pattern of the family as such. Even if – leaving aside idiosyncratic developments in the ascetic and monastic wing of the church – a reconciliation of the Christian message with the family seemed inevitable, this could happen only at the cost of a profound subversion of the family model. With the triangle of a nuclear family consisting of Mary, Joseph, and Jesus – whether in the stable in Bethlehem or on the flight into Egypt – the unbanishable phantom of the Holy Family appears on the stage of the old European imaginary, and Albrecht Koschorke has shown how far-reaching its modifications of profane family life were.[23] This second modification not only institutes between husband and wife a novel tie, asexual or beyond sex, which imposes on the husband a restraint up until then unknown even in marriage, while for the wife new degrees of freedom open up as a result of her special relationship with the divine pole. At the same time an incomparable psychodrama between mother and son starts to form within the Holy Family; and this psychodrama promotes a matriarchal renaissance. At the end of it the mother – overprotective to begin with, then rejected – places the dead son again on her lap; and this *laptop*[24] scene in the absolute, represented in fine art in the genre of the *pietà*, offers the basis for a limitless exaltation of the woman who gave birth to God and generates tendencies toward a global Marianization of femininity in areas with a Christian heritage.

As far as the male "axis"[25] of the Holy Family is concerned, it is being jolted more than anything by the subversive effects of the early Christian concept of dual fatherhood:[26] by establishing a relation to a modest earthly quasi-father while on the other hand he identifies with a glorious divine über-father, the son knows he has been placed virtually outside the order of familial descent. "The Christian identity of the Son with the Father does not establish a genealogical continuum but breaks it."[27]

*

The son must make sense of the fact that God has one day begotten an extramarital child upon Mary, like an exuberant oriental potentate, while the retroactive legitimation of the transcendent offspring could be testified to only with a special effort. Certainly, to save appearances, the unclassifiable child was to grow up in the household of a regular, though somewhat disturbing, married couple. However, a mother who could have an affair with the divine Word and a father who could accept this are not your run-of-the-mill people.

Hence, within the sphere of influence of the Holy Family model, every son brought up in the Christian faith is instructed that, by virtue of his empathy with the position of Jesus, he should understand his own existence as potentially that of a bastard begotten by God: in his veins flows the blood of the transcendent Lord; his soul bears the imprint of an enigmatic and inexhaustible nobility of descent; his mind is aglow with the spark of a calling that exceeds the interests of any empirical family.[28]

This formulates in principle the dilemma of genealogical processes in the space of Christian civilization: no matter how much of a fight the ruling clans and family systems of old Europe, controlled as they were by genealogical magic, put up against an abstract, sibling-oriented Christianization, insisting on the precedence of kinship over ties to the pneumatic commune called church, the infiltration achieved by the Christian model could not be undone. Christian personalization pushes the son – and later the daughter, inasmuch as she is a "spiritual daughter," *filia spiritualis* – out of the genealogical continuum; it positions him or her in an immediate relationship to God that has an explosive psycho-political dynamic, bypassing all descent. There would be no exaggeration in calling Christian personalization one of the most important sources of western individualism.[29] It acquired power above all in the sectarian movements of the late Middle Ages and early modern age, as the Catholic Church was ultimately unable to reabsorb completely the surplus of wild subjectivization. The fundamental theorem regarding the dynamics of civilization, according to which, while processes of transmission immanent in a system are in progress, many more energies are released than can ever be reintegrated by the functions and form-giving powers of existing institutions, makes itself felt nowhere more dramatically than in the ecclesiastical and sectarian history of the modern age – and, later, also in the history of art and forms of expression in modernity.[30]

*

Where this condition has been reached, the Christian subject understands itself not only as a chosen bastard of God but, as a general rule, literally as one of the last human beings: whoever has once fully identified with the son of all sons will not return into the genealogic series, but will renounce all progeny in view of the impending kingdom of God, to be ready when the hour has come.

The consequences for the dynamics of civilization of a social order partially shaped by the pattern of the Holy Family show themselves in a profound split of the old European ideas about legitimacy. While from the point of view of Jewish, Greek, Roman, and Northwest European cultures legitimacy is primarily the result of patriarchal acts of transmission, apostolic succession introduces a second source of legitimacy. For long stretches of time, European intellectual history was nothing but the product of an effort to force the antagonistic legitimacies of secular hereditary succession and apostolic succession into some congruence, particularly among Christian ruling dynasties – where the failure of such attempts was in the nature of things. Whoever equates patriarchy and filiarchy should not be surprised if one day the roof over the allegedly common habitation is being blown up.

The beginnings of the second system of legitimacy can be traced back to the escape of the absolute son from the lines of the local histories of genealogy. No matter how much, after the transition of the original communities into the early church, the second order was recoded with the help of neo-patriarchal terms, the anarchic energy of the Christian world of sons and daughters could never be entirely forced back under the leaden blanket of political patristics. With it a paradox was transmitted that was to become constitutive of the European dynamics of civilization: in the name of the son, the legitimacy of the illegitimate was rendered unforgettable, while at the same time a suspicion arose that could constantly be actualized, according to which at the heart of that which is officially legitimate lies hidden an abyssal illegitimacy. How else could Jesus have said that the stone that the builders rejected had become the cornerstone (Matthew 21:42)? How else could Augustine have dared to claim that, *remota iustitia*,[31] earthly realms were nothing more than enlarged robbers' caves (*magna latrocinia*), and robbers' caves nothing more than small realms?[32] And how could Rousseau still dream of a "society" in which positive law and the "religion of mankind" would once again speak the same language, instead of continuously talking at cross purposes, as is customary in Christian Europe?

All this became possible once the son of all sons had managed to present his palpable illegitimacy as a higher form of legitimate authentication, thanks to his intimate unity with the father. Ever since, a contradiction that cannot be pinned down has been at work in the super-id of old European processes of transmission. The cloth from which filiarchal transmissions are cut is made of anti-authoritarian authority and authoritarian counter-authority. As if it had been a matter of proving that only the impossible has a future, this contradiction secured Christianity its persistence as a movement of incurable irritation.

The church as a vehicle of alternative legitimacy may well have succumbed, temporarily, to states of internal corruption, but its function as transmitter of the human right not to belong to a subjugating body – be it called family, kin, or people – could not really be affected by that. Indeed, even if the church itself, while it was a ruling ideology, became guilty of the enslavement of the psyche of many generations, inherent in its foundational documents was an inextinguishable impulse to release human beings from inherited captivities. Modern human rights are based, first and foremost, upon the individual's freedom – claimed by Christianity and reaffirmed in baptism – from the pressures of one's earliest descent, and certainly also upon early philosophy's commitment to the spirit's cosmopolitan freedom to move and its distancing itself from the polis and from Mother Earth. In the history of ideas, the basis for the "sacred nature of the person," recently witnessed again in the preambles of constitutions and in the tables of value of modernity, lies in these partly productive, partly illusory teachings regarding freedom.[33]

*

Transmission of souls is the first politics. According to it, every human being, from birth on, has an incontestable claim to be "in the wrong" in the face of most relatives, no matter how many they may be. Nobody has to agree with the customs, opinions, and lies of the people of origin, just because the ancestors didn't know any better. In addition, whoever performs the fundamental operation of Christian personhood that one calls "faith" turns instantly into a child of the supreme being born out of wedlock.

That ordinary mortals descend from profane parents is a rule to which exceptions are hardly known. But where the wind-dispersed seeds of the spirit spread, procreation beyond what is common becomes conceivable. How, then, if in your case, too, a vertical factor had intervened? In the era "after Christ" no human being can be denied the right to lead his life as God's bastard. A river Jordan can be found anywhere. In any arbitrary place a human being, emerging from the water, can hear a voice from above that says that this is his dear child, beloved by him, the supreme being.[34]

6

IMPROVING THE HUMAN BEING

Philosophical Notes on the Problem of Anthropological Difference

It is only with hesitation that contemporary philosophical anthropology takes up the challenge of reconstructing the distances that the hominids covered in becoming human beings. To be sure, ever since the 1960s, foundational research and excavations have moved the field significantly. However, from the side of philosophical anthropology, a more or less awkward silence has reigned – and I believe that one can say precisely why.

I would like to begin here with a few sentences on the real quandary of being a human. It is reflected in the fact that we live in a situation dominated by egalitarian criteria, where we find it hard to characterize the human as a being that lives constitutively in vertical tension, that is, as a being consumed by the pressure to be different, as far as her own ability to be and to become is concerned. As they say, the human being is never identical with herself. She relates to herself as to a slope on which there is a more or less, an up and down. Vertical forces affect and permeate her. In the 1990s our American friends brought a wave of political correctness[1] into our country. Along with this came a superb phrase to characterize people of small stature: in the United States, the politically correct call them "vertically challenged people."[2] As for characterizing *conditio humana* as a whole, this expression hits the bull's eye. It is a coinage of high conceptual energy that will prove to be indispensable for us. Indeed, human beings qua human beings are always already "vertically challenged"; they are beings who have to relate to their own vertical tension, hence creatures who can never be relieved from the pressure of their ability to make more or less out of themselves.

We are here placed on the front lines of a battle that we cannot avoid fighting, although we mostly try to evade it. It is well known that we live in an epoch that has given itself the task of implementing egalitarianism in theory and practice – and there has been a precise formulation for this task ever since the eighteenth century: the aim of all politics is to transform the vertical differences between human beings into horizontal differences. This is, likewise, the ultimate level of meaning in the formula *liberté, égalité, fraternité*. We are no longer allowed to categorize in terms of higher and lower, better or worse. Rather we must describe humans as beings who are still distinguished only on the horizontal plane – no longer according to rank, let alone existential value. Concepts of rank have disappeared from contemporary reflection on the human being. This justifies the conclusion that, at bottom, modern anthropology amounts to a science of struggle: the science of abolishing nobility in every sense of the word. This is the first characteristic of this unmistakably modern discipline. It emerged in the eighteenth century, under the banner of an attack carried out by the third and fourth estates against the leisured nobility. On this class Figaro in Beaumarchais's play *The Marriage of Figaro* made a decisive statement – one that could in truth go down as the key sentence of the age: "What have *you* done to deserve such advantages? Put yourself to the trouble of being born – nothing more."[3] Unfortunately da Ponte did not incorporate this sentence from Figaro's monologue into his libretto; hence Mozart still owes us an ironic aria on the words "Put yourself to the trouble of being born." This formula contains the declaration of war that the moderns issued against an outdated age, a declaration in which discourse on the human being was inseparable from reflection on what I am here calling the anthropological difference: whenever the thesis of difference was advocated seriously, the conviction was in force that humans can be different from one another – and not in the sense that any Jack is different, and thus only different by degrees, but in the sense of being fundamentally and dimensionally different.

*

In the history of premodern anthropologies, there were at least four configurations in which the anthropological difference – in other words the substantial vertical difference – was located. In the earliest times, the figure of the god-man or, better still, god-king emerged together with the arrival of Mesopotamian city-kingdoms and of early empires. This figure, which presented itself to its fellow human beings in the form of a qualitatively or metaphysically different creature, has been very powerful in the history of ideas.

Meanwhile we, contemporaries, live in a time in which people no longer wish to hear of a difference between the god-man and so-called mere humans – even if otherwise we are prepared to consider the Dalai Lama to be a sympathetic man, or to learn a thing or two about the two natures of Christ in a theological seminar. To most of us today, the difference on which theocracies were once based seems so preposterous that it becomes unnecessary to demonstrate in detail that this could never have been a difference encountered in reality but only one engineered – and, if it comes to the worst, even a deceptively contrived difference.

We have likewise got rid of the second form of anthropological difference, namely that between saints and profane human beings. We are persuaded that saints were basically only athletes who subjected themselves to very uncommon routines of spiritual training. In India, for example, some tried to stand on one leg for a decade in order to make spiritual progress. In the West, some spiritual athletes tried to perfect themselves by whipping themselves daily and loving all humans to boot. All the great saints were ascetics who attempted to live as people without qualities – abnegating their first nature, their affects, and their body.

I would like to assume that such exercises have practically ceased to generate universal interest today. Only in a rather marginalized mode of intellectual Catholicism is the idea of waiting for the saints still current. In accordance with its own logic, modernity has done well to bestow emeritus status on the saints. Incidentally, the painters of the Italian Renaissance already pointed the way to this situation when, at the end of the fifteenth century, they began to paint figures in sacred history without the hitherto obligatory halos. Perhaps one could even consider this omission of aureoles as the defining criterion of the Renaissance. The loss of the aura, of which Walter Benjamin spoke in his own time, is of course quite directly connected to the ebb of transcendence that became manifest in the images of the burgeoning modern age.

Yet even more significant – and in a certain way also more tragic for us, as people of learning, *homines academici* – is the fact that the third form of anthropological difference, that between the sage and the ignorant masses, has collapsed. Here too, leveling and secularization are to be observed across the board. In fewer than 200 years, the tension between the *sapiens* and the *insipiens vulgus*, the knowledgeable and the senseless crowd, which had been constitutive to the intellectual history of humanity in the past, was eliminated. It was especially the anthropologists who showed how this happened: they attached a second *sapiens* to the first one and transferred the adjective from the individual to the species. On top of that, eighteenth-century philosophers issued the slogan: "Let us hasten to make philosophy popular!" With modern skepticism, with conventionalism, with deconstructivism, we have toppled the concept of a positive knowledge that is based in evidence and makes itself sovereign, and in doing so we have brought about a situation that Richard Rorty summarized when he proclaimed the priority of democracy over philosophy. This implies that there is no longer any transcendent evidence for us, and thus no sage of considerable importance who would have a share in it. Consequently the sage can no longer enter the sphere of the unenlightened individuals like some visitor from another world, someone from a dimension illuminated by rare enlightenments, and spread the truth there. Rather we must find our way into a commune of half-knowers and half-enlightened individuals, at a table of half-knowledge or absent knowledge. Only very few of our contemporaries – theologians among them – have declared resistance to this liquefaction of postmodern knowledge and hold fast onto certain non-negotiable and thus transcendent basic doctrines. At the risk of being labeled fundamentalists, they would not abandon certain forms of orienting knowledge. They would not put their revelations up for debate, even if the world were full of conventionalists.

Finally I wish to identify a fourth leveling, with which the last form of anthropological difference is also eliminated. Generally we have long forgotten that, in its struggle against the nobility, the bourgeoisie adopted a specific title of nobility for itself when it appealed to "nobility of spirit." This is not merely a random book title, under which Thomas Mann collected his lectures and essays on great authors of the bourgeois era. It is at the same time a programmatic title, which expresses the values and the perspective through which the natural aristocracy of talent was able to succeed in its uprising against the nobility of blood and office. The self-creation of the bourgeoisie in aristocratic shape [*Selbstaristokratisierung*] was evidently a condition of possibility for the success of its emancipation. But whoever participates in slaughter is no longer, in future confrontations, the same as he was before; and it was precisely the success of their own slogans that made the bourgeois grow tired of their initial slogans. After 200 years of a winning religion of talent, in our times they parted with their catchwords "talent" and "genius"; and this is a rip that runs palpably through our life stories.

We see today, as if scales were falling from our eyes, that even nature, that great conferrer of talent and ally of bourgeois ascent, was itself conceived of rather like a court in which there were still protégés and favorites. Thus, when exposed to the light, nature is as unjust and capricious as the absolute ruler, nay, even more: it is the absolutism of chance in its purest form. With this insight, talent and genius become offensive to all those who, as Niklas Luhmann

so finely (and maliciously) put it once, must also live off their looks.
First there is discontent, then comes hatred, and hatred, as always,
is followed by a codicil of good reasons.

The phenomenon of crowds, of which Elias Canetti provided a
classic description, can then appear on the scene as a broad center,
as an *aurea mediocritas* – a golden mean. It puts the liquidation of
the nobility of nature and talent on the agenda of political ideas.
Today we live in the final phase of this process. Consequently the
watchword is not only priority of democracy over philosophy but
also priority of democracy over art. As indicated, the project of
modernity is based on the resolution to revalue all values in the
direction of horizontal differences: all human beings are primarily
equal, differentiations are secondary. This new equality does not
signify the traditional equality of all human beings before God.
With an eye to the medieval estate system, one could speak of an
infinite egalitarianism, insofar as no relation can take place between
the finite and the infinite, as is well known. The relevant dogma in
scholasticism had been *inter finitum et infinitum non est proportio*
["there is no proportion/analogy between the finite and the infinite"].
Meanwhile, what we are dealing with is an entirely different form of
equality. It is not God in relation to whom – as the infinite – all finite
differences are null. Rather what is at issue now is an equality before
nothingness, the equality before the indifference of equal value,
which puts everything at the same level. There is, at best, an equality
before the genome, which indeed even at its own level, demonstrates
an overwhelming preponderance of the common over the distinct.

*

We have likewise learned from philosophical anthropology that
the human is precisely that being who has no properties of her
own, except for those that she creates for herself. The concept of
anthropotechnics designates nothing but that no *Homo sapiens* has
yet fallen from the sky, that this creature is therefore attained only
by means of technogenic effects, which react to their own evolutionary drift. Thanks to anthropological research, today we know
that the body image of *Homo sapiens* can be explained only by
recourse to an evolutionary effect that anthropologists after Alsberg
call the "deactivation of the body." This means that, early on, the
burgeoning human being withdraws behind a distancing shield,
which allows him to deflect the immediate selective pressure of
nature. Behind this shield, this being steps into a special, luxurious
evolution, which biologists call neoteny – literally a retention of
youthful, partly even fetal forms into the stage of adulthood. To

put this clearly, *Homo sapiens* is a human–monkey fetus developed to sexual maturity yet biologically frozen in a state of chronic early arrival, a fetus that profits from the remarkable privilege of not being able to grow up – and of not having to grow up. He emerges from a unique phenomenon of retardation, and whoever speaks of *Homo sapiens* without speaking of his neoteny, his organismic immaturity, his immobilization in a semi-fetal state, and *eo ipso* his precarious relation to time has missed his theme from the get go.

*

I would like to sketch here the anthropotechnic problem in six or seven vignettes. These vignettes will bring to light what things are at stake when human beings work on human beings – and hence when human beings make human beings themselves an object of production or of conscious and intentional modifications. I would like to begin with the most notable example: a thought experiment that a French author named Didier van Cauwelaert has enacted, not so long ago, in a macabre novel titled *L'Évangile de Jimmy* (*The Gospel according to Jimmy*). This book is about some American research scientists who get close to a fundamentalist evangelical sect and come to the conclusion that the return of Christ is too important an event to be abandoned to our passive mode of waiting for him. Americans occasionally distinguish themselves by being able to tackle even metaphysical questions with technological expertise, and hence this event, which in the terminology of the expectant is called "the Second Coming,"[4] must inevitably become a technological project. Aside from genetic engineering technology, three things are needed for it: first, access to the Shroud of Turin; second, access to the Sudarium of Oviedo; and, third, access to the seamless robe of Jesus in Trier.

It is easy to explain why this is so. Famously, there are several scientists – I don't know whether they are nested scientists working for the Vatican, for the other side, or for other, obscure interest groups – who assert that the same blood can be found on these three pieces of cloth, even though they stem from different centuries. Moreover, according to certain authors, all signs point to this blood's being genuine – because evidence suggests that these pieces of cloth were once wrapped around the corpse of Christ. Thus there are also indications that the Americans are replacing the outdated European search for the Grail with the project of reconstructing the blood of Christ at DNA level. If anthropotechnics is ever to take place at high-tech[5] level, then it is probably best to begin with the most ambitious object. If there is to be cloning, then without further ado one will clone Jesus Christ himself. We have lost the patience to wait for his return – and rightly so, since we have come to understand the cunning of reason according to which several material bearers of Christ's original DNA were preserved precisely up to the point where the complete sequencing of the human genome and, in consequence, a technological restoration of the body of Jesus through cloning have become possible.

*

This is, in a few short words, the content of that techno-Gnostic cock-and-bull story that sprang from the pen of a French cartoonist and novelist in 1994. Significantly, after the great success of the novel, the same author attempted a second blow when he published a report about the real consequences of his fiction. In this report he claimed – this time in the style of a docusoap – that, after he had published his Jesus-book, he was visited by an American professor who purported to have been really working on the same project for quite some time and to be on the point of a breakthrough. This example shows what anthropotechnics could mean at its peak: the human being manufactures God – a handsome techno-Gnostic blasphemy that, for the time being, we will have to swallow in science fiction format.

We have far less blasphemous sentiments toward the narrative with which the biblical Genesis opens – where the project of making humans proceeds from the other side. In our cultural environment, it seems normal that God would manufacture the human being. Why, though? In Christian anthropology, we have always connected the concept of the human being with the idea that we are dealing with something manufactured. We are not at all pained by this theologically, and certainly not anthropologically. We raise no objections to this story, even though the myth of a manufacturer is present here with its own, firm manual grip. When we read the biblical narrative of the sixth day of genesis closely, it becomes clear beyond any doubt that God is a ceramicist and that the creation of the human being occurs in two strokes, first ceramically, then metaceramically; metaphysics begins as metaceramics. First there is pottery making, insofar as an empty form is manufactured. Then, in the second act, personal life is blown into it. Thus, whenever we speak of the human being in Christian terminology, we are always already standing on the soil of producer and manufacturer fantasies. Consequently we should not complain when new figures are shaped from the same grammar later on, even if by means of other agents. These figures follow the schema according to which a powerful agent actively works on human material – thus the anthropotechnics of God serves as a model for human work on the human being.

*

A third example illustrates in its own way the connection between Christian semantics and modern techno-Gnosticism. Only a few people in the West know that, during the Russian October Revolution, there was a group of metaphysically ambitious anthropotechnicians who reached the high point of their activity probably around 1920, being inspired by an author named Nicolai Fedorov. They called themselves "biocosmists" or "immortalists." Their guiding idea was that communism could not be realized as long as private ownership over one's lifespan was not eliminated. They believed to have discovered the deepest cause of the inequality between human beings, namely that every individual is each time allocated a completely unique temporal pattern [*Temporalisierung*] of her existence. These allotments came from an intolerable generator of chance or fate that one calls history. Even as Martin Heidegger attempted to think the essence of existentiality against the background of imminent death, which he then wanted to extrapolate to human historicity as a whole, the Russian techno-Gnostics developed a program for the most radical realization of communism – namely on the basis of a demand for the immortality of all participants in the great experiment. In fact, according to them, any genuine communism must establish this premise, because otherwise there will always be a relapse into the terrible privacy of owning one's lifespan.

*

If we go back one step further into the history of the anthropo-technic motif, we will come across an intellectual configuration that could be described as the early humanist doctrine of human autoplasticity. Here one should mention in the first instance the Hermetic thinker and polymath Pico della Mirandola, who has gone down in history as the author of an *Oration on the Dignity of Man* on everyone's lips when they are trying to reconstruct the origins of the bold idea that human beings are creatures who, all by themselves, set things in motion and thus generate new effects in the world. Pico inspires this idea by having the highest creator distribute to his creatures every possible attribute. When he finally turns to Adam, the *Homo* he has created from the earth, he realizes that he has already used up all the available attributes.

Everything that was supposed to be allotted has been allotted. One creature is left without any attributes. God makes this defect into an advantage, by telling this to Adam: 'Among all creatures, you will be the one who fashions himself. You will have the dignity of being your own inventor.' It is at this point that we find the decisive formulation. 'From now on you will be the *plastes et fictor* of yourself, your own fashioner and creator, endowed with the capacity to operate upon yourself as you will. You will be the one who decides what will come of you. If you elevate yourself to the level of divinity, it is you who will be responsible. But if you lower yourself to the level of animals, you yourself will likewise be responsible.'

*

This is one of the first passages in which the modern ideology of the human creature without qualities emerges. It defines the human as a dowerless animal. Thus the human is handed a complete auto-demiurgic competence, born of the dialectical unity of deprivation and endowment.

Pico della Mirandola's text came out at a time when the demiurgic conception of the human being was still in complete minority. This is the late fifteenth century, at the zenith of the reception wave of Thomas à Kempis's only just redacted *Imitatio Christi*. It is precisely *not* the creativity of the human being that is addressed there – this treatise focuses instead on human passivity, which was driven to its utmost extreme under the banner of "mysticism" and imitation of Christ. This tradition speaks uniquely to the lust for passion among middle class people in cities, which were again on the rise at that time. In the early modern age commoners were asked to step in as experts in their own suffering, to the extent that they had the model of imitating Christ as an ideal path through life imposed upon them.

Here, too, the human being is seen completely as a creature that should transcend itself. Only, in this case, it uses *imitatio Christi* to interpret its vertical tension. However, this is not to be understood as a program of creativity, as Christianity hardly ever speaks of creativity. It has no creative, or rather creativist image of the human being. It doesn't find the human being interesting because this being is aesthetically virulent or has the tendency to compose operas and paint pictures. The only thing that counts is that humans measure themselves by the task of becoming like Christ, who for his part became like God by giving himself fully to God – no time was left for art as such. *Imitatio Christi* amounts to a comprehensive training in passion whose goal has been described with the Greek

words *theōsis*, "becoming god," and *henōsis*, "becoming one," for
which the Romans supplied *unio*.

*

When we enter the realm of flatter anthropotechnic self-operations,
we will encounter a field that has long encompassed the tribal
territory of humans operating on humans. This is the territory the
Greeks called *paideia*, whose modern equivalent is "paedagogy." In
the founding era of modern educational science in the seventeenth
century, when the great Comenius was active and the first anthropo-
gogues came on the scene – significantly, the early paedagogues
called themselves leaders of human beings, not merely leaders of
children – using education to make human beings was proclaimed
the first obligation of citizens and teachers. Under the headings
"cultivation" and "education" were placed the procedures by which
the children of the bourgeoisie and of the nobility were to liberate
themselves from the class-based narrow-mindedness of their provenance, to become human beings and nothing but human beings,
absolutely and for the first time. One of the most interesting paedagogues of the seventeenth century, a certain Becher, proclaimed that
the nobility's educational practice up to that point had not advanced
beyond breeding "noble beasts." Why beasts? Because the dressage
offered to their caste made them mere reflections of their forebears,
in the absence of the dignifying alchemy of the early bourgeois
humanistic and cultural education. Here again the thesis that the
human being is not yet as she should be is completely obvious; first
she must be skillfully produced through a paedagogical process of
elevation.

If at this point we reflect back on the project of cloning Christ, we
will see how far we have already descended into the pragmatic realm.
Anthropotechnics is now supposed to mean nothing but paedagogy.
Nevertheless, paedagogy is and remains an activity that, at least
when it is exercised in a sophisticated way, dignifies the human not
only as a being who is able in principle to go beyond herself, but as
one who actually and justifiably does so; for her purpose consists in
unfolding and elevating her powers. My life would thus be nothing
but my transformation into the best book I can be.

If at this point we go one step further again, we end up in the very
shallow waters of anthropotechnic self-treatment. Under this rubric
I group things that perhaps do not always go together: prosthetics,
athletics, and cosmetics. With these three concepts we give expression
again to the fact that human beings operate on human beings – in
self-relations as in relations with others. Yet, although we are dealing

with trivial or flat forms of anthropotechnics here, nothing is being said about their dispensability.

When I use the term "flat," I mean it in relation to the stark vertical tensions that I mentioned in the introductory examples. However, it contains no judgment about the dispensability of these things – for what would the human being be today without his prostheses? What would we be without our artificial teeth, without our false hair, without the glasses that first let us live as *homines academici* – let alone as "wise persons from Tübingen," *homines sapientes tuebingenses*. The human being, in other words the neotenized primate fetus, depends on cultural technologies of supplementation for becoming impressive and capable of appearing before himself and others. What is proper to prosthetics is valuable to athletics – and the same holds at the level of cosmetic operations. They quite literally make the human being *plastes* and *fictor* of his appearance. Then the envelope is pushed, and many people come to the seemingly blasphemous, yet today well-established idea that they no longer wish to accept themselves as they were delivered from the hand of the creator. One glance in the mirror and they are persuaded that they have grounds, indeed even a right, to work on themselves by means of plastic surgery; and Pico della Mirandola looks on approvingly. This becomes more understandable when we think about the fact that the human being is a creature condemned to go on stage, to appear, and to be perceived. When we further take it into account that, for both men and women, there are body parts that become uncomfortably conspicuous more than others, as subjects of gravity, opposing gravity with something stands to reason. The intervention of plastic surgery imposes itself as soon as we come across the idea that gravitation and human dignity are mutually contradictory.

*

Only at this late point in time, when the anthropotechnic curve has already become quite flat, do I wish to bring the concept of *eugenics* into play. Just recently, this term has generated a lot of contrived excitement. Literally eugenics designates the art of being well born. If this were different, then countless mothers and fathers of the bourgeois and the pre-bourgeois era would not have christened their daughters with the gorgeous name "Eugenia." And if the art of being well born had carried connotations of blasphemy at some earlier date, Christianity would not have had popes with the sonorous name Eugene. (There were, however, four with this name between the seventh and the fifteenth centuries.) Eugenics, as the art of being well born, zeroes in on the attempt to improve the conditions of human reproduction. In the previous history of humanity, technology, if we may call it this, was not able to go beyond the threshold of mere facilitation – and in essence this pertained only to the modalities of bringing reproductive partners together. Today, by contrast, it seems for the first time that in the near future certain smaller modifications could be made in the style of direct eugenics, too. Eugenics came on the agenda as soon as the Enlightenment began to occupy itself with the popular subject of procreation; and it is the most legitimate child of the Enlightenment when it comes to the question of what happens when humans are confronted with the problem of procreation in broad daylight. Here as everywhere, the Enlightenment votes for more light.

The first to utter these thoughts was none other than Plato, who contented himself with the requirement that the choice of a partner should occur with eyes wide open. The act of love must not take place in the dark. When people have reached the point where they cannot refrain from the well-known preliminaries to conception, they should not close their eyes. Plato marshals the remarkable requirement that conception be a *tokos en kalōi*, a bringing forth in the beautiful – and here we have the complete definition of eugenics. It expresses the following thought: when one has the feeling that something beautiful will emerge, one may do what one will. This measure should in principle suffice to make people want to continue to proliferate successful impressions of beauty. Only, in choosing their partners, people have the same sort of experience as in everything else: for the most part one doesn't get what one wants, for which reason one takes something else instead – and then swerves into dimness or complete obscurity. We may surmise that the bringing forth in the not-so-beautiful or in the unbeautiful that results from this also deposits itself in the bio-aesthetic profile of *Homo sapiens*.

To the extent that it became explicit at all, eugenics is a theme that has been practiced for centuries, above all within the framework of an aristocratic politics of difference. In the days of that politics, there actually was something like an aristocratic natural selection and an incestuous practice among the upper classes. Since the nineteenth century, however, eugenics changed political camps and became a favorite theme of socialism. One should take the opportunity to note here that, essentially, there never was an effective Nazi eugenics – what one hears about it to this day is, for the most part, simple misunderstandings. What was actually in place on a massive scale in the context of the National Socialist movement was overtly euthanasist programs, which have incorrectly been associated with the concept of eugenics. In their tendency and effect, they were programs of obliteration. Even the concept of euthanasia became thereby estranged from and opposed to its traditional meaning. A wide trend within the history of ideas proves, however, that from the nineteenth century on there was a tendency toward eugenic socialism. This tendency extended to the foolhardiness of demanding beauty for all, even intelligence for all – a demand that should nevertheless be appraised as revolutionary. One must insist on the historical fact that, in the main, eugenicism has been a motif of the left – and all the National Socialist literature does not counterbalance a single page from the relevant writings of George Bernard Shaw, or from the communist eugenicists.

*

Perhaps you will have noticed that I managed not to make use of the concept of the superman [*Übermensch*] in this speech – and I hope you will recognize this as an accomplishment. There is good reason to avoid it. I am persuaded that this concept has simply disintegrated itself, in the enumeration I offered above. It has unfolded its meanings and tendencies, more or less completely, in the examples given, such that there is no essential semantic remainder that would not have been treated here by implication. This means only that the concept of the superman belongs in the oldest, inalienable stock of the Christian tradition. Only in the contemporary age, where a postmetaphysical reformation of Christendom has begun, will one produce a purely human form of Christianity; thus one would like to release the faithful from the vertical tensions that previously grounded one's dignity.

7

EPOCHS OF ENSOULMENT

Suggestions for a Philosophy
of the History of Neurosis

My soul is weary of my life; I will leave my complaint upon myself; I will speak in the bitterness of my soul. I will say unto God, Do not condemn me; shew me wherefore thou contendest with me. [...] Remember, I beseech thee, that thou has made me as the clay; and wilt thou bring me into dust again? Hast thou not poured me out as milk, and curdled me like cheese? Thou hast clothed me with skin and flesh, and hast fenced me with bones and sinews. [...] Wherefore then hast thou brought me forth out of the womb?

Job 10:1–18

The soul is always inhabited by some power, whether good or bad. Souls are not ill when they are inhabited, but when they are no longer inhabited.

Pierre Klossowski, *La Ressemblance*, 1984[1]

The subtitle of these considerations immediately brings together the expressions "neurosis" and "philosophy of history." This provides the occasion, if not the reason, for the thesis that I do not mean to suggest here just an external amalgamation, but rather the development of an internal connection. As will be shown, a psychoanalytic doctrine of neuroses is, in itself, a historical–philosophical undertaking: by analogy with the defeudalization of society and the democratic revolution, psychotherapy is the "medical" variation on the typically modern order of procedure in the trials conducted by the individual against the prevailing life circumstances, which are of a grievous nature. In its highest political form, the philosophy of history was the cognitive model for the transition from a feudal to a bourgeois society. It formulated the matrix for the processes of emancipation that were supposed to lead from the reign of peoples to the reign of law, from the psycho-politics of command and obedience to the psycho-politics of the self-determination of equal and free individuals. We can thus understand why the protagonists of this way of thinking were able to emerge as custodians of a society of political adolescents, as it were, or, say, as tribunals and lawyers for an emancipatory cause nationwide – nay, humanity-wide. They wished to advance this cause with such persuasiveness and such a powerfully inclusive universality that even their opponents would basically have to acknowledge their claim. The guiding word of the Enlightenment was the one that Immanuel Kant invoked, namely *Mündigkeit*. It was defined as the capacity to make use of one's own reason without the guidance of others – especially when it came to religious matters.

Now *Mündigkeit* is a concept that no psychoanalytically trained reader of historical texts can accept any more without reservations. To translate it simply as "autonomy" or "self-determination" would be unwarranted naivety – even if this would be most welcome to those academic philosophers who are anti-psychologists. *Mündigkeit* – a "third ear" hears *Mund* [mouth] in it from the outset – is a phantasm of an orality that has extended into the political sphere. Behind the ideal of *Mündigkeit* is the idea that a subject has taken possession of her oral abilities – especially of language – to such an extent that she can speak for herself, indeed even for humanity, in her own voice. A pedagogical program is articulated in the idea of *Mündigkeit*. This program encompasses an educational and cultural history of the mouth that spans from the first gulp to the last will and testament, from the primal scream to parliamentary discourse. Hence the oral destinies of human beings are intimately tied to the global course of modern epochs.

The philosophy of history is always, by nature, also a philosophy of cultural education, insofar as it describes and helps initiate normative processes that are supposed to lead from speechlessness to the summit of a universal language, from helplessness to comprehensive self-help. At the vanishing point of the idea of *Mündigkeit* is a fantasy of radical self-sufficiency and a definitive decoupling from the material and psychic influence of others. Bourgeois education consists in influencing others in such a way that the idea emerges in them that they would always have sought their *Mündigkeit*, even without any external influence. Incidentally, in this context it is easy to understand that – and why – psychotherapists misunderstand themselves when they take the basic trait of their profession to be medical. To any unbiased eye, they should be treated as educators.

And if they must indeed be educators of some sort, this is because
they are dealing with post-cultural formations and post-educations
– like teachers at a special needs school of life. At the most, the
educator profile is completed by the lawyer profile, insofar as
psychotherapists support their clients in their lawsuits for the restoration of those life opportunities that in regular biographies foster
a fulfilled human existence, as one would call it. With the model
of the *mündige* [mature, responsible] subject, an ideal of maturity
is envisioned that – by virtue of a doubly oral autarchy – should
be in a position to speak for itself and to keep itself alive by its
own efforts.

In both of these aims of education, tightly interwoven as they are,
it is not only remnants of the Stoic ideal of wisdom that survive;
basic figures of the old European grammar of philosophy that have
become problematic also find expression in them. Know it or not,
whoever speaks of *mündige* human beings takes out a loan from the
Aristotelian concept of substance and its dynamized continuation in
the modern concept of the subject. I will attempt in what follows to
show that the philosophy of history, in its basic political form as well
as on its therapeutic wings, is laden with a questionable inheritance
of false abstractions. Its translation into modern psychotherapy had
to lead to consequential deformations of the psychological domain.

*

Here is another way of putting it: the crisis of the philosophy of
history and the crisis of the subject that gave the second half of the
twentieth century its character also affects the therapeutic domain.
Bound up with the recognition of this crisis is the thesis that philosophical psychology is steering toward an upheaval that will reform
its basic approach to concepts – with unforeseeable consequences
for everything to do with the ideas of *Mündigkeit*, mouthliness, and
orality. The doctrine of the human as the being through which there
is speech inevitably assumes a radicalized mediumistic form. With
the conversion of a substance or subject theory of the psyche into a
media psychology we will arrive at a critique of oral substantialism
– and at prospects for a medial or mediumistic theory of personality
with a new sort of quasi-pneumatological payoff.

In order to characterize this transformation, we should avoid
the fashionable phrase "paradigm shift." For it is precisely not the
paradigm that is here the model for thought – which, by changing
course, would lead to another view of things. Rather a conversion of
the thinker is necessary before a revised experience of psychic space
can open up for him. Here I am pointing to a sort of meta-noetic

procedure that rivals a philosophical training analysis; it can only come to light under a philosophical supervision of the psychological conceptual work. A logical training analysis of this sort[2] carves out the universal in the processes of psychological assistance by establishing an analytical mediumism – one could also say a school of knowledge of transformation and of boundary transgressions. In this context we cannot emphasize enough that psychology is not possible as a "bourgeois science," if to think in a bourgeois fashion means to think under the premise of the semblance of well-defined ego demarcations between *mündige* private persons. From the perspective of its object, psychology requires an eccentric and indiscrete logic, because the "soul" can itself be adequately thought of and discussed only as the effect of an intimate penetration and tuning; the object of psychology is something intangible, something that really exists only as the breathing of the mental into the mental, as it were, as an overreaching or overleaping of one psychological sphere into another.

In what follows I would like to suggest a spherological definition of the mental and characterize the object of psychological discourse as a medial magnitude that "emerges" only insofar as it can be occupied, penetrated, and shaken by what is like it.

Thus, metaphorically speaking, souls would be houses whose inhabitants are not to be governed by bourgeois laws of tenancy and private property but rather are taken in and cleared out by squatters, along with other occupying and inspiring spirits, in a fluctuating game of coming and going.[3] This medial perspective on the mental field presupposes two things that, for the moment, can only be postulated, not carried out: a historical ontology of the human as the being that cannot *not* come to the world; and an anthropological kinetics that describes the human as a being that changes elements – in other words as the animal that always already, wherever it "emerges," transposes itself from the fluid into the fixed and from the unsaid into the said.[4]

It follows from the first presupposition that human beings, because they cannot *not* come to the world, have been burdened with a high risk of psychological miscarriage ever since the beginning of "hot history" – which Lévi-Strauss speaks about – and of imperial class societies. Humans who have failed to enter into the house of the world would be stillborn in the ontological sense – if the old holistic suggestion of characterizing the world as a house obtainable by all members of an imperial whole was ever valid. The problematic tenants of being are stillborn; they are hurt entities, which have problems with their stay often before they move in. In their brittle world enclosures, they will cultivate – culturally, nationally, and personally – typical styles of defective and begrudging being in the world – styles whose meanings are "symptomatic" in the technical sense of the word. The concept of symptom is broadened here beyond the dialectics of manifestation and resistance, so that it may include the ontological tension between seizing the world and fleeing the world, and also, one could say, the double dimension of presence to and absence from [*Dasein und Fortsein*] the stages of life-determining dramas. Neurotic styles of human existence [*Dasein*] are compromises in which individuals submit their accounts of the advantage and disadvantage of being born. Hence we can interpret neuroses as negative balances in the experience of the world.[5] It follows from the second presupposition that human beings, as creatures of risk that change the elements, can fail in the transition, whether because they do not learn a language properly and thus cannot symbolize their passions in a sufficiently lively way, or because they do not reach the shore of the real world, the *terra ferma* of mature actions, and remain persistently inundated and stranded.

Against the background of such intimations, it is evident that psychotherapy must be an art of discreet indiscretions; its medium is a tactful shamelessness or a restrained intrusiveness. This bipolarity or paradox in its approach is inevitable, because, in substance, between therapists and clients there can be no bourgeois relation, of the kind that occurs in the use of physiotherapeutic services. If psychotherapy were like reprogramming malfunctioning computers, it could be transferred without remainder into the ambience of bourgeois services. (Incidentally, the rudiments of this have been in place for a long time now.) It could be performed in as disengaged a manner as endoscopy, or as continued education paid for by one's employer. But, since psychotherapy is essentially the practice of rectifying an ensoulment through the introduction of a soulfulness that is successful and common, it is self-evident that such a co-psychological or medial practice can come into its own only when it sets in motion a true miracle of good intrusiveness and energizing boundary transgression.

*

If one looks at constellations of the history of ideas in classic Viennese psychoanalysis, one will notice that the latter has a threefold religious–philosophical character. We could express this with the terms "postexorcism," "post-idealism," and "post-Judaism." In each of these expressions the prefix "post-" marks a revisionist stance on a model, while the nouns mark spiritual–historical formations of the highest psychological competence. Common to all three is their mediumistic character. We will see how, in the closest relatives of psychoanalysis – and thus in the exorcist, idealist, and Judaic traditions – an extensive knowledge of the mysteries of inter- and intrapsychic circumstances of spiritualization and ensoulment wandered through the ages. It is as disconcerting as it is understandable that these at once awkward and fascinating relations are still not part of the basic knowledge that goes into psychoanalytic training. To the extent that the older psychoanalytic movement attended upon the myth of Freud's epochal originality, it was initially forced to cordon itself off from the continua in which the older knowledge of medial processes was transmitted. Only a psychoanalytic movement that is sufficiently recognized culturally and broadly secure institutionally will be able to afford a demythologized image of its macro-historical circumstances and typological affiliations, without fear of condemnatory associations.

The best reason for unease with the affiliations of psychoanalysis may be related to exorcism. Insofar as it is moved by the demiurgic idea of gaining independence, modernity shies away most of all from the thought that the individual could be the scene of some intimate occupation, that is, of some foreign domination or possession that works from within.[6] This is where the Catholic tradition of exorcism, itself rooted in pre-Christian shamanism, has a strong point. In its conviction and experience, souls are essentially "housings" or ravines that spiritual entities and forces of all sorts wander through and that, in unfavorable circumstances, offer themselves as outposts and fixed abodes for demonic occupying forces. Exorcism took refuge in the idea of a spiritual hierarchy whenever it detected a malign occupation of a soul or, in traditional terms, a demonic or diabolic possession. For, if there are relations of rank among the occupants, it becomes possible for a higher occupant to expel a lower. In exorcism, healing was launched like some kind of temple cleansing. The soul was conceived of neither as a theater nor as a factory, as is typical of the modern age, but rather as a sanctuary in which no image was allowed to be on display except that of the god-man – whose imago, in turn, had to represent an undescribable God. It is decisive that, under such premises, healing must never be thought of as something negative, as the mere evacuation of a disturbance. Driving out evil spirits always had to be supplemented with and completed by the entrance of a bright principle, which, as warden of the purified soul, became its new monitor and source of inspiration. The most noteworthy moment in the exorcist tradition is given by this circumstance: the possessed human being is never left despiritualized after exorcist cures. When the spectacular spirits of torture have moved out, times of disorientation or "self-determination" in the modern sense do not begin; it is, for the person who has been healed, the dawn of the discreet regime of a higher spirituality, which makes itself perceived exclusively through an inconspicuous success in life. In view of these circumstances, it can be said that the truth of exorcism lies not so much in driving the demons out as in the effective establishment of a spiritual hierarchy within the possessed soul. As the most indiscreet of all cures, exorcism puts itself forward as able to organize the power relations inside another self. Exorcism remains discreet and respectful with regard to the individuality of its clients; however, insofar as it works to implant a super-personal spiritual motive in the sick soul, it acts, as a rule, like a Christological cure. In view of the premises of exorcist catharsis, one could say that healing always presupposed a shift of "possession"; here an obscene occupant of the soul is replaced by a discreet and generous spirit. The latter does not bring into effect any perverse private interests in this individual soul, but rather declares a manumitting goodwill toward it. The "true God" is one whose abstinence can be relied upon. When we admit that a similar healing power of discreet sympathy is asserted and required in the ethics of psychoanalytic countertransference, we will clearly see how the psychoanalytic approach profiles a postexorcist field – on the one hand, at the bequest of a strictly monotheistic conception of spiritual hierarchy, on the other, being marked by the modern rejection of positive religion. As postexorcism, psychoanalysis refrains from adopting only one motif from its predecessor's work in the field of saving souls – or, better, in that of pastoral magic – a motif that takes on psychological significance even after the departure of doctrinal metaphysics. It is the motif of re-ensoulment or respiritualization, which promises to replace crippling obsessions with passions worthy of life.

*

I will refrain from discussing here the hypnotism intermezzo, which lasted for more than a hundred years and whose significance for the development of the typically modern awareness of transference as the medium of therapeutic interpsychic relationships can never be overestimated. It may be enough to say that an established magneto-pathic and hypnotic practice between Mesmer and Puységur on the one hand, and Freud on the other had provided evidence for the effectiveness of the postexorcist position. On this position it became evident that even in post-Christian culture the operation of souls in other souls need not be anything horrific or fantastic. And yet hypnotism remains the bad conscience of psychoanalysis, as it were. It has the unsettling privilege of having introduced undeniably the most effective probes into the mode of being of the psychic realm. The problem of why Freudianism had to emerge, however, not only as postexorcist but also as posthypnotic will stay out of the picture for the time being.[7]

When we consider the second headwaters of the psychoanalytic system, namely the philosophy of German idealism, especially in its Fichtean and Schellingian configurations, we can see how the model of the soul to be ensouled and of the spirit to be inspired appear at the highest level of universalization. For the sake of hyperbole, we could say that, according to idealist logic, it is only the invasion of the psychological by the psychological that constitutes the region of the soul or spirit as such. Thus the logic of indiscretion has attained a level of universality that can no longer be surpassed. In the idealist conception, "thinking" or "being a spiritual soul" means nothing but opening up to the invasion of a principle that works through me and devoting myself to it. Idealism in this sense is a procedure of devoting oneself to an overpowering – or, better, diapowering – principle that thinks, gives soul, gives life, and inspires. This principle has been addressed, in its various hypostases, as spirit, life, idea, and God.

To this day, whoever is interested either in the general logic of boundary transgressions between personal "units" or in the general form of encroachments between psychological systems can do no better than bend over the theories of inspiration developed in the venerable tradition of German idealism. There, in the form of a philosophical theology, we find the maximum encroachment, in amply explicit forms. The highest thinking task of idealism, the so-called absolute reflection, consists in the obscene trick of grasping oneself as a local symptom of God – whereby "grasping" should be understood quite seriously, as playing along in a cognitive theodrama. Thinking in the eminent sense refers to a grasped grasping, a seen seeing; here too we could replace the participles "grasped" and "seen" with the stronger forms "grasped through" and "seen through" in order to mark the middle-voice character of the occurrence of grasping and sight. It is not I who see and grasp; rather a power of seeing and grasping welling up from the absolute works through me. If I were to let myself fall completely into God, in the final instance I would no longer be me, but entirely he through me. Complete theopsychosis would be the ideal case of successful ensoulment.

As the highest form of philosophy of religion, German idealism draws the ultimate consequences from metaphysical mediumism.

From Plato to Hegel, metaphysical mediumism had placed all individual souls under the monarchy of God, the One. In monotheism, all individuals, as *personae*, are character masks of God. Absolute spirit – let us say, God or life – realizes itself as a principle of total indiscretion; it is a wellspring of unreserved intrusiveness and penetrability that is at home with itself (only or above all) in others and through others. Life, idealistically understood, is pure penetrance – it is more indiscreet than a hypercaring mother whose child would be continually transparent to her at an emotional level, without any blind spots.

It is easy to see how extraordinarily momentous this monotheistic psycho-theological thought model is for the post-idealist conception of the region of the soul. Two concepts emerge from it that are essential for understanding psychological thought in the nineteenth and twentieth centuries: on the one hand, the idea of the unconscious as the forgotten, yet reappropriable shadow of conscious psychic life; on the other, the conception of subjectivity as a double subjectivity of the ego and the self.

After what has been said, the latter can be easily explained. If the ego is really a local function of an absolute spirit, the soul can be thought of only from the side of what ensouls it and the individual spirit only from the side of what inspires it. Insofar as subjectivity, idealistically understood, is intrinsically constituted as a double subjectivity, we can investigate the function of the ego in light of the question as to whether and to what extent it makes itself available to irradiation through the self. Seen in this way, idealism would be a sort of philosophical psychoanalysis hot on the trail of egohood [*Egoität*] as a form of resistance to the depths of the self – where the resistance can itself be interpreted only as something divine that has been purloined, perverted, and made unconscious, and thus as a forgotten piece of property, like a symptom in a history of alienation.

Owing to the basic approach of her system, the idealist's communication with her fellow human beings must be of an indiscretion that can hardly be surpassed; she looks into the demonic side of other souls and becomes their confidante in matters of death during their lifetime. This necropsy of one's fellow human beings is the harshest psychiatry. Any emphasis on and by the ego, even if it fancies itself as healthy energy, would be the trace of an occupation by deadness.[8] The ego that emphasizes itself would always be already perverse, in a specific sense; perversion, interpreted theologically as egoism within the absolute, means being diabolic. The deadness that fancies and privileges itself is diabolic; an idealistic therapy would be the recall of the egoist back to vitalizing life and the appeal to

resurrection from the deadness that he already is. The ego, idealistically described, would turn out well only as a non-emphasized
function of the self. A successful ego, to paraphrase Fiche freely, is
an inconspicuous twinkle in the eye of God.[9]

In recent times it has been shown – by Gehlen, Marquard, and
Macho, among others – that psychoanalysis is a disempowered
or "deteriorated" form of German idealism.[10] The late nineteenth
century understands by "deteriorating" the act of coming off the
high horse of absolute reflection and of giving up exalted pretensions, to characterize bourgeois individuals through theological
mediality, without further ado.[11] In fact psychoanalysis finds itself
for the first time in a post-idealist and *eo ipso* post-theological
position. Its typical public is largely made up of despiritualized
clients who have outgrown the continuum of classical metaphysics
and religion. From this there emerges, as if by itself, the new task
of reformulating the ego–self duality in a non-theological fashion.
As is well known, Freud intended to acquit himself of this task by
naturalizing the self under the name of "drives." Other psychologists, Jung above all, sought their salvation in reformulating manifest
theology into crypto-theological doctrines of the self in the style of
Gnosticism. Then again, the representatives of prenatal psychology
derive their concept of the self from the aftereffects of intrauterine
pre-existence.[12] On the best path seem to be those analysts who
interpret the self as an inner sedimentation of successful interactions
of children with mothers and other good spirits – therefore interactions through which adolescent life experiences and acquires the
dynamic unity of differentiation and integration. This, by definition,
includes the prenatal legacy. Under post-idealist conditions, the
word "self" would then be an abbreviation for the expectation that
a sufficiently ensouled child can emerge through interaction with a
sufficiently good mother, in a culture with sufficiently good intentions. Yet, however the relationship between ego and self may be
interpreted in a non-theological culture, a quandary still persists for
psychotherapeutic practice, namely the activation of that discreet
indiscretion that is indispensable for a successful post-ensoulment
of stunted ego–self structures.

*

As for Judaism or Mosaism – the third source area of the psychoanalytic movement, taken in a narrower sense – it does not put on the
agenda the logic of a deeply anchored transferential indiscretion,
as did the two factors previously discussed, so much as it raises a
question about the implicit overall promises of psychotherapeutic

practice. An element of boundary transgression is concealed in these promises too, insofar as therapists of Freud's school of thought, by virtue of the Mosaic implications of their occupation, get extremely close to their clients in an ethical arena, often without being able to provide an account of what is going on that is sufficiently clear to themselves.

Here one touches on the most fervently denied and most radically misunderstood feature of the Freudian undertaking. Admittedly, both the denial and the misunderstanding can be understood in part as a result of the integration of psychoanalysis into the twentieth-century upheavals of anti-Semitism and fragmentation of Jewish identities. Because he feared his project would be characterized as Jewish science,[13] Freud himself contributed in no small part to the obfuscation of the Jewish profile in his work. Decades of clarification were required before these connections could be discussed calmly.

Ever since the work of Yerushalmi and others, it has been reasonable to assume that the label "Jewish science" would sooner or later be accepted as a sort of humorous self-description by the members of the fraternity. Freudians of all nationalities will one day present themselves without complexes, as honorary children of Israel – Israel offspring *honoris causa*. The reason for this turn is only a little mysterious. Despite all its Hellenizing and Aegyptianizing aspects, Viennese psychoanalysis is to be ultimately deciphered as a psychology of exodus. It transposes a people's founding myth – the myth of the Jews' exodus from Egypt – into every single analytic therapy by interpreting clients' previous lives as neurotic–Egyptian and by depicting future life as a case of heading in a big way toward a libidinal Canaan. There is no guarantee for the attainability of the Promised Land apart from an obscure pledge brokered in earlier times between God and Moses.

Psychoanalysis is an individualized practice of exodus. With each of its clients, it repeats a schema that marks the history of the Jewish people even to the present day. Every patient indeed reproduces, more or less discreetly, a private exodus from Egypt under the guidance of psychotherapists who as a rule do not admit that they stand, legally, in the Mosaic line of succession. Every patient is Israel on the forty-year march through the ego-forming desert – a desert that, as a space of suffering, is at the same time a zone of purification and hope. Of this desert it is said that it is better to traverse it in agony than to remain in the comfortable psychic death of Egypt. Patients who register doubts about the success of their cure repeat the grumblings of the children of Israel against the inconceivable duration of their odysseys. And when, on occasion, modern analysands categorically deny their therapists any competence, they are unwittingly invoking those Israelites who, after decades of wandering, let their doubts come out about Moses's ability to lead. In terms of the history of ideas, the famous grumblings mark the discovery of resistance. Incidentally, no one can deny that the way Moses dealt with his subordinate officers is reproduced with great precision in Freud's behavior toward dissident collaborators. At that time as in the twentieth century, the undertaking of exodus was too important to be abandoned to the whims of outsiders, however talented they may have been.

As a model of analytic departure, exodus involves the guiding idea of a radical difference between true and false life. The false life is being possessed by déclassé mother goddesses and indiscreet demons; the true life is drawing your breath under the law of the one breath-like God. The false life is Egypt's intoxicated complacency with death; the true life is the soberly energizing effort to move through the inner desert. A psychotherapy conceived of on a more or less veiled analogy with the monotheistic ethics of holy disillusionment will not hurt its clients' integrity too much when it explicitly acknowledges the greatness and rigor that characterize the anthropology of a religion of exodus. On the contrary, it gets too close to its clients when it has no idea what it's doing when it initiates them into the discipleship of Freudian ideas of healing, which for their part are already encrypted. It gets to be an unconscious boundary transgression when therapists blunder with their clients into Mosaic space, which they neither recognize for what it is nor seek. Psychoanalysis can become an unconscious form of seduction when it emboldens its clients to take elitist pride in their newly won vitality, without reckoning that psychoanalysis in the great Viennese style brings de facto a cryptic form of chosenness into the world. Whoever has decided for the "great analysis" makes company with the chosen people of former neurotics, who will live with an erotic–psychological consignment among those who have not undergone treatment – not unlike the way in which the suffering pious, energized by their god, lived among Babylonian zombies during their years of captivity.

The double nature of modern Judaism is unmistakably reflected in psychoanalysis. On the one hand, its people is, more than ever, a persecuted and chosen people; on the other hand, it wants nothing more to do with its special role and would like to leap out of its theological script, as a completely normal nation state. The psychoanalytic movement is both – consistently, one would almost say: on the one hand, a completely normal therapeutic professional organization, just like the Deutsche Psychoanalytische Gesellschaft

e. V. [German Psychoanalytic Society, registered association], with a
secular self-image and a lay therapeutic mission; on the other hand,
an exodus community with Mosaic rules of succession and a latent
pathos of chosenness. In this ambivalence, which as a rule is relayed
to the clientele in a vague and unmarked fashion, there is considerable potential for overreach and seduction – admittedly a potential
that one can hardly criticize and hardly avoid, because it remains
bound up with the existence of the movement itself. Besides, the
"exodus" of modern therapy has become so abstract that nothing
is left of sacred history but the formula: an amorphous clientele is
accompanied by an amorphous leadership in an amorphous target
zone, where it is supposed to enjoy the fruits of an amorphous
chosenness – this added value of a health earned on its own.

*

To conclude, I would like to move the focal point of our reflections away from the psychoanalytic movement's sources in the
history of ideas and toward a real history of psychological forms
themselves and of their types of deformation. The idea that a
philosophical history of neuroses is possible implies the thesis that
souls are historical structures and that their structural shifts need
not lie entirely outside the range of vision of historical psychology.
In order to make this thesis conceivable, I suggest dividing the
universal history of the psychological realm into three epochs or
regimes, distinguished from one another by typical differences in the
prevailing processes of ensoulment.
    The first psycho-historical regime would be that of horde civili-
zations, in which human beings experience their ensoulment
immediately, by participating in the life of their collective. The
horde is the primary human-forming group and, as a physical and
psychological locus of perception, it regulates its members' endow-
ments. In the regime of the horde, "to be ensouled" means to
resonate with the life of the micro-totality of the group; one could
describe hordes as the first uterine configurations of social order –
with their help humans, as beings who have "come to the world," are
assimilated into a common "inside," into a collective psycho-sphere.
Any half-successful psycho-group proves it: as incorrigible horde
animals, human beings have to this day retained the tendency to
immerse themselves into the sphere of a music group collective and
to enjoy conspirative euphorias inside this horde-like soul sphere, as
a model of successful communal life.[14] Falling out of this life-giving
psycho-sphere is the prototype of immemorial human neuroses;
and they have shamanism as a method of healing. No matter how

extremely different its cultural variations may be, the basic model is that the shaman or shamaness brings free individual souls who have become lost back into the psycho-spherical continuum of the horde society.[15] For this reason, aspiring shamans in all cultures must train the motility of their soul in order to be in a position to follow the stray and lost souls of their tribal companions into their solitary exile and to move them from there back home, to the spiritual house of the community.

If we are to believe ethnographic reports, there is hardly a modern training analysis that could compete for harshness with the initiations of the shamans. The shamanist's activity of bringing migrated souls back home is located on the register of a major treatment for psychosis. It stages a psychosomatic healing ritual that cannot yet be distinguished from a socio-somatic operation. The uterine quality of the psycho-sphere of the horde as a whole has a sense of threat when individual members suffer mental damage, and hence the whole has a well-justified interest in reintegrating its endangered members. In this respect, the art of healing begins as a socio-somatics: it proceeds as a psychological surgery, performed on the wounded collective body. Under this order all spirits are public spirits, and ensoulment can only be the effect of the whole in the individual. The form of thinking displayed in this formation is unabashedly mediumistic. Spirits and gods get into individuals and depart from them like old relatives and wise ancestors; hence we should call this regime "ancient mediumism."

*

The second psycho-historical regime emerges from the synergy between political empire formations and monotheistic (or universalist) abstractions. With its arrival, neurotic disturbances reach epidemic proportions, at the levels of both state and empire. This becomes easy to understand when we interpret neuroticism in two ways – on the one hand, as a form of loss of soul that can occur when individuals fall out of the psycho-sphere of their primary groups; on the other hand, as a psychological overload, which typically occurs when several incompatible inspirations or doctrines make claims on the same individual.

Indeed, when entire populations in large political entities are sucked into the slipstream of monotheist abstractions, an unparalleled psycho-spherical shock occurs. It asks great numbers of individuals to undertake a sort of re-ensoulment – one could also say a shift in what one is possessed by. Here a previously governing local reason for possession and motivation is to be replaced by another principle, a "higher" one (as we say today). The older history of religion handles this evolution by forming a hierarchy in the realm of spirits; high gods begin to overlie middle and lower worlds of spirits – as though the principles of hierarchism and feudalism were also implemented in the second world, that is, in the sphere of ensouling invisibilities.

Historians use Karl Jaspers's term "axial age" to refer to the period in which these tendencies began with incontrovertible evidence to be implemented.[16] It dissects the continuum of human evolution into that "before" and "after" that Europeans, even the atheists among them, still presuppose today when they divide their world calendar into the years before and the years after Christ. Ever since the axial age, all human beings on this globe, with or without their knowledge, live in this dramatic temporal structure, which recognizes the opposition between the before and the after of an X; and what functions for us as X is an epoch-making, world-turning event that reconfigures the meaning of the world. The essence of all Xs is that rationalizing spiritual revolution, which stamps a new shape on the souls of the subsequent period.[17] One could call "meta-enthusiasm" this neopsychism of high cultures after the axial age, to convey the idea that souls of post-axial-age human beings, especially in Israel, Egypt, Persia, and Greece, could take hold of themselves only through a process of respiritualization. Platonism – together with its Socratic bequest of spiritual midwifery – is the enduringly effective monument of this reversal.

Of course, from a pathographic perspective, the past 2,500 years also represent the great realm of monotheomorphic pathologies – that is, of sicknesses that, with the re-ensoulment of horde-like and tribal–ethnic psycho-spheres, had to develop into high theologies of an abundantly religious and political philosophical nature. If one understands the psycho-spheres of the new empires and great worlds, formally, as *ecclēsiai* – "churches" in some unspecific sense – the age of cities and empires is *eo ipso* an "ecclesiopathic" world. In this world souls make the setting for wars among gods, be they wars between equal divinities, as among Greeks of the heroic age, or wars between a central high god and a rebellious world of demons, as among late Greeks, Jews, and Christianized Romans and Germans. Incidentally, there can be no doubt that even Freud's placement of the ego between the powers of the superego and those of the id is a remote reflex of this high-culture scenario of divine warfare.

Consequently during this period the art of healing takes the form of a theological psychagogy to begin with; and it leads to success when it proves able to make a new constitution plausible for souls, in which the high god has been able to subject the spirits that came before him and to force them to pay a tribute peacefully, or at least not too reluctantly. The history of Judeo-Christian civilization has, however, shown that, when seen as a whole, the monotheization of the psyche is a project that cannot be completed. The construction of a successful and philanthropic psycho-sphere of worldwide inclusivity will always be long in coming; owing to its inner paradoxes, it is from the start an impossible project, when we consider it properly. Not even the churches wanted persuasive communities of saints to emerge – to say nothing of the rest of profane humanity, with its innumerably splintered zones of local spirits.

In the high culture of the post-axial age, the principle of ensoulment is an all-encompassing God, the One, who is able to enforce his claim only by expelling previous gods and other ensoulments; in consequence, we should call the period of his psycho-historical regime "intermediary mediumism." This points to that order of ensoulment in which orientation to the one divine being does not purport to be a new state of being possessed, but rather comes out as liberation from all prior inspirations and pre-obsessions. Of course, we must think of the monotheistic principle of ensoulment as an influx that passes through the souls of individuals; this is also why we can understand monotheism only in mediumistic terms. Where individuals think that they have been penetrated by the One totally, without a residue of resistance, there cultures of this type speak of illumination or enlightenment. Such expressions are supposed to symbolize the fact that ensoulment by the One does not have the paradoxical quality of an unrealizable task in all circumstances; in special, blessed cases it is realized during one's lifetime. In the age of intermediary mediumism, the threshold value of the ensouled psychic realm is therefore illumination as mystical theopsychosis. Curiously, it does not wish to be understood as a pathological phenomenon but as an extreme form of healing.

*

Ever since the late eighteenth century, new forms of psychiatry have heralded a further psycho-historical regime. As a natural nucleus of the process of transitioning to the post-monotheistic psycho-sphere, psychoanalysis also bears, at its point of emergence as throughout its historical development, the symptomatic trait of a stage transition to the third age, that of neurosis.[18] What leaps out first is something that could be described as a sort of implosion of the psychic space; in a manner that is not quite understandable yet, the new souls appear to have become non-mediumistic and uninhabitable, as though no orderly spirit, be it of the old demonic sort or highly theological, could move in or pass through. All of a sudden, the post-monotheistic psycho-sphere appears to narrow down radically, as though the automatic had begun to outstrip the psychological. In one of her books – one that bears the distinctive title *Les nouvelles maladies de l'âme* (*The New Diseases of the Soul*; Paris 1993), Julia Kristeva speaks of a new set of symptoms, which seem to act in concert with most of the recent forms of psychic malaise: a mutism, a thoroughgoing difficulty of the mental to describe itself and form spaces of expression. What had fallen under the concept "soul" in previous traditions of humanity always distinguished itself through a special power to produce inner space. The spaciousness of the shamanist universe manifested itself in the well-qualified ability to take an inner journey, which presupposed a sort of psycho-cosmic marketability of the free soul. Remainders of this have been preserved all the way up to the "tripping" and drug subcultures of the late twentieth century. By contrast, souls of the high-culture type were characterized by having to win, in themselves, the expanse of an arena where gods of various stripes could battle it out. They were familiar with the inner spatial feeling of the world temple, of the inner forum, or of the parliament of parties of drives. In this arrangement, the word "soul" designated the capacity to internalize a universe of antagonistic forces and to foster them, as though in a palace of conflicts. This is why, in the era of intermediary mediumism, there is always a pull to greatness in the idea of psychic vitality.[19] The soul is a pathetic entity – or, better, megalo-pathetic. In order to keep fit, it needs the power to form hierarchies as well as the power to balance. As far as the "soul in the technological age" is concerned – to pick up a well-known phrase by Gehlen – it is above all an anti-mediumistic tendency that preponderates. It wants to be everything, just not a "theater"; hence coolness is the meta-symptom of the epoch.[20] The "media" are no longer understood as personal magnitudes, but rather as technological systems by which messages are transported, in endless reproduction, to as many recipients as desired. The recipients, for their part, do not wish to be mediumistic authorities but rather "themselves." Being a self can be understood as the uninspired consumption of one's own experiential possibilities – the end use of opportunities and resources by their owners. At best, modern subjects, as bearers of creativity, still arrogate mediumistic properties to themselves, although they do not do so as media of thoroughgoing inspirations that are not their own, but as original creators – and this means beginning with themselves.

What, then, does psychotherapy mean in an age in which a media revolution of an unknown type is unpredictably affecting all inter- and intrapsychic relations? Hardly a therapist today – regardless of her school of thought – would come up with the idea of defining healing as the attempt to connect people to streams of ensoulment that come from intact psycho-spheres, cultural continua, and great traditions. Almost all of them have in some way consented to serve the desire for a substantial, *mündig*, and oral–consumptive selfhood. As an illusion of health, despirited vitality has hazardously broken into the psychotherapeutic market. In view of these tendencies, it should not be superfluous to emphasize that psychotherapy always already implies an opinion about the reigning vitalistic nihilism. Psychotherapists worthy of the name would have to resist the temptations of a psychology of automata and the pull of mass culture to deplete the inner world in all its manifestations. Every therapeutic encounter with the other remains a test of individuals' ability to be ensouled by the invitation to an expanded psycho-sphere.

8

LATENCY

On Concealment

8.1 Emergence of the *krupta*

In historical anthropology, people have been working for a while with the assumption that concepts are lexical sediments of actions. The farther a concept spreads intraculturally and transculturally, the more universally does the action that has sunk down and been schematized in it appear to have been present. In what follows I will proceed on the following supposition: ever since the crystallization of the species *Homo sapiens*, there has been no culture on earth (culture being understood as an intergenerational process of copying ethno-semantic contents), not even among traditions now extinct, that did not have at its disposal some notion of concealment, withdrawal, and invisibility. In this sense, all cultures, qua cultures, would be "cryptological" – not because they had secret writings from an early age, but because they were condemned without exception to tamper with concealment in the broadest sense of the word. *Ta krupta* [secrets, hidden things], conceived of as a comprehensive concept for concealment, forms a universal category of primitive thoughts[1] – we cannot imagine things without it. It is the flipside of the illuminated world in which the everyday sojourn of human communities takes place.

Stillbirths provide a crosscheck of human existence in the light of the manifest. They present early observers with a puzzling ontological question. What should we make of these beings, who pass from their first concealment in their mothers straight into their second concealment in their graves, without reaching an illuminated path in between? If stillbirths are possible, what does this mean for the mode of being of those mortals who have not been born still? It evidently means that the beings who are able to gain a foothold in the light of existence are positioned between two obscurities, despite their orientation toward the sphere that has been cleared for them. Samuel Beckett: "They give birth astride of a grave, the light gleams an instant [...] Down in the hole, lingeringly, the grave-digger puts on the forceps."[2] Beckett's day is the bright expanse between two ontological nights. Without doubt, the highest proto-metaphysical achievement of early human reason consisted in linking the two obscurities, that of natal provenances and that of mortal disappearance, into a single, coherent sphere of invisibility. Long before the articulation of explicit metaphysical concepts, the archaic logos draws together the concealment of "whence" and the concealment of "whither" into a domain of communicating obscurities. By hot-wiring the mystery of woman with the mystery of the grave, the elemental thought that wishes to think itself in human wit generates a comprehensive, fascinating yonder. Later on philosophical metaphysics and the high religions will rationalize this yonder into a tidy beyond – be it Plato's supra-celestial place, whose contents resemble a lexicon, or the kingdom of God, which is like a council of saints. Such a yonder, loaded as it is with creative forces and death threats, forms the dark cloud from which the lightening of the Enlightenment comes. It is no coincidence that the key saying of Heraclitean wisdom is *phusis kruptesthai philei,* (true) "nature loves to conceal itself." In the early philosophical concept of *phusis,* concealment is thought of *as* concealment for the first time. All of a sudden, the crypts that are filled with the treasures of coming to be and passing away have a name that appears to be legible as an address. As soon as this address is made known, grave robbers know where they need to look.

8.2 Maximally invasive operation

The activities that lead to the notion of a field of concealment are identical with the actions of the first [*sc.* Pyrrhonian] *skepsis,* insofar as the adjective *skeptikos* originally described an adult who investigates something in great detail, and *skepsis* initially designated the act of hanging around an unexplained matter and inspecting it probingly. Such activities consist in an ambivalent witnessing of the proto-dramas of nature. Concealment is discovered, qua concealment, through the action of autoptic investigation into births and generally into beginnings, as well as through the actions of not turning our eyes from the extinction of life and of looking

back to see what has disappeared. Thus thinking in limit situations is in the first instance a martyrdom of the incomprehensible
(compare the Greek *martus*, witness).

Popular familiarity with concealment emerges even earlier,
though. It does so mainly in everyday situations where human
intelligence begins to be mindful of the difference between looking
at the same thing for the first and for the second time. Such situations occur preferentially in hunting and cooking, since in both
these fields of activity there is room for collecting experiences that
harbor some disparity between a first appearance and a later result.
Hunting and cooking are maximally invasive operations, whose
agents do not content themselves with the status quo. Hunters do
not rest until they have successfully contested the animal's aspiration
to live in concealment. They "expose" the deer by dismembering it,
and pull out of it what was invisible – the muscles, the inner organs,
the bones; indeed they see the creature's skin from the inside. The
gesture of skinning belongs among the most archaic gestures of an
intrusive enlightenment that wants to have seen everything from the
other side. From this point of view, turning something inside out
and consuming it boil down to the same thing. It is not an accident
that myth sees this atrocity of exposing the muscular structure as
the most extreme evil when it is practiced on a human being. If the
skin is the organic veil over the organs, unveiling and death amount
to being one and the same. The maximally invasive operation of
the hunters continues in the activities of cooking. The agents of the
hearth also insist on showing us how something entirely different
comes to be drawn out of what was initially given. In the oldest
pots, what was inedible when raw is made edible when cooked. In
mortars, grain is exposed as flour – pulverization looks like another
way of making edible what is inedible. The hardest shells are cracked
open for the sake of reaching the hidden fruit. One sees through
nature's game of hide and seek; the non-mysterious ways of violence
lead inward.

8.3   Boxing in as latency production

Civilization is a process in which the fabricated concealment
outstrips the concealment that is found.

For idols and kings at the beginning of high cultures, a man-made
invisibility is invented that keeps up the mystery, with help from the
fabrications of nature.

Concerning the summer residence of the Persian Great King, the
mountain stronghold Ecbatana, Herodotus reports:

These ramparts were laid out so that each circle was elevated above the one in front by the height of the parapets. Although this arrangement was aided in part by the hill on which the site is located, it resulted more from human design and construction. There are, altogether, seven circular walls, and within the innermost one are located the palace and treasury. The outermost wall is about the length of the wall that surrounds Athens. The parapets of the first circle are white; the second is colored black; the third, crimson; the fourth, dark blue; and the fifth, orange. All these circles are painted thus in different colors, but of the innermost two, one parapet is plated with silver, the other with gold.[3]

The Great King resides in the throne room of the innermost building, sitting motionless on the throne like the statue of a god, his gaze disconnected from the world as he embodies the really existing mystery of his kingdom. His disconnect corresponds to the high rank of the quality of his majesty: as the Great King, he rules not only over his people but also over kings who rule over peoples. He pronounces his earth-shattering decisions in such a quiet voice that his chancellors and ministers have to put their ear to the mouth of the monarch to be sure they understand his enlightened remarks.

The mystical thesis takes its point of departure from this artificial concealment of great power. It holds that seekers of God must rise up into the innermost divine mysteries by traversing numerous levels. Even in the sixteenth century, Theresa of Ávila will espouse the late Persian doctrine that the soul can achieve union with God only in the seventh chamber of the "interior castle," *castillo interior*. Even Augustine's supplication to God, "You are more inward to me than my most inward part" – *interior intimo meo* – is indebted to the political topology of the palaces of the Great King and their technique of boxing in, which generates inwardness [*interio-genetischen*]. The more sublime the idea of majesty, the longer the corridors that make the visitor feel the shortness of her steps; the more the monarch has the power to save, the higher the number of forecourts and anterooms designed to humble the newcomer. The imperial architecture of crypts culminates in the erection of burial sites for those rulers who cannot give up on their delirious dreams of power-protected concealment even in the beyond. Among them Qin Shi Huang still stands out. He was the first emperor of China, and had himself buried, some 210 years before Christ, in a tremendous subterranean burial site. About 700,000 laborers are supposed to have worked at it, for thirty years. The corpse of the monarch lies under an artificial hill, walled into a dozen massive rectangular boxes, the largest of which measures 2,500 by 1,000 meters. Each rectangle features a defensive fortification, whose garrison appears to be ready to repel invaders. In several neighboring precincts complete armies of terracotta warriors have been set up for final battles. Each armed box is followed by another, deeper, more withdrawn one. In the innermost quadrangle, the corpse of the emperor rests in a sealed coffin – which to this day has remained untouched, purportedly because archeologists still do not have techniques that may be safe enough to salvage the undoubtedly embalmed body. In truth, the political archeology of China is in league with an imperial–cosmological tradition that fears messing with the still influential hermetic center of legitimation of its own culture. Not unveiling the mortal veil of Qin Shi Huang maintains China in the charismatic state of a latent empire.

8.4   Wadding up and unfolding

The Enlightenment draws its élan from resistance to artificial concealment: what one class of people concealed, another class of people can unveil. Psycho-political modernity begins with an indignation about subjecting oneself to fabricated mysteries. It is above all holy texts that get to experience it, when whistleblowers come along to claim, with fierce honesty, that these writings are the work of human authors. No transcendent dictation lies at their foundation, no unfathomable mystery manifests itself in them. "We know the way, we know the text, we know even the masters who authored it." The epoch of the most powerful metaphor of the world, which molded the western way of being in the world, comes to an end with *reductio ad auctorem* – the reduction to the author. After it, the world lies open to us like a book written by God in code. We have learned to read several passages, but most of it remains undeciphered. For a very long time, it appeared as though humans had to content themselves with producing exact copies of the legible parts of the book of the world, just as the scribes of the Holy Book used to, in the scriptoria of medieval cloisters.

The book, however, no longer resists profanation – the modern extension of zones of writing and reading makes this inevitable. A suspicion arose that everything that appeared to be concealed in the form of a book could be a concoction. Modern people are those who, for good or bad reasons, are convinced that when we write, we do not copy a holy text that has been imposed upon us once and for all. If our texts are worth something, this is only because they push forward, into something new. This is possible only because there is no first edition of being itself – just continuous rewritings, in which the ongoing rejuvenation of beings is articulated. But, if the world is not a book to be leafed through, forever submissively, by some catholic intellectual, how else should we conceive of it? It could be a piece of paper, folded in an infinitely complicated way and crumpled together in an infinitely compact way, which, after the original rumpling, is gradually stretched again. On the suggestion of the baroque thinker Leibniz, we can represent the occurrence of the world as an ontological and cognitive drama where the original, immeasurably compact interfolding of beings is pulled apart thanks to a complementary unfolding. What one takes to be the music of the spheres could be the rustling of the world-paper being progressively uncrumpled. Every time folds that had previously been pressed together open up in the bundle, new clearings, new signatures, new objectivities, and new public data appear on the extended surface of the crumpled body.

Research science is inevitably included in this developing trend. Authors are occasionally of the opinion that they are in a position to note something new here and there, paying all due respect to their predecessors. Now, by attending the work of unfolding, they can, as researchers, produce evidence for their assumption. For what was previously implicit, what was not yet visible and never yet said in such and such a way, is here brought into the light of explicitness. If we hold fast onto the image of unwadding what has been folded up, taking it as a basic statement about human existence defined by research, we can understand how scientific prose ends up as a medium in which the prose of the world continues to be written.

8.5   Intuitive integral calculus

Etymologists have pointed out how languages of ancient peoples arrived at pre-philosophical concepts of the world by creating metaphors out of concrete images. Thus the Russian word *mir* would stand for the transference of the idea of village to the idea of world. The Greek *kosmos* transfers the concepts of adornment, jewelry, and order to the entirety of the universe. In the Latin *mundus* one will hear the round sacrificial pit raised to the higher power of a symbol of the world. The German w-word [*Welt*, "world"] takes us back to the Old High German *waltan*, "to prevail," as though the universe should be represented as a larger countship.

In truth, pre-philosophical notions of world have more in common with philosophical concepts than can be demonstrated through etymological derivatives. They are not only results of metaphorizations and amplifications by virtue of which the far-reaching imagination makes the leap into totality. In every concept of world we can find the trace of an archaic integral calculus that could not be carried out without a concept of latency, however vague. Whoever says "world" conducts, *uno intuitu* [in a single grasp], several mental operations where we typically mark only the result, without specifically making explicit the path taken to arrive at it. In the light of proto-ontological analysis, the word "world" designates the product of a spontaneous calculus, in which one takes into account that even the human intellect, saturated with experience as it is, cannot know everything that is the case. What is manifest to this intellect always amounts only to a limited horizon of perceptions and skills. The phenomenon of wisdom would have begun, in the ancient times of humanity before classical antiquity, with an awareness of the fact that the continuum of things that can in principle be experienced continues beyond the horizon. Since the realities behind the horizon cannot be manifest and present, the wise consciousness is obliged to reckon continually with the possibility that something not yet manifest may be actualized. A first pre-concept of latency emerges from a sketch that marks off the vague field of this non-actual, non-present, yet in different circumstances actualizable X as a magnitude with its own legitimacy and as an incubator of unknown powers. This X begins at the edges of the cleared zone. All the same, it sends signs indicating that this unknown is not a nothing but rather a something in the state of having turned away from knowledge. We know of gods and dangers from advertising signs. The operations by which X is sketched cannot be expressed by the basic figure in identity philosophy, A = A, whose task lay in tracing the difference between the left and the right members of the sentence back to identity through the magic power of the equal sign. The original integration of the world emerges from an ontologically richer operation, by virtue of which what has been cleared, become known, and made manifest (A) is counted together with the obscure, the unknown, and the latent (X) and summed up in a compact symbol of totality (W, world): A + X = W. A primary epistemo-ethical injunction resonates in this sum, which is actually already a primitive integral calculus: remember that, when you know something, you don't know enough to see the whole. Once the religious injunction "Fear the gods!" is translated into the language of philosophy, what is expressed through it is the maxim "I know that I know nothing." The Delphic maxim "Know thyself!" is also articulated in this register, since in substance it means "do not be presumptuous but put yourself in-between what is hidden on high, which is manifest only to the gods, and what is

hidden down below, which is accessible only to animals and demons."
At the same time, ancient thought had already paid attention to a
continuous displacement of the zone of latency. Thus one reads in
Xenophanes: "Yet the gods have not revealed all things to men from
the beginning; but by seeking men find out better in time."[4]

Here comes to light a first indication of the occurrence that, after
the discovery of the technology of discovery, the moderns will call
research. Heidegger defined technology itself as a mode of uncon-
cealing, but not without suggesting that it is, at bottom, synonymous
with an organized crime against latency. Heidegger's suggestion,
which is skeptical when it comes to research, has often been interpreted as a reactionary renunciation of the benefactions of modern
rationality. In actual fact its constructive sense reveals itself as soon
as we interrogate the primitive ontological integral calculus about
its immunological sense. This calculus became almost explicit in
Heidegger's way of thinking, which paid heed to the play between
concealment and unconcealment. The formula $A + X = W$ implies
not only an epistemo-ethical admonition to respect the unknown
that is not nothing. It reveals a universal occurrence of integrity
in the concept of the world itself. It thinks of being as self-healing
mediation. The operation "A plus X" signifies no simple addition;
it designates a "completion" in the literal sense of the word. The
world, which is replenished by the obscure, is everything in which
the possibility of a successful life remains contained. The product
of A and X stands for a totality promising immunity at the highest
level. Thus we can reformulate classical metaphysics as a general
immunology. If still so many cases of failure become manifest in
the A-sphere, the X-sphere holds ready the antidotes to excessive
increase of miscarriage. The philosophy of latency is the last bid on
the belief that evident disaster does not have the last word.

9

THE MYSTICAL IMPERATIVE
Remarks on the Changing Shape of Religion in the Modern Age

9.1 Martin Buber's *Ecstatic Confessions* as an epochal symptom

A. is a virtuoso and Heaven is his witness.
> Franz Kafka, *The Zürau Aphorisms*, Aphorism 49

When, in the year 1849, Søren Kierkegaard wrote down his reflections under the title "The Difference between a Genius and an Apostle," he succeeded, with a felicitous level of explicitness, in drawing a difference that is decisive for the spiritual economy of modern civilization. We call a society "modern" when it allows a plurality of sources of inspiration – let's say, a market of confessions. In this market place, people enthused about and inspired by different things can encounter one another. We call "medieval" a culture that is defined by singleness of inspiration; in such a culture, the one thing that's necessary holds a monopoly on what counts as a source of legitimate enthusiasms. As long as the Middle Ages reigned in Europe, all enthusiasms tended to be condemned to appear as Christian apostolates – that is, as post-Pentecostal speaking ministries [*Sprechämte*] fed ultimately by the only authoritative source for the promulgation of truth: the Gospels and the Christian commission of Matthew 28:19. Hence there is no medieval genius, if "genius" means speaking out on the strength of a zeal other than evangelical.[1]

Post-medieval circumstances first emerge when extra-Christian inspirations are thrust on the market under the Latin heading "genius." Then, on its own territory, faith in Christ forfeits its privilege of not needing to bank on an external observer.[2] Before the Enlightenment, only the devil had the freedom to observe Christians in their belief. With the modern age a true epoch of the devil breaks out. In the aftermath of what historians usually call "the Reformation" and "the Renaissance," more and more Christians end up in a position of devilish external observers of other Christians' faith. The period of religious wars gives us a sense of the cost of implementing the pluralist inspiration of western culture; only after the catastrophe of the sixteenth and seventeenth centuries is the demonization of the external observer, if not annulled, then at least hedged in at a religious–political level. With the 1555 Augsburg Settlement's formula *cuius regio, eius religio* [whose realm, his religion], a historical compromise is made between the demonization and the toleration of those who believe or are inspired otherwise – a compromise whose distant effects extend into the twenty-first century.[3]

Under the banner of confessions, the no longer suppressible manifestations of holding, or being inspired by, different beliefs forge paths into coexistence. At the same time, the early book and science markets prepare a pluralist inspiration that, since the eighteenth century, has presented itself aggressively as an "enlightenment." From then on, the Enlightenment offers itself as a *via regia* [royal route] of supra-confessional tolerance. A market of relativistic enthusiasms dissolves the civil war of absolutized confessions. Enthusiasms that step out on the market must brace themselves to face external observers who do not agree. The pathos of tolerance, which has accompanied the Enlightenment ever since the eighteenth century, is grounded in the modern effort to pronounce certain propositions of faith in such a way that everyone already knows that they will be unable to command the observer's assent. Bourgeois enthusiasms are subject to the rule that the confessor ought to believe in herself and her program, without being permitted to anticipate the assent of others. Thus one acknowledges the difference between the public and the community; applause and creed part ways, and a confession's candor and impressiveness take on a value that is independent of its "truth." Through "enlightenment," public religious passions morph into private religious interests – and into poetic talents. Thus, in the end, "confessions" can also assume the form of collected works. At the same time, quasi-religious functions pass over into the literary market; the latter represents the one and all of every inspiration, to such extent that it succeeds in making space for every pronounceable confession, like a pantheon. The special character of the modern bourgeois confessional market shows in the fact that, in principle, no one can be prevented from proclaiming his faith, or be forced to join a cult. Hence religion

"after the Enlightenment" is based on the interplay between confes-
sionally tamed forms of positive religiousness and a pious atheism
in critical mode. We could speak straightaway of an organized
match between civil religion and civil atheism, if by civil religion we
mean enclosed confessions and, by civil atheism, resistance to the
"medieval" imposition of being permeated by a doctrine without
reserve. Only confessionalism and atheism, together, grant modernizing societies the continuity of their successes, as they produce
psychological forms in conformity with the world.

When, in the middle of the nineteenth century, Kierkegaard set
about redefining the difference between the genius and the apostle,
he was dealing with a bourgeois society that had already traversed
the longest stretch of the path from a culture of apostolate to a
culture of ingenuity. In consequence, it comes as no surprise that the
distinction between the apostle, who speaks by dint of an imperative
assignment, and the genius, who leaves samples of his own artistic
force, fell like ripe fruit into the hands of an astute "religious
author" – as Kierkegaard called himself. Apostles are possible
only as messengers of God – geniuses are media of themselves. If
apostles are driven by a simple mandate and serve a serious "for the
purpose of," geniuses celebrate their productivity for its own sake;
they live by reason of their own strength, in the enjoyment of their
"nature" and of their humorous sufficiency. In all circumstances the
apostle's god is superior to the apostle; with the genius, it is only the
person's own creativity that is, at best, superior to the person – a
creativity that doesn't know today how it will surprise itself and the
social world tomorrow. There is no doubt that Kierkegaard's sympathies are with the apostolic type, in whom the gravity of the teaching
function of the church would be unconditionally at work; there are,
however, sympathies here that do not hide the fact that Kierkegaard
knew he was condemned to be a genius – a mere author who did *not*
feel the authority of the apostolic mandate.

It is food for thought that the author who had carved out, with
decisively shining clarity, the opposition between genius and apostle
was not in a position to implement this difference in his own
person. With this distinction, a new sort of undecidability comes
to the fore rightaway. The Christian–post-Christian hybrid of the
"religious author" enters the stage with Kierkegaard. A paradoxical
mixture of tendencies takes a shape in him that the later philosophy
of life will celebrate under the description "religious genius." As a
"genius," Kierkegaard becomes a witness of his inability to be an
apostle; as an author, he makes it his mission to contest the right
of the dispirited Christian churches to preach the gospel. We see
in Kierkegaard the exemplary case of how awareness of genius

stood in the way of the apostolate, while a frustrated apostolic ambition had to corrupt the author's self-satisfaction in his genius productivity.

The life's work of the Jewish philosopher of religion Martin Buber (b. 1878, Vienna, d. 1965, Jerusalem) represents a later act in the drama of paradoxes of religion whose headline was provided by Kierkegaard's reflections. Buber's early writings – especially his famous collection of mystical world literature, which was first published in 1909 by Eugen Diederichs Verlag in Jena under the programmatic title *Ekstatische Konfessionen*, then went through five editions by 1984 – are a landmark in the history of problems surrounding the typology of this author, who made his way to the proscenium in the nineteenth and twentieth centuries as a "religious genius." There is no better phrase to characterize the essence and aura of Buber's authorship in the years before his dialogical "turn." Buber's early fame was based on his ability to stand as a virtuoso of eclectic devotions before a religiously musical[4] public ready to applaude bravura performances from the heart. Of course this was the same public – made up of supporters of life reform movements, of theosophy, of Nietzscheanism, of anarchist philosophies of community. Such a public had long been primed to get excited about the message that the detail of what one believed did not matter as much as it did to hold open the human inside, like a screen for variable projections from the other world.

For the young Martin Buber, the Jewish virtuoso of religiousness in the decade of art nouveau, moving freely back and forth across the languages of Polish Chassidism, Zionist modernity, and bourgeois humanist classicism, as if living parallel lives, may have seemed at first the obvious thing to do. If one were to proceed solely on the basis of the impression given by Buber as editor of *Ekstatische Konfessionen*, one would conclude that one were dealing with an author from whom all forms of theistic religion, whether Jewish, Islamic, or Christian, were equally remote. His collection helps an apparently metareligious cult of psychological liveliness to find expression – where liveliness, as is typical of any vitalistic and youth-inspired thought, is placed in opposition to anything related to society, institutions, hustle and bustle, and business. Lived experience is the keyword of cults of "religion of life," which criticize civilizations; their inescapable qualifiers are "genuine," "deeply inward," "truly felt," "primal." When people said "lived experience" in 1900, they meant deliverance from the mechanized world.[5] "Lived experience" is liberation from the bourgeois curse of having to be a "secluded human being"[6] who no longer lays claim to a soul.

For the 31-year-old editor of *Ekstatische Konfessionen*, too,
all that was at issue was deliverance through lived experience, it
seems. His voice gets lost almost beyond recognition in the choir
of pantheists and mystics of all-encompassing unity who, in the
midst of an increasingly hardening and chilling bourgeois world,
spoke of the fusion of the I with the cosmic whole. Buber's own
touch can be found at best in a certain Ahasverian religiousness,
which in the name of a genuine "lived experience" joins the belief
of the foreign creeds and blends in with remote mystical unions.
A religiousness that has become a matter of genius proves itself
by means of its congeniality with witnesses "from all times and
peoples." Had we not known from independent sources that Buber
had simultaneously emerged as an early proponent of cultural
Zionism[7] and had made a name for himself as a rediscoverer and
popularizer of Chassidism – an ecstatic pietistic movement that
flourished among Polish Jewish communities in the eighteenth
and nineteenth centuries[8] – we would have to take the author of
"Ekstase und Bekenntnis"[9] ["Ecstasy and Confession"] to be an
advocate of the pantheist monotheistic neopaganism that, around
1900, was seeking to gather the building blocks for a post-Christian
"world picture" from medieval German mysticism and Nietzsche's
Thus Spoke Zarathustra. This is supported by the Hellenizing core
vocabulary of Buber's text, where words such as "enthusiasm,"
"ecstasy," and "myth" determine the horizon, in an elevated and
thoroughly solemn tone.

As a religious genius, Buber evinces the paradox of an apostolate
devoid of specific content; his status is that of an envoy without a
sender – an apostle, plain and simple, of what is generally beyond.
He presents himself in the bizarre position of being the messenger of
an anonymous transcendence whose only plea is to recall that there
can be witnesses for transcendence "even today" – although here
we are no longer dealing with a particular type of transcendence,
for instance that of Muslims, of Yogis, or of Mormons, but rather
with transcendence generally – "transcendence *sans phrase*." "We
hearken unto ourselves – and know not which rushing sea we
hear."[10] Seen from the mystical angle, all statements of the heart are,
inevitably, no more than inadequate "projections" of the ineffable
into the externality of language; measured against the inexpressible,
all languages are like foreign languages.

At the intersection between the inexpressibilities of all peoples
and ages we find the modern individual – loquacious and
indefinable, *ineffabile*. To be sure, there are hardly any contents
left to this individual's belief, yet in the dimension of interiority he
knows himself to be related to all the positive witnesses of mystical

inspiration. By preempting faithless external observation and by observing himself in the process of "believing" and confessing, he discovers himself as the abyss in which preconceived dogmas come undone and from which projections gush out. In this sense, individuality becomes synonymous with religiousness. Empty and enormous, the modern religious "I" settles in the vicinity of the greatest meanings – it now understands everything. By virtue of her emptiness, the individual becomes the diaphragm of "transcendence pure and simple"; everything that comes wholly from within can find resonance in her. An invisible order of aristo-crats of the innermost life is formed even as mass society is rising. Every member of this impossible order knows, in select solitude, that she dwells near the inexpressibilities of all ages. The religious virtuoso, trembling before his own ability to be inspired, relates to the abundance of witnesses of "transcendence tout court" as a musician does to a keyboard: he makes himself the sounding box for even the most remote inwardness – reason enough for the adherents of orthodoxies to scent a rival in Buber.[11] In doing so he is like the representatives of "new resoluteness" who attempted to make the affliction of modern polyvalence into a virtue: the virtue of deciding on a single position to be defended with one's whole existence. The new, twentieth-century representatives of this decisionist party took no pleasure in letting themselves be rolled into a single realm of primary experiences of the "world spirit" that all claimed to be equally true and equally valid. The philosopher Franz Rosenzweig, who would later become Buber's collaborator, is reported to have said that a decent person does not play with the ninety-nine possibilities that exist, but seizes the one possibility that she is. This was certainly also said *pro domo*, as Rosenzweig was an example of the Jew who has "converted" to Judaism, which was not atypical in that century.[12] It could also have been said against Buber himself; indeed, one knows of Rosenzweig's aversions to the presumed "mystical subjectivism" of the already famous author, as well as of his devastating judgment about the "dreadful book" – as he characterized *Ekstatische Konfessionen*.

When Rosenzweig became acquainted with Buber, he under-stood that Buber's ingenuity was more substantial than he had initially guessed. The apparent "mystical subjectivist" turned out to be a man of integrity, a witness to a momentous religious situation, a genuine Jewish medium of his time.[13] Precisely as a naive virtuoso of religious polyvalence, Buber, in his early work, announced nothing less than a structural transformation of revelation that had to accompany the entrance of positive regional religions into the age of universalized reciprocal observation. Even monotheists are no longer able to avoid adapting God's multilingualism. Once the new situation of revelational pluralism is recognized for what it is, the external observers of my religion who were previously diabolical turn out to be partners in fate, given the global dilemma of "religious humans." Buber's development mirrors exactly his receptivity to the new sort of problems that emerge in the history of ideas. The much invoked turn from mysticism to dialogics shows how Buber grounded the connection between one's own religiousness and foreign religiousness: "the human" always already goes beyond toward her other, and only in the state of "inter"-humanity – in which, as it were, a reciprocal creation occurs – does the individual win over herself.[14] On the basis of such findings Buber reformulates his Hellenized Judaism into a "Hebraic humanism." After his "turn," Buber was able to declare "dialogue in general" to be the essence of the religious and to make himself its promulgator. Now we no longer listen exclusively to the choir of mystical confessors but also to the voices of *the* other, insofar as there is a "genuine encounter." Religious talent expands from the mystical into the dialogical, from the solitary state of exception to the ordinariness of life that keeps its ears to the ground.

At this juncture, a later victory of the apostolic over the ingenious comes into view for Buber; the virtuoso of religiousness ceases to be a shimmering witness of his eclectic excitability and turns into an apostle of the doctrine of dialogue – not only between one person and another but also – and even more – between the individual and that which gives her transcendence: the other in general. As promulgator of a quintessential Judaism understood this way, Buber makes himself the exemplary representative of his people, who *eo ipso* become apostolically virulent.

Today his ideas about a Jewish renaissance in Palestine that he assumed to be necessary to humanity as a whole read like bitter parodies of the real Israeli state.

While I am "genuinely in conversation" with others, it is impossible for me to fail to encounter those who "believe otherwise," who have developed other language games of dealing with transcendence, in other nations and times. As soon as I am aware of substantive forms of "believing otherwise," I am condemned to let people look over the shoulder of my own confession. Either the adherents of other faith are diabolical parodists of my religion, in which case they are not worthy of being recognized; or, conversely, they merit attention, in which case I must go beyond the niche of my own confessional, toward the open field of "religion in general" – just as it is necessary for me to be a democrat first within the parliamentary system before I espouse my party.

Buber's collected *Ekstatische Konfessionen* remains in this regard a great document in the more recent history of mentalities and ideas, in spite of people's reservations about his method of selection and his textual interventions;[15] regardless of certain insufferable touches in Buber's presentation, *Ekstatische Konfessionen* marks a stage on the way toward the de-devilization of the external observer of faith. It claims its rank as a witness of the resistance against the depletion of one's inner world in modern media culture. With its impression-istic and inclusive tendency, it allots mysticism an eminent role in the structural transformation of revelation; after Buber's collection, one grasps mysticism's potential role of an avant-garde in the encounter with the foreign.

9.2   Religion in the age of the experiment

Most unbearable would be a god who was as one wished him to be.

Elias Canetti[16]

In a dictum of considerable weight in the history of philosophy, Hegel, the metaphysician with Gnostic tendencies, reportedly said that the Middle Ages were in substance an era of "unhappy consciousness"; in those days the human spirit saw itself condemned to look toward the Highest as though toward a promised, unattainable beyond. The mind's stipulated unhappiness during its Catholic phase would have consisted in having the divine be an object of terror and longing, outside oneself. However, from a systematic perspective, the European Middle Ages must be described as an epoch of happy consciousness; neither before nor after has Christianity made such conscious use of its privilege to see without being seen and to pontificate without having to be instructed. The voices of critique from late antiquity are largely silenced; they lurk about the premises only as remote pangs of the Christian apologetic conscience. The new atheists do not yet stand at the door, let alone in the house. Theologians can still sleep well, in the certainty that everything that is to be said about Christianity is said by Christianity itself, in definitive formulae, thought through from all sides, that promise to remain true until doomsday. The tunes of those who, as aliens or alienated people, would one day tell Christianity off have not yet been printed.

The happy ages of medieval self-centering come to an end with the dawn of modernity. The old citadels of belief now offer exposed flanks to all sorts of external observations and descriptions. In modernity, religion is characterized by its inability to defend itself against observations made by non-members.[17] It thereby becomes apparent that religions are constructs sensitive to being observed; the icy breath of external perceptions can easily destroy the tender flowers of easy credulity. As a rule, belief flourishes best when it can get acclimatized. It is precisely this protection secured by the medieval climate that peters out in the age of the book market and stops completely in the age of media pluralism.[18] The belief, by no means incontrovertible, in the sum total of improbabilities that go under the name "Christianity" must now hold its own against a universal, childlike alertness that has not already been ensured against. From here on, only what survives the skepticism of external perception – which is increasingly built into one's self-perception – belongs to the "substance" of belief. Hence the great retrograde movement of the modern confessional toward theological axioms and anthropological "cores." Under the pressure of skeptical external scrutiny conducted by philologists, mythographers, psychologists, and sociologists, Christian religion becomes downright skeletonized. Two centuries of modernity – of cool external descriptions of Christianity, plus new admissions of alternative enthusiasms, above all in the name of art and humanity – have sufficed to turn a two-millennia-long, omnipresent power into a residual value that is well advised, if it is so willing, to settle as a "subsystem" among subsystems, in a functional niche of modern society – alongside school, legal, educational, and medical systems. In the core countries of the modern world, the great religious denominations find themselves reduced to the role of service providers that meet the vague needs of their clientele through specific means – above all when it comes to making sense of limit situations. Today church is, it seems, a company for the self-management of the melancholy feeling that church is itself impossible. The great majority of modern populations go along with the contemporary civilizational process of a comprehensive individualization of forms of life and gear up for informal and private manifestations of residual religiousness.

In his late work of philosophy of religion, the American philosopher William James gave classic expression to the tendencies to individualize religiousness. James signals the new status of belief in the title of his essay "The Will to Believe" (presented at the Yale and Brown Universities' Philosophical Clubs in 1896). In the future, belief will no longer be able to be delivered to individuals in massive dogmatic packages[19] – at least not with any prospect of broad success. When unconnected individuals continue to opt for religious hypotheses, they do so as if they were trying out promising pharmaceuticals – treating them as tests of the positive effects of a therapeutic measure. Whoever makes an issue of the will to believe does not do so because he is grounded in firm convictions, but rather because "grounds" have become a scarce resource. Moreover, the "ground" has shrunk so much that one can stand on it only by oneself. For this reason, an individual religion is the adequate form of relating to transcendence in a world that subjects all existing stock to experimentation – that is to say, to an exercise of ungrounding and reshaping. As James admits, belief has to do above all with humans in an age of skepticism and of trying things out. The skeptical subject who has outgrown a dogmatic state of affairs recognizes an existential advantage in the cultivation of a vague religious sensibility. Whoever has experience of the impetus-hampering effect of skepticism – and, here, that refers to feelings of meaninglessness thanks to self-observation – will know that belief in anything at all unblocks the individual and unleashes her energies. *In hoc signo vinces* ["In this sign shall thou conquer"]: when you believe, you too will be among the victors. With the help of psychological rules for prudence, the doubting modern soul can rowel itself on.

The Americanization of the religious realm begins with William James, already at the end of the nineteenth century, although it is still wrapped up in noble thoughtfulness. Religion becomes a metaphysical vitamin, a mental diet, an antidepressant, and a heart tonic – a factor in a comprehensive self-medication and self-mission. From there to meditation tapes and to apparatuses – mind machines[20] – that artificially induce states of "mystical" deep relaxation there's barely one hundred years. Under the banner of auto-hypnosis and neurolinguistic self-programming, a striking incursion of technology into the psycho-religious field comes about. The process makes public something that in earlier times had been known, to various degrees, only to monks and other athletes of religiousness: that even belief is a matter of exercise; that, over long stretches, belief and training to believe amount to the same thing.

This secret cannot remain hidden from psychological modernity. In the future, transcendental fitness will be a part of the self-management of liberal white Anglo-Saxon Protestants – and of those who wish to emulate them. Today self-generating streams of new religions are dawning worldwide; meanwhile, those interested can find the means to build their personal religious diet anywhere. All the reserves of spiritual traditions are offered to combat the pain of being a modern person – be it Sufism or the Cabbala, Gnosticism or the Upanishads, Tao or the Great Spirit. Anything that allows the religiously inclined soul to hum the corresponding melodies of belief of foreign cultures is welcome.

As these reflections show, not even religiousness remains unaffected by the experimental and constructivist spirit of modernity. As a result, even the most venerable function of human consciousness comes under a new paradigm – one could call it reflected autohypnosis or endogenous illusionism.[21] Because one can no longer rely, in the conditions of modern life, on the old heritage, in religious matters one must get assistance by new means. Religion – understood as "general religiousness" – is thereby brought into extremely close proximity to the strategic ego and its machinations. Toward the candidates of transcendence, our contemporaries with an interest in religion no longer behave like acolytes, or like subjects who remain loyal because they know no better, but rather like voters, or like customers who assess several items and retain the best. Most of the players on the western religious scene, a few ultraorthodox aside, are actually subject to what Peter L. Berger has called the "compulsion to heresy": if "heretical" originally referred to the behavior of those who took only pieces – *hairesis* in Greek meant "choice" – from a "catholic" – in other words complete – canon of dogmas, then the moderns are almost without exception damned to heresy, even before they realize how this happened to them.[22] Those who look for the possibility of joining a persuasive orthodoxy are precisely the ones who readily end up on the sectarian, idiosyncratic, eccentric path. Adherents of liberal and lay societies are for the most part already born into an atmosphere of fundamental rejection of prejudice, canons, and dogmatism; the experience of being sheltered in a cave of orthodox traditions is no longer available to them. If someone in such a position looks for something that could grant him stability, he must construct it himself, out of the abyss. To employ a notion of the Japanese philosopher Nishida, he is forced to build on the open sea the raft he will float on.

The principle of romantic irony, which was discovered by poets in the early nineteenth century, has meanwhile reached the state of a religion. Only those who have found a way to let themselves believe with eyes wide open can remain religious today, under the sharp light of a chronic state of being observed, from the outside as well as from the self. General religiousness is the gradual manufacturing of belief in the course of experimenting with belief. Yet it could be that someone who lets herself believe becomes in the end someone whom belief leaves in the lurch.

9.3   World arena and unmarked space

The best is to become thoroughly dead while you are still alive
and to do what you want.

Shido Bunan[23]

With the reduction of Christianity, Judaism, and other historical
traditions to general religiousness, the components of the construct
of belief that are not further reducible come to light like pure
elements or radicals, with a new sort of clarity. Among these
radicals, mysticism has long drawn particular interest. In circles of
connoisseurs of the supernatural, it is seen to be the material out of
which religions have emerged; once we strip mythological layers and
regional particularities, mysticism seems to be the ultimate content or
the deepest enzyme of religions.[24] This is the source of the pull toward
mystical ecumenism, even beyond incorrigibly positive religions.

Recourse to lived experience of the mystical sort does in fact offer
the advantage of cutting the ground from under all forms of dogmatic
pronouncement. This accommodates quite well the individualism of
modern conditions. Ideal-typically, the person who reports on mystical
states in the presence of a third party speaks of his lived experience
neither as a genius nor as an apostle, but as witness to an incident
on the front line of transcendence. Reporting on a transcendence
that is (so to speak) fresh, the witness's discourse responds to the
very sharp need for a contemporary general religiousness: it provides
evidence that the doors of revelation were not finally closed two
thousand years ago with the final redaction of the Gospels or other
holy texts. The mystical religiousness of experience gives expression
to the fact that it would be unacceptable if all those who came later
were made mere epigones of the classical self-presentation of God to
humans – those future generations, to whom no original experience
of "truth" would be accessible. Mysticism represents the claim of
current generations to equality of birth with those of the golden age
of revelation.[25] It protests against the privileged position of the past
vis-à-vis epiphany – a position upheld by all orthodoxies. Back then,
so say the canonical conventions, the absolute appeared undisguised;
today one must make do with transcripts of an unrepeatable manifestation. Mysticism is the wager on the continuing revelation of what
earlier, here and elsewhere, unforgettably "made an appearance."
Without *revelatio continua* there is no mystical position. If there were
a motto on which mystics of all stripes should agree, that could only
be "Apocalypse now."[26]

From the idea of a continuing revelation one can draw a second
advantage to mysticism, one that is particularly suitable to the

religious radical in a post-confessional period. If traditional religions of all sorts had to deal with the intercourse between mortal inhabitants of this world and powers and entities of a second world, it is obvious that positive religions end up in crisis mode as soon as the second world as a whole becomes an object of doubt. This is the characteristic of modernity. For numerous reasons, members of modern civilizations see less and less why they should continue to perform the basic metaphysical operation of humanity in the past – namely the duplication of the world into this world and its beyond – as though there had been no process of "enlightenment." What exactly is "enlightenment," if not a progressive elimination of the beyond (beginning with the Platonic reformation of the heavens and the Buddhist explanation of Nirvana, and ending with the introversion of metaphysical "projections" in deep psychology)? Nietzsche's metaphysico-historical telegram "How the true world finally became a fable" (in *Twilight of the Idols*, 1888) sums up the result of all enlightenments masterfully. Plato's "true world" dissipates like fog in the modern sun; even the longest ghost story – the discourse of the one god who communicated with this world through sons and prophets – has been told to the end. The metaphysical drowsiness of the human being must give way to a post-historical clarity, at long last; all paths of impartial intelligence lead sooner or later to the point at which the world becomes, again, everything that is the case: "We leave Heaven to the angels and the sparrows."[27]

Against this background, mysticism, that religious radical, stands out especially clearly, with its irreducible tenacity. After the depletion – indeed cancellation – of the positive beyond, the evidence remains in force for watchful life that it exists only together with everything else that is the case. It may be that I am not all there is; it is undeniable, however, that I am included in something that is all there is – I am, as John the Evangelist and the existentialists after him say, "in the world"; from where I am, it is obvious that the incident of the world persists unfinished. As long as I exist, things that are the case have the opportunity to appear to me. No special revelations to my address from a second world are necessary to remind me of the risk that I could be claimed by the evidence of a something in general. Once ideas of the beyond have been cleared away, everything that is the case can in principle, in some special sense, become exalted in appearance and pregnant with revelation. "Not *how* the world is, is the mystical, but *that* it is."[28]

The clearest consequences of this situation have been drawn by the great modern artists; even those who rank second and third on the speculative art markets participate in this new state of affairs, which allows the revelation of "being" to be pulled into every present thing. This must be taken seriously: the individual is now the heaven into which world and things come when they appear to her in their "that." Every individual, conceived of in modern terms, is indeed a child of the world and of nothing but the world, down to the last fiber of her being, but she is at the same time the place in the world before which the world both disappears and dawns. For this reason, the genuine mystics of the present – especially artists – speak above all of the disappearing of the world and of the naked, impenetrable appearance of things. That the rest, namely the mystic tradition-alists of the old European school, continue to seek their salvation in citations by Meister Eckhart or Jan van Ruysbroeck is another story.

If, in modernity, mysticism must be conceived of as the threshold of a normal experience of the world – and not as the break-through of a full beyond into our world, beckoning with a spooky gesture – then a description of the human being that calmly recog-nizes mystical states as a universal birthright must be possible and attempted. An anthropology of the mystical would have to explain the naturalness of mystical states together with their rarity. This presupposes an analysis of human memory that plausibly explains why human beings, although "born mystics," typically forget their fundamental endowment in the course of acquiring their egos; indeed they forget it all the more radically as they entangle themselves more deeply in vulgar versions of adult life. Besides, it would be necessary to show that certain individuals reconnect with this "endowment" when, going past what they have acquired, they reoccupy the state of the brain *before* the learning processes were directed toward the world. This occurs, for example, after shock, under the influence of drugs, or through meditative exercises designed to make the everyday world of representation pass away. The ominous "mystical death" is a metaphor for the awakened brain, when it is in the state of recollecting its pre-linguistic stillness – something that the noisy and excited personality would take to signify sheer downfall. Empirically, mystical states can be distilled into two groups. There is a mysticism of states of exception. These take the subject outside its normal state in moments of extraor-dinary transfiguration and wondrous emotionality or state of being affected [*Berührtheit*]. They also prepare for the embarrassment of having to communicate afterwards the displacement the subject experienced. In addition, there is a mysticism of continuity. Here every waking moment in the life of subjects is shot through with the radiance of an unvarying sameness.

This binary ought not to be made the object of a controversy over genuine and phony mysticism; the appearance of both phenomena is informative for an anthropology of the mystical. If the theory of memory is to furnish an interpretation of mysticism with the desired explanatory power, it would do well to situate both types of the mystical brain – the one tipping over into the state of exception and the one that is continually capable of remaining undifferentiated – on a common scale. Thus we need both a continuum concept for the mystical recollection of nothing – that is, for the recollection of the state of the brain before the inscription of radical differences – and a catastrophe concept for the ecstatic and sudden recollection of the other state.[29]

These requirements are most readily met by a theory of the human that recognizes in *Homo sapiens sapiens* not only a learning and somehow maturing animal, but also an animal that shifts elements: an animal that is destined by the fate of its species to pass from what flows to what is firm.[30] The primary direction of learning, from the sea to firm ground, finds expression, at the species level, in the establishment of relatively firm ego structures. In the myths of high cultures, heroes represent the typical struggle of members of a species to assert themselves "on firm ground," which in historical time turns out to be a theater of war and toil. The world is an arena of ineluctable passions. The need to go from childish fluidity to land is, typically, a hard lesson for the adolescents of high-culture periods. To exist is to play a role – the "role" being that of subjects capable of conflict and who behave heroically, cum grano salis, vis-à-vis their "great works" and in their unavoidable struggles for chances in life. In the brain of such individuals a certain state is established, which is marked by keeping the theater of conflict and one's position with respect to it permanently in view. For human beings in the arena, the inner picture of the state of the conflict passes for the world itself; if someone were to come up with the view that the map is not the land – a picture of the world not the world, one's self-image not one's self – that would be total news to them. Such a message[31] would come like an invitation to climb out of the arena and end the war of ego bearers in combat. Whoever wishes to deliver such a message should muster the proof that "in reality" the world is no arena and no theater of war that we must enter wearing our best ego armor. She would have to show that, in spite of all our illusions about a mainland arena, the something on which we live has remained a homogenous river, an oceanic continuum, in which differences impress themselves no more powerfully than does writing on water.[32] Exactly this would be the mystical message – now delivered no longer as a report from a positive beyond in the sense of a two-world ontology, but rather as elementary anthropological information. Mystics are the contra-heroic informants on the human being; they do not abet ego assertion in the reality of the arena. They try to rebut the arena ontology as such. They do so by showing that the something in which we "reside" is in truth an unmarked space in which there can be no difference that makes a difference – and first of all no difference that justifies struggles for life and death along the line of fighting for the position of one's ego.

For its very impressive witnesses across history, the unmarked space bore names that belong with the greatest picture puzzles of humanity: paradise, kingdom of God, white land – in ordinary language, sky and ocean. These designations will retain their dignity when cooler descriptions have taken their place. Put differently, the mystical state turns out to be the brain's recollection from its state before the struggle for the identification of the something in which it is destined to reside. The peaceful brain's hovering state of being in something recollects itself in the fluid beginning of its history, as it were. Whoever experiences this is, in a heartbeat, well versed in the other state, even if he is also shaken by the evidence that this is possible in spite of everything. For this reason, mysticism becomes more impressive the more powerful the existing stock of mature adult consciousness is, in defiance of which mysticism asserts its claim. "Mysticism for beginners" is trivial, since beginners cannot but be mystics – any fetus will confirm this. Mystical recollection is impressive when its subject is an adult fully under stress. Then the individual becomes the incarnation of the improbability that the endowment of the most ancient inner state can be as vital at the peak of societal tensions as in the intrauterine cave. In the original fetal state, "to exist" means to hearken enstatically[33] to the "sound of the world"[34] and to grow in the torrent of the double bloodstream of child and mother.[35] – The fact that echoes of this state and mode of being return even in duly grown-up adults is a psychological disgrace for this species given to mysticism. Once recollections of the old innermost state can rise to the surface in a soul able to circulate worldwide and, like a compass for salvation, show it ways out of its entanglement, we get a notion of what was to be required of an ideal–typical, spiritually mature adult in high culture. To give structure to the experience of wavering amid fixity, to be a form for the formless: it is with such and similar formulae that mystical teachers in the East, as well as in the West, have established a norm for adult illuminations. To explain mysticism as a mere "regression" of the subject to states that precede the formation of the ego would itself be regressive – a capitulation to cultural tendencies to reduce and lock up interior space.[36] When it comes to mysticism, what gives much food for thought, especially in a society that lets itself go ever more, is the progressive elevation of the remotest "recollection" to the status of full-blown awareness of reality. Perhaps this gives us an idea of what education might mean in a world of barely educable people.

10

ABSOLUTE AND CATEGORICAL IMPERATIVE

Ladies and Gentlemen,

By way of introducing the brief remarks that follow, which deal with the dramatic accentuation of the dangers that loom over the current world process, allow me to make a confession: I am grateful for the extraordinary opportunity, offered to an author of philosophical works – moreover, one who, for all his Francophile leanings, is at home in a non-French tradition – of addressing a circle of political personalities as eminent as the one assembled here. Of course, my gratitude goes first of all to the host of this event; but it also extends to the circle of my colleagues, who encouraged me to take part in this presentation of the Collegium International before the French Senate.

In fact I would not have ventured to address you here, had I not taken part in an initiative that was brought into being a few years ago by Michel Rocard, the former French prime minister, and whose participants included such outstanding figures of contemporary intellectual and political life as Fernando Cardoso, the erstwhile president of Brasil, René Passet, the initiator of the World Social Forum at Porto Allegre, Edgar Morin, the grand master of European sociology, Michael Doyle, advisor to the former UN general secretary Kofi Annan, as well as leading social scientists and economists such as Amartya Sen and Joseph E. Stiglitz – to name just these individuals.

To clarify from the outset the perspective from which my intervention comes, I would like to propose the view that politics and philosophy, today as in the age of their foundations in the Greek world, have a strong common ground: politics and philosophy, each in its own way, are arts of worrying about the world as a whole.

This is true today more than ever. We have extremely good reasons to compare the current situation with that of the post-1945 period. Looking back on the catastrophes that people suffered, a few of the great intellects of those years spoke of an "age of anxiety," as is confirmed by the British American poet W. H. Auden in an eponymous poem; but they also spoke of an age of reconstruction – which had become indispensable after the desolations of the two world wars. By analogy with these important and consequential diagnoses, one should make two points concerning our time. In its own way, it, too, is, unmistakably, an age of anxiety – an age of global concern and, what is more, an age of disorientation. At the same time, however, it must be interpreted as an age of constructive provocations, an era of the boldest oppositions to the ordinary course of things.

As regards the philosophical side of the art of worrying about the world as a whole or, better, of letting oneself be affected by the great worries of the world, what is at issue initially is overcoming the climate of demoralization that has spread into the life of countless of our contemporaries. This demoralization has its sources in the daunting size of current challenges, in the unsettling disproportion between ends and means in politics, and in the staggering inconsistency and incoherence that we find in the language and actions of the classes in charge. Philosophical reflection can oppose demoralization only by way of articulating a guideline for action whose power to orient is strong enough in spite of all pragmatic confusions.

I may remind you that, toward the end of the eighteenth century, Immanuel Kant believed he had found such a straightforward orienting principle. He expressed it in his well-known categorical imperative, which in one of its formulations reads like this: act in such a way that the maxim behind your action could serve, in each case, as law in a universal legislation. With this principle, Kant wanted to reconcile the egoism of private interests with the requirements of the common good, and thereby to make possible the coexistence of all rational beings within the juridical framework of bourgeois society. Half a century later, Karl Marx – who had witnessed the devastating hardships of the working classes in Europe – modernized the liberal categorical imperative with the revolutionary thesis that it is the imperative duty of every human being to abolish all conditions in which the human would be a poor, suffering, contemptible, and abandoned being. One is justified in interpreting the antagonistic synergies of liberalism and socialism in the nineteenth and twentieth centuries as the expression of a common effort to realize this powerful imperative.

The question of the proper formulation of an ethical principle was revived once more a good hundred years later. In the face of the imminent ecological crisis, in the 1970s, the philosopher Hans Jonas updated the categorical imperative by charging it with the futurist energies of a political ecology: act in each case in such a way that the consequences of your action remain compatible with the continued existence of authentically human life on earth.

I content myself here with the observation that this series of redactions of the categorical imperative allows us to identify an increasing dramatization. Both Kant and Marx are still the offspring of Europe's faith in history: they are imbued with the conviction that the human is a historical being capable of accomplishing what is ethically required of her within the apportioned time – and against any obstruction, which would stall what is morally and politically right. In principle, in a Kantian and in a Marxist world, one always knows exactly what has to be done – and one is allowed, by the way, to wait until the conditions mature. What is right is delayed only for a while; it can never be out of date.

Things are completely different in Hans Jonas's new version of the imperative. In the world of ecological alarm, there are deadlines that must be met via external physical processes. Unlike in human history, where one may always wait for a second or third chance to make good on what was previously neglected, here the law of irreversibility reigns.

Allow me, ladies and gentlemen, to recall a recently composed document that will give us a sense of the impermissibility of delay when it comes to the new ecological imperative. At the end of May 2009, a group of Nobel Prize winners convened in London to discuss how the ecological imperative could be put into practice. At the end of their meeting they presented the "St. James's Palace Memorandum" (so named after the meeting place), which renewed demands that had been well known for decades – demands for a new climate politics and for a resolute agenda dedicated to the protection of global nature reserves. What makes us pay special attention to this document is its disquieting, indeed impatiently demanding tone: a group of scientists of the highest stature, who cannot be suspected of any propensity for hysterical pronouncements and apocalyptic exaggerations, have taken the risk of addressing those in charge of the world in a manner that can only be interpreted as unconditional alarm. The authors of the London Appeal are concerned not only with the well-known list of demands for measures that are supposed to lead to a great transformation – or, in the language of Edgar Morin, to a metamorphosis from which a new cultural model could arise – measures such as the formulation of a universal climate contract, the shift of our entire civilization to carbon-free technologies, and the protection of the rainforest. What is most impressive about this document is the emphasis placed on the need to act *now*. Thus the key phrase in this most recent redaction of the ecological imperative reads "the Urgency of Now."[1]

Such a move toward globally responsible action can succeed only when we formulate a new concept of concrete solidarity with universal implications. I will attempt to indicate how such a concept could be formulated – and indeed formulated in the language of a general systemic immunology. General immunology proceeds from the axiom that all life is the successful phase of an immune system; here the term "life" is applied not only to biological organisms but also to the historical existence of cultures, peoples, and institutions. "Immunity" refers originally to the protection of the right of those who have functions relevant to the community. This points to the deep connection between community and immunity. The Roman legal system already recognized that there could be no *communio* without suitable structures of *immunitas*. Every immune system is an embodied expectation of injury or an institutionalized defense against harm.

When we are dealing with human beings, we must therefore take into account the existence of three synchronized levels of immune systems. Biological immunity protects the individual organisms from species-typical invasions and injuries, while social immunity is guaranteed by simple systems of solidarity (such as hospitality and neighborly assistance) and by the legal system. These institutions bring home the insight that humans are beings who can flourish only in the element of reciprocal support, and only under the protection of laws that defend them against injustice. In most cultures, symbolic or ritual immune systems accompany these formations. In Europe, these immune systems are conventionally called "religions"; they furnish human beings with words and gestures that tide them over at times of helplessness and hopelessness. Symbolic immune systems compensate for death and secure the transmission of common norms to successive generations.

Human systems of solidarity and immunity of the juridical and religious type obviously go beyond the horizon of organismic egoism. To be sure, like all immunitary structures, they, too, practice the distinction between what is foreign and what is one's own, but they define the latter not merely biologically, but culturally – whether it be as a people or as a group of peoples, as a community, or as a succession of generations within this very community. Thus, at this level, immunity always already involves a strong element of cultural altruism. To the extent that individuals learn to proceed as agents of their culture, they set aside private advantages in order to serve the advantage of the larger group. Cultures or peoples can assert themselves in the flux of time only when they bring individuals to the point of grasping that their private immunity can be obtained solely within the framework of an effective social co-immunity.

For this reason co-immunity is the keyword in the effort to understand any story of political and social success. It enables us to grasp how human beings can cooperate in larger groups in the first place. Co-immunitary calculus explains why one must sacrifice something at a lower level if one wishes to attain something at a higher level. This is the basis of all sacrifices and taxes, all manners and services, all acts of askesis, and all virtuosities.

The current state of the world is obviously defined by the fact that it offers no efficient co-immunity for the members of world society. At the highest level, there is no operatively convincing system of solidarity; there is rather only the classic war among interest groups – and, for the time being, even the existence of an institution such as the United Nations and other global forums can do nothing to change this. Today as in ancient times, we can still find efficient unities of co-immunity in smaller formats: they are familial, tribal, and national. Even the current empires follow tradition in obeying the law of exclusivity, insofar as they continue to make the conventional distinction between what is foreign and what is one's own. In this situation, the familiar contest prevails: war of all against all. Partial systems compete according to an implacable logic, which consistently turns one's immunity profits into another's immunity losses. Every partial system seeks its own advantage, but the whole remains unprotected and exposed to the plundering of combatants.

The catastrophic drift of global processes makes it necessary today to contemplate the creation of a comprehensive unity of solidarity, which should be strong enough to serve as an immune system for the defenseless whole – that unprotected whole that we call nature, the earth, the atmosphere, the biosphere, the anthroposphere. We must for this reason intensify Hans Jonas's updated categorical imperative even further. In consequence, here is the basic principle of action in our times. Act in such a way as to promote the emergence of a global system of solidarity, or at least not to hinder it through your action. Act in such a way that the practice of plundering and externalizing, hitherto common, may be replaced by an ethos of global protection. Act in such a way that what you do may not generate any further delays to the indispensable reversal that serves everyone's interest.

One must admit that it will not be easy to follow this imperative. It requires that every individual be as impatient as possible and as patient as necessary. But what is world history, if not the result of getting used to suffering and of demanding happiness and satisfaction?

11

NEWS ABOUT THE WILL TO BELIEVE

A Note on Desecularization

Almost 110 years ago, before the philosophical clubs of the Universities of Yale and Brown, the Harvard philosopher William James gave a lecture that would become famous; in it, at this evening gathering of peers, he defended the basic right to believe. His argument was not about that freedom of belief that makes the subject of constitutions in the modern nation states. What James wanted to convey was rather a justification for contemporary individuals' right to take the leap into a deliberately adopted attitude of belief for the sake of a moral–practical direction in their life; and here James coins such stimulating phrases as "our right to adopt a believing attitude in religious matters" and "the lawfulness of voluntarily adopted faith."[1] In a later paper – published under the title "The Will to Believe" – he summarizes his reflections in this lofty thesis: "Faith thus remains as one of the inalienable birthrights of our mind."[2] James is looking for a liberal response to a dominant intellectualism, which had declared it immoral, on the basis of insufficient evidence, to adopt any dogmas of beliefs. James, by contrast, holds that all people are more or less "absolutists by instinct" and that, when it comes to practical everyday living, even rigorous theoretical empiricists will follow their personal dogmas like "infallible popes": "they dogmatize like infallible popes"[3] – a sentence that illustrates how a Protestant American could make creative use of the scandalous dogma of infallibility twenty-five years after the First Vatican Council. James was the first one to recognize that not just the pope, but every self-respecting human being who lives in the modern world is condemned to a sort of infallibility. However, as James emphasizes, instinctive absolutism for the most part goes together with a lack of logical evidence. Because, when it comes to matters of life and belief, people cannot wait until the clock of evidence within themselves strikes twelve; they have the right, indeed in some sense even the duty, to bridge the gaps between the dubious and the certain with a leap into the most credible assumption or, as James says, the most vigorous hypothesis and to build their happiness on it.

In the light of this analysis, what one calls "belief" appears to be a form of enlightened precipitousness in formulating one's axioms of conduct in life. Anybody can, at will, hear in these theses a transatlantic echo of Nietzsche's investigations, an echo generated in the space of a new sort of cybernetics of individuated human existence. In his reflections on the art of living for post-Christian individuals, Nietzsche, too, was concerned with the precedence of the will over knowledge and with the supremacy of immunitary interests; however, he crossed his own approaches to the biologization of the truth function with a Hyperborean ethos of bravery in the face of unwelcome truths – thereby defending the primacy of knowledge over vital interests, in the best old European philosophical tradition.

In what follows I would like to develop the hunch that the new religious discourse that is spreading throughout Europe nowadays amounts to nothing less than a way of bringing Europeans closer to the American standard in matters of regulating our personal system of convictions. The psycho-political framework for this rapprochement was furnished by the nascent denationalization of the insurance industry, which we have now witnessed for a while in Europe as well. From a sociological perspective, the striking religiousness of Americans reflects the fact that the United States was never shaped as a social state that safeguards everything. For this reason, its citizens remained forever at the stage of insuring themselves privately. It is enough to understand that "God" – if one may utter this label with sociological detachment – represents the highest authority among private insurers to see right away why, in an age of debilitated social state services, the demand for religion is on the rise even among Europeans.

Now if one asks whether there is a "post-secular society" and whether we live in one, the answer (provided that we are European, read the newspaper, and live in 2007) would immediately suggest itself: "It's quite likely." For at the present we are receiving from all sides, media and academia alike, signals of a reactualization of the religious element – especially in the commercial form of "world religion." But such an answer would bear witness to journalistic behavior, not to the intellectual virtue known as distance, namely distance from suggestions. Insofar as they ride the wave of probability, journalists are always "embedded journalists," even when they do not go into the field with American troops. By contrast, intellectuals – who are like scholars in this respect – typically champion a disembedding[4] of the theses that emerge from the current state of affairs. It is part of journalists' ethos to think that what is current is always right; so why cannot this hold for the religious currency of today, just as absolute historicism's motto – "the time is always right" – held for the communist and nationalist revolutionaries of 1917 or 1933? For intellectuals, however, answering leading questions directly should never be allowed, just as it is never permissible to go along with the flow just because it is flowing. They have to ask questions in return. Why do you want to know this? Next, what are the assumptions and presuppositions embedded in this question? And, finally, in what social group does one end up by opting for the pro, the con, or the undecided?

It should be obvious that I would like to speak out on behalf of an intellectual answer. Hence I will put the term "post-secular" in brackets and, for now, register firmly only this feature – that it belongs, quite evidently, in the vocabulary of a grand story told by contemporary orators who wish to be dated after a palpable mental watershed.

I begin my substantive reflections with the thesis that we live in a thoroughly hysterical "society" – if by "hysterical" we mean the talent for experiencing metaphors physically, for somaticizing rumors, and for acting out suggestive grand stories as though they were our own convictions. Hysteria is the inevitable psycho-political condition of thoroughly mediatized populations. As a result of national lifestyles, hysteria has prevailed where people have had to learn to live in the stream of media-constructed constant communications and to orient themselves to the rhythmic subject matter changes of our zeitgeist. If hysteria – the paradigmatic neurosis in the nineteenth century – has largely disappeared from the practices of psychotherapists today, this is due in no small measure to the fact that its motivation – the more or less inauthentic production of oneself before the eyes of a powerful observer that has to be beguiled – has become the norm in a mediatized world. Suggestibility is now the first civic duty. The same dispositions that a hundred years ago were reckoned to be clinically abnormal are written off today as media savvy.

In this context it is necessary to realize that the moderns' ability to become hysterical involves a modification of religiousness that is typical of the most recent period insofar as it implies the modernization of credulity – one could also say the flexibilization of dogmatic behavior. In substance, what the beautiful and canny German word *Zeitgeist* has described ever since 1800 is just the reflection of the psycho-semantic modernization we generally discuss under the name "romanticism." (It is no doubt appropriate to recall Rüdiger Safranski's sonorous definition here: romanticism is the continuation of religion by aesthetic means.) Life in the zeitgeist implies converting the disposition of so-called firm belief into free-floating suggestibility. On the one hand, this process is expressed in the moderns' dangerously elevated readiness for ideology. On the other hand, it is expressed in the development of an invasive aestheticization, at work everywhere in the manifestations of their culture – high culture and mass culture alike. Thanks to the aesthetic education of civil society, if not of the human species as a whole, countless individuals have learned during the past two centuries to develop a higher inner mobility and to gear themselves up for an increasing mass of organized sensuous presences – in plain language, artworks and fabricated environments. In these presences they experience continually changing micro-gospel intensities.[5] Against the backdrop of this current, a specific countermodernity has been developing ever since the nineteenth century. This countermodernity specializes in resisting the liquefactions of credulity, indeed of religious faith tout court, in the fluctuating zeitgeist. Here I would like to characterize it as the position of good, orthodox belief.

So then, if the concept of post-secular society is put forward for discussion, the first comment to be made can only be that we are here dealing with a classical expression of the zeitgeist drawn from the hysterical matrix of liquefied religious convictions. It invites those who would use it to act out a grand narrative, in which the present marks the turning point in a historical drama that reaches us today from the depths of time. As in all myths of the modern age, a narrative schema is performed here that prompts us to place ourselves in a three-act chronological sequence of states of order and disorder. In the present case, the narrative path leads from the pre-secular world, in which religion was the alpha and omega for human beings, through the secular world, in which religion was ostensibly repressed and forgotten, to the post-secular world, whose beginnings we have the privilege to experience and in which religion would return from exile. For those who avail themselves of this kind of schema (and it doesn't matter whether they use it explicitly or covertly), at issue here is, evidently, what is always at issue in hysteria: the possibility of connecting one's own existential feeling with some strong source of meaning. Such a source becomes available when the lived "now" can be interpreted as the pivot of an epochal turn or as a cultural revolution.

As is well known, when Karl Marx advanced the myth of the return of a classless society, he provided the most effective schema for a hysteria that could be acted out. Here again there was a typical three-act structure in which the originally classless society was ousted by class-based societies, only to return in the end at a higher level, in the form of a new classlessness. Nietzsche's myth of the rebirth of tragedy was built in a formally similar fashion: according to this myth, the ancient Greek foundations of the tragic arts were subverted thanks to the concerted efforts of the leveling powers called Socratism, Christianity, Italian opera, and modern optimism – finally to return as German music drama, thanks to Richard Wagner's masterstroke.

The treatment of the second act is decisive in such triadic narratives. As a rule, it is supposed to feature as a fallen middle period, and we, the hysterical collective, find ourselves at its end as soon as we give credence to the appointed interpreters of the signs of the times. Third acts in the mythical schema, acts that one describes as returns and rebirths, fall under a class of events that, in accordance with their logic, can take place only after the end of middle periods – and it makes no difference to the narrative structure whether a formal middle age lasts 5,000 years, like the Marxist era of class societies, 2,000 years, like the period without tragedy, 1,000 years, like the stretch from late antiquity to the modern age, or 200 years, like the age of dominant secularity. Several of today's outspoken myth tellers assure us that we have reached the end of this last middle age and that the subsequent era, the third age, has already begun.

At this point I do not wish to speak any further about the uses and disadvantages of triadic narratives for life. I will content myself for the moment with the observation that here the so-called secular society, which the post-secular society has purportedly ousted, re-enacts in its self-image a congeries of narrative bodies – though the narratives it uses are of a completely different structure from that of the romantic and dialectical three-act narratives.

Undoubtedly the most important narrative of secular society still is, in our context, the historical account of the constitution of forms of knowledge and life that prevail today in our part of the world; we summarize these forms under the collective concept of Enlightenment.

This account does not merely tell a myth; it holds fast to the chronicle of a struggle for emancipation, in the course of which citizens of late absolutist "societies" liberated themselves from the tutelage of representatives of the first estate (the clergy) and second estate (the nobility). This struggle went hand in hand with a change in cognitive climate toward supporting individuals' ability to undertake business ventures, as well as their claim to political and moral self-determination. To the extent that religion was perceived as the natural ally of feudalism and absolutism in this conflict, it was inevitable that the antifeudal front of republican Enlightenment would also form an antireligious line.

If people think they recognize today a certain return of religion, not to mention a turn to post-secular "society," this speaks at first only to a change in the global strategic situation. Because modern "society" has meanwhile taken on a thoroughly post-clerocratic and post-aristocratic structure, the older animosities of the Enlightenment's polemics against religion could – and had to – give way. Over the course of the twentieth century, the combative "Enlightenment" has worn itself weary in its victory; thanks to its consolidation, it can afford to grant its debilitated opponent a return to the center of good society. While in his *Dictionary of Accepted Ideas*, under the entry "Conversation," Gustave Flaubert noted that "[p]olitics and religion are to be excluded from it" – thereby tactfully stating the norms of civil communication for his own century – today we are observing numerous symptoms that testify to a new dignity afforded to religious themes in conversation. I doubt, however, that these observations suffice to support such a bold thesis as the return of religion.

In spite of everything, the primary narrative of the contemporary culture of rationality remains indebted to the principle of progressive research and critical accumulation of knowledge. And, even if the polemical side of "Enlightenment" may have come to rest, there are no serious indications of an interruption of the continuum of research and reflection that connects us with the intellectual pioneers of the modern age, and in a certain way even with the patriarchs of the philosophical enlightenment of the Greeks in the fifth century BC – for all the changes in grammar and vocabulary and all the paradigm shifts.

In these continua of learning, an abundance of knowledge has been collected that decisively changes the status of religious lore. Beyond all Enlightenment polemics, there have been reliable increases in knowledge that force religious dogmas to coexist uncomfortably alongside findings that contradict them and compel them to be reformulated. By dogma I understand here a statement that gives authoritative status to the human relationship with transcendent matters. I do not wish to get bogged down in the swamp of discourses that deal with the tension between belief and knowledge. Rather I content myself with two observations that I will not justify any further. On the one hand, it is necessary for human beings, today as in the past, to remain, in the interest of their cognitive stability, within the continuum of the knowledge of their times. On the other hand, in view of the finitude of knowledge, it is rational to compensate for the realism of positive knowledge with a certain surrealism – let us say, with a sense of the possible, the extraordinary, the wondrous, and the absurd. In any case, it is certain that in modernity the realm of knowledge has expanded at the cost of religious behavior toward transcendence – which is why the religious worldview of the past had to surrender irrevocably, to secular thought and mundane science, broad swathes that were once in its possession.

*

In what follows I will name, provisionally and without systematic intentions, seven aspects of the phenomenon of transcendence, of which at least the first four can be translated critically into mundane categories without causing the religious side to lose more than what is normally lost with the acquisition of better knowledge. I distinguish four false interpretations of the state of affairs regarding transcendence from two further aspects. I do not wish to claim that these two are completely secure from misunderstandings, but, owing to their objectively enigmatic character, they do resist a simple mapping onto pragmatic and natural contexts. Regarding the seventh aspect, I will establish that, owing to its undecidability, it lies beyond the difference between knowledge and belief, although, saliently, it is for the most part belief that takes advantage of this circumstance.

*

Let us begin with a thesis that Heiner Mühlmann recently formulated in an essay on cultures as learning unities; to be sure, he put it as a resolute question followed by a lapidary answer: "How does transcendence emerge? It emerges from the misapprehension of slowness." The author continues: "A movement is slow when it lasts longer than a generation. To observe it, we rely on the cooperation of people who lived before us and of people who will live after us."[6] Since in earlier human history instances of cooperation with preceding and following generations were attained only selectively, or were structurally impossible, or in any case remained precarious episodes, it is understandable that in the more distant spiritual history of humanity a large part of slowness was relegated to transcendence, which in this case means unobservability. There it could be explained as a matter of transcendent design by transhuman or divine minds – and no good refutation would have been possible. However, as soon as civilizations produce effective methods for observing slowness, the concept of transcendent design crumbles – regardless of whether this design is called creation, providence, predestination, or salvation history – and room is made for immanent procedures of interpreting the longue durée, be it via biological or socio-systemic theories of evolution or via wave theories and theories of rupture that allow one to describe oscillations and mutations within the realm of the longue durée. In orthodox circles, where there is still an intense identification with the edifying concept of a transcendent design, one can register resistance to the means of thought that lead to the secularization of transcendentized slowness – most plainly among US creationists who, as is generally known, come up with all sorts of things in order to immunitize their doctrine of sudden, intentional creation against the new sciences related to a slow, self-organizing emergence.[7]

In the next step we reach the finding that transcendence also emergences from the misapprehension of fierceness. To elucidate this state of affairs, we must again turn to a concept that Heiner Mühlmann introduced into cultural studies: the connection between stress theory and the theory of determinant symbol formation, as Mühlmann explained it in his epoch-making book *The Nature of Cultures* (1996). The phenomenology of the great stress response in *Homo sapiens* makes us understand that the states experienced by the subject exposed to stress often appear to be of a transcendent nature – and why this is so. The fierceness of the body's own processes, which initially are determined in a strictly biological mode, may reach such a degree when all the reactions have been fully deployed that what one experiences can plausibly be attributed only to external forces. Within our traditions, the paradigm for this is Achilles's rage as sung by Homer – that *mēnis Achileōs* that has been invoked for millennia in old European warrior camps as the numinous source of a sublime and gruesome calling. It is reasonable to place this heroic rage in the series of manifestations of battle frenzy demonstrated by numerous cultures, and also comparable with prophetic ecstasies. From a physiological perspective, the finding one can recognize in these episodes of heroic fury is an offensive identification of the warrior with the driving energy that floods him. This belongs in the spectrum of manic enthusiasms, which also includes the well-known amok syndrome of Polynesians (which western mass culture has eagerly taken up and superficially copied), as well as the ecstatic rapture of Vedic warriors and the German heroes' battle fervor, which swells up to becoming desire for destruction – we could even associate it with Giordano Bruno's phrase *heroici furori* ["heroic frenzies"], were the latter not already too strongly elevated to the spiritual meaning of philosophical mania. With psychological quasi-necessity, the fury we are talking about here appears to its bearer as an obsession given from on high, in which energy and the objective of battle coalesce into a firm intention. As long as the transcendent misapprehension of fierceness predominates, it is impossible to see that what is experienced as a gift of power comes from a storage fund, psycho-semantically codetermined, of the organism in extreme stress. This should also hold for a large part of the prophetic arousals that express themselves in excessive discourses and commentaries on holy texts. Incidentally, the great stress response manifests itself not only explosively, but also implosively. An example was provided a few years ago during a bullfight in one of the largest arenas in Madrid. Three times in a row, the matador failed to deliver the fatal blow to the charging bull – and then fell into a sort of rigid state, in which the wounded animal would have stamped him down or killed him, had the petrified bull fighter not been pulled out of the arena by his colleagues. The scene is best elucidated when we recognize in it the polar opposite of the great stress response: here we have a shock of self-denial. There is no question that, for the bullfighter, the disgrace revealed itself at that moment as a transcendent force. The physiological side of the event may not be all that mysterious; its spiritual aspect, however, is not completely transparent. From a religious perspective, it reminds us to what degree the god who judges human beings also has the power to reject them. In any case, it is certain that the connection between guilt, disgrace, and stress without which many religious subjects' raging against themselves is not conceivable is rooted in endogenous mechanisms that are open to psycho-biological explanation.

A large part of what Rudolf Otto has named "the holy" in his well-known book[8] thus falls *de iure* under the domain of stress theory. On the whole, Otto's book is to be seen as a formal type of misapprehension of fierceness, despite its much praised services to the formal clarification of its subject.

A third transcendence emerges from the misapprehension of what I would here like to call the independence of the other. I will explain this briefly with an example from the classics of modern literature. Toward the end of Part 2 of his four-part novel *Joseph and His Brothers* (1934), Thomas Mann depicts Jacob receiving the news of the supposed death of his favorite son, Joseph. Jacob falls into an excessive ritual of mourning – sitting, as Job would later, on a pile of trash in the courtyard and assailing God for days and weeks on end with lamentations, accusations, and backtalk against his fate. After the mourning has subsided, Jacob becomes aware of the indecency of his behavior. Now he begins to see it as a great advantage that God did not react immediately like an offended lover to everything that Jacob had brought against him in the heat of passion, but rather concealed himself in his silence – Thomas Mann speaks subtly of Jacob's provocative "sport[ing] with his misery," which, fortunately, God ignored "in silent forbearance."[9]

It is evident that the sovereign silence of God, about which many a theologian makes a fuss, could initially be interpreted, here as elsewhere, in a more plausible fashion. For one, we are dealing with nothing bigger than a bad case of inaccessibility, and a series of challenging requirements must be fulfilled before one is allowed to conclude that whoever does not react must be a sovereign opponent. One would not always accept such a conclusion. If one were to tell a deaf mute one's life story, one would not conclude from the deaf mute's silence that that person prefers to keep his commentary to himself. In such cases, transcendence is an over-interpretation of the lack of resonance. It results from the circumstance that the others are, first and foremost, independent from us, and hence they usually remain unreachable to us. For this reason they stay outside the fantasies of symmetry that mark our traditional ideas of response, understanding, retribution, and the like. When given its proper due, this discovery prompts the birth of rational relations between concrete persons – relations marked by a hygienic distance.

The madness of dating puts an end to such agreements. Hence gratitude for the independence of others is naturally the first emotion in the encounter with an intellect that remains free even in close cooperation. In this sense, we should understand God as a concept that supports human beings as they get practice in dealing with the opponent's withdrawal, which is beyond manipulation.

Finally, the emergence of transcendence can be traced to the misrecognition of immunity functions. Immune systems in general constitute embodiments of expectations of injury. At the biological level, these show up in the capacity to build antibodies; at the juridical level, in the form of procedures designed to compensate for injustice; at the religious level, in the shape of chaos-overcoming rituals that show people how they can carry on when things no longer work according to human estimates. From a systemic perspective, religions should be defined as psycho-semantic institutions specialized in the manipulation of disturbances of integrity. In their midst we find the meaning-making processing of suffering, death, and disorder. This performance, which links consolation for individuals with the ritual stabilization of groups, is often achieved at the price of a problematic side effect. The consoling effects of religions are inevitably tied to ritualized speech acts, and thereby affixed to the level of symbolic generalization. What is supposed to function as a cure must at the same time envisage itself as a symbolic order or as a worldview. This is where the approach to a categorial mutation of dangerous momentum lies. It rivals the temptation to explain a painkiller as a manifestation of divine power. Moreover, it is probable that several symbolically stabilized immune systems bring their generalizations into orbit at the same time. For this reason, these systems call one another into question without fail – indeed they cancel one another partially or completely, depending on the intensity of the aspiration to generalize, which is inherent in a religious project. When such systems collide, the need to be right is superimposed on the task of imparting salutary confidence, giving consolation, or generally setting orderly rhythms and rituals for endangered forms of life. In order to appreciate such conflicts, one would have to imagine users of Prozac and users of Valium accusing each other of heresy in order to put into perspective the otherwordly punishments that await the person who does not convert to the opponent's medication.

I name here sedatives that are well known for falling short of their primary effect on occasion and giving rise to manic impulses instead. There is a comparable risk in what, ever since Paul, has been called "belief." The welcome psycho-semantic effects of belief – the believer's psychological stabilization and social integration, not least in extreme situations – are bound up with symbolic effects that correspond closely to the manic response. (For this reason we should not take lightly the fact, well documented historically, that the expansionary monotheisms emerged from their founders' manic–apocalyptic states of excitation. Thus the failure to recognize the immune function directly affects the understanding of truth. While pragmatic conduct can make do with the proposition that whatever helps is true, theoretical conduct presses on with the proposition that truth can befit only what demands universal submission. The polemical danger here comes from the bigoted tendency of a misunderstood theoretical pretension.)

These arguments obviously stand within the tradition of David Hume's *The Natural History of Religion* (1757) – although they no longer follow the classical Enlightenment in tracing religious ideas to "hopes and fears" but rather propose a natural history of wrong conclusions. Now I will add in their trail a fifth aspect of transcendence, which in my view cannot be subjected to any compelling critical redescriptions. Many authors have pointed to the fact that the human intellect has the capacity to imagine an intellect that towers over it. This upsurge, even if it is carried out only pro forma, is an irreducible movement of intellect beyond its own real level. It attests to the fact that this intellect understands itself correctly when it sees itself included in a vertical tension within which its specific growth takes place – provided that it decides to take the risk of learning. The intellect always lives in a "more or less" of its own, and orienting itself to the pole of the "more" is a gesture by which it confesses to its peculiar transcendence. In the current context, we need not occupy ourselves with the variety of such gestures in monotheistic religions (where they are typically expressed as a requirement to study the Holy Text) – or in classical philosophy either (which equates living, suffering, and learning).

We touch on another irreducible aspect of religious conduct when we consider the answers that human beings have given when stirred into thinking under the influence of death. It is above all the topological aspect of the problem of death that opens up the prospect of a transcendence that, in my view, is irreducible. Since time immemorial, mortals – to call them by the ancient Greeks' appellative for them – have been compelled to come up with ideas about the place to which the dead have "gone" and to which they, too, will "relocate" after death. It is indisputable that the imagination has produced powerful blooms when it comes to this theme, not least in its detailed depiction of otherworldly places of a paradisiac or hellish quality – yet this remark has no tendency to exhaust the problem on our hands. We must admit, without further ado, that we cannot simply assume a simple continuum between the way the living understand space and place and the way they imagine otherworldly "places." Because there is a stark discontinuity here, the place of the dead remains transcendent, in a sense that needs to be clarified. This place forms a radically heterotopic magnitude – if by that we mean that the dead "tarry" in an "elsewhere" that escapes the empirically understood alternative between somewhere and nowhere. The tradition provides quite disparate encodings for this elsewhere. These extend from the phrase "in the presence of God" to "in nirvana" or "in recollection." These characterizations may be polysemic and metaphorical; they are, nevertheless, idiosyncratic enough to resist flippant reductions.

Finally, I would like to refer briefly to a seventh meaning of transcendence. Typically this is associated with the idea of an otherworldly authority, typically God, who, out of compassion or in grace, turns to human beings in extraordinary moments and makes them recipients of messages that one interprets as revelations. Here is not the place to discuss the implications of the concept of revelation. What is certain, at any rate, is that this expression makes sense only within the framework of a very presupposition-laden mode of thinking, which we could call the metaphysics of the strong sender.[10] The idea of revelation implies the dramatic notion that a lord keen to communicate turns to a group of recipients; he does so with the help of dictates that are gifts or gifts that are dictates; and these are sent through the privileged media of prophets, legislators, and visionaries in order to move this group to receive his message. "Revelation" thus refers to the kind of message that, owing to its special mode of conveyance, obliges its recipients to assume the posture of grateful submission. Seen in this light, the concept of revelation belongs in the world of *Homo hierarchicus*. It implies an analogy between the feudal relation of lord and vassal and the epistemological relation of object and subject, clear emphasis being placed on the primacy of the lord and the object. On this model, receiving a revelation resembles the highest option for vassal passivity. In other contexts one would speak of an offer you cannot refuse. Under such auspices, the will to believe appears as a search for service and submission. One understands right away how this model loses epistemological and social plausibility in cultures characterized by de-vassalization. The idea that there are purely receptive subjects turns out to be logically and empirically untenable. As a result, the concept of a revelation that issues dictates does plunge into crisis. No matter what is made manifest to subjects or through whom, that thing is no longer conceivable without these subjects' contribution. Whether this can lead as far as to a primacy of the recipient, as many constructivists believe, may remain an open question.

This turn to the subject de-passivizes revelation; what is more, it constitutes a departure from the preference for a religious context. Revelation is no longer perceived only in the isolated pronouncements of a transcendent sender, as we find it for instance in a holy text; it occurs permanently. This happens on the one hand by virtue of an accommodating openness of the world itself and on the other hand on the basis of the forced disclosure of what was previously concealed, which in more recent times has been called Enlightenment, research, and the progress of knowledge. (In the phrase "sacredly open mystery," Goethe attempted, as though for the last time, to give expression to a compromise between respect for the treasure of wisdom in the religions of the book and participation in the continuing revelation of nature, no matter whether it comes about spontaneously or through technology.) The moderns' scientific research gives expression to the fact that the era of merely receptive revelations is over. In the modern, activist culture of rationality, a strong antithesis to ancient and medieval passivism has emerged that awaits to be integrated by the apologists of the older concept of revelation. This also bears, both indirectly and directly,

on the idea of "belief," insofar as the active factor – as opposed to
the traditional, passive factor – comes to the fore increasingly here;
this is what William James emphasized with his voluntarist re-inter-
pretation of belief. As for the suggestion that the phenomenon of
Reformation was triggered by the intrusion of activist motifs into
religions, I cannot develop it here any more than the suggestion that
the phenomenon of Counterreformation begins with the hysterical
pretense of passivity.

*

The preceding reflections should have made my argument clear: it
would be a fatal misconception to understand the talk of post-secular
society as if "the Enlightenment" – or, to choose a more neutral
term, the culture of rationality that had crystallized in Europe since
the seventeenth century around its concept of cumulative and cross-
generational learning curves – had been just a middle period that
came to an end in the present. What could in fact expire now, what
deserves to come to an end, is the period in which a certain ration-
alist skepticism was able to emerge as a dogmatic power. Under
its reign, there was an abundant multiplication of metaphysically
unmusical and religiously illiterate people, cooped up in the prefab-
ricated constructions of despiritualization. Unfortunately today we
must often count the universities, too, among these constructions –
together with their philosophy departments.

We, however, are no longer concerned with Margarete's famous
leading question to Faust, about how he feels about religion. (It is
a leading question because it contains the covert invitation to enter
into marriage with her.) It is not this question that gives us pause.
What does is rather the reverse. How do we feel about the binding
nature of what we have learned in the meantime outside religion, as
heirs of the Enlightenment and actors in the contemporary civilization under its technological, political, psychological, and artistic
aspects?

It seems to me that the only way we can provide an answer
worthy of the subject matter is by reproducing the venerable relation
between the Old Testament and the New Testament on the basis of
modern global knowledge. It would be pure nihilism – and civilizational defeatism to boot – if one were to assert that, in the 1,800
years that had elapsed since the redaction of the New Testament,
the Christian Europeans and the remaining fractions of humanity
had experienced nothing new and had created nothing new that
would be on par with the older holy texts. This would be tantamount to sacrilege against general intellect. In fact the reproduction

mentioned here has long been accomplished. We know, in calm self-awareness, that we are not merely composing commentaries on a 2,000-year-old revelation. We are rather taking part in a continuing illumination of the world, both on this side of religious themes and beyond. The archive of modernity wells over with works and documents that have as much evangelical status as the most sublime witnesses of the older tradition. Even more, we live for the most part as if the New Testament had been ousted by a newer testament. It is essential for this testament to maintain a low religious profile and to speak, at most, of human rights, sciences, and arts, without showing any intention to form a church – unless it be the community of those ready to learn. As usual in intertestamentary relations, there are rich typological resonances between bodies of writing. The newer testament is naturally composed of numerous elements that fulfill and confirm the New Testament, just as the New Testament fulfilled and confirmed the Old Testament; but it also contains an abundance of innovative formulations that must be read as an abrogation of earlier establishments. If I had to summarize the content of the newer testament in one sentence, I would say that it encloses the record of everything that humanity, which has been split into cultures, must not forget if it wishes to place its future fates under a wholehearted concept of civilization.

12

CHANCES IN THE MONSTROUS

A Note on the Metamorphosis of the Religious Domain in the Modern World, with Reference to a Few Motifs in William James

Those who undertake to comment on the fates of religion and the religious domain amid the rise of modern world conditions find themselves immediately confronted with a concept that numerous authors have wielded as a master key, to gain access to every room in the common house of modern Euro-American humanity: secularization. Initially "secularization" was a legal term, which designated the more or less violent appropriation of church property by organs of the modern nation state, after the French Revolution. In the nineteenth century it developed into a term that appeared to express the direction in which the world as a whole was moving – a true direction, in the eyes of the progressives and the laity, a false direction, as the losers of the modernization process believed. In Catholic circles one spoke of secularization as of a momentous crime, committed by the narcissist–humanist modern world in its revolt against God-given origins. For the progressives, by contrast, the discourse of secularization contained the promise that, through work and self-determination, humanity would be able to free itself from its unworthy prehistory, shadowed by religious patronage. The enlightened bourgeoisie believed that it had license to dispossess the unproductive masses of their spiritual holdings and to deliver them into the hands of an industrious worldly humanity. By transforming sluggish church treasuries into active capital, secularization in the narrower sense carried out the modernization of riches that had become historically due. In the end even the Vatican had to follow this trend. It earned the reputation of being an exceptionally fast learner by throwing itself into the practice of finance capitalism and catching up. The transition from wealth in the form of treasury to wealth in the form of capital necessarily affected all the other domains of value. As a result, secularization became the cue for a technologically and commercially powerful society to depart from all modes of thought that had been built on axioms of passivity and subservience. A modern is any person who believes that one can do something other than devote oneself to God and higher powers, even in extremis. The modern human being does not want to endure the higher power; she rather wants to be that power herself.

As a program for becoming worldly in a broad sense, the discourse of secularization heralds the deployment of a human type that has committed itself to a threefold program: one of all-encompassing processing, of continually expanded self-activation, and of increased self-enjoyment in the unfolding of one's powers. As the natural scientist Laplace said in his famous reply to a similar question by Napoleon, self-mobilizing human beings of this type see God as a hypothesis they no longer need to conduct their business. In a well-constructed world of activity, procedure, and volition, the god who had been worshiped in the theological tradition as the original source of the fact that humans were endowed with existence and attributes indeed becomes superfluous. He was the unavoidable sovereign pillar that a constitutively weak humanity was facing, in pain and hope. As we realize now, the weakness of the human being was the true reason for God's strength. This was a super-strong god who, as lord of the higher power and as the primary cause of contingency, held humankind in heteronomous clutches, in spite of all the pretty words on human freedom that we hear from theologians. In the age of entrepreneurs, self-helpers, and mobilizers, such a god was bound to become the great unusable. Precisely because omnipotent, he became a stranger on earth, an extraterrestrial invader of willful, civilizational enterprise. In order to stay tuned to the frequencies of the real world's flow, a contemporary god would have to present himself as an accomplice to activation and to transform himself into a transcendent business resource – otherwise he would become a mere god of recess, a god of relaxation, a god for the weak and for bad hours. When the things we do take place everywhere as if by themselves, God either degenerates into an idle hypothesis – and this indeed holds for the broadest domains of modern organization of life – or has to undergo a metamorphosis from which he emerges as a transcendent sponsor of immanent successes.

From a historical perspective, these metamorphoses are connected, above all, with that Anglicization and Americanization of religion to which William James has remained one of the most distinguished and informative witnesses. Whoever follows his suggestions can, today more than ever, gain valid insights into the dynamics of the manufacture of belief in the spheres of the power and influence of English-speaking empires.

Alongside the primary, legal sense of the term "secularization" [*Säkularisation*] and its metamorphoses during the cultural revolution of the nineteenth and twentieth centuries, we can also ascribe it a philosophical meaning. This meaning comes to light as soon as we understand the process of secularization or becoming worldly [*Verweltlichung*] not only as an expropriation of spiritual treasures and gradual transformation of passive liabilities into active assets, but also as an elevation of the world into a paragon of being without an opposite. Secularization in the philosophical or ontological sense means the absolutization of the *saeculum* [generation, age, world] and at the same time the elimination of the two nonsecular, transmundane, or supernatural magnitudes that were to be distinguished from and opposed to the world, on the ontological model of classical metaphysics: God and the soul. As soon as one attributes this radical feature to the component -*welt*- [world-] in the term *Verweltlichung* [becoming worldly, secularization], the latter designates no less than the impossibility of tolerating ontologically unauthorized forces such as the soul and God alongside the world. Thus the classical metaphysical triangle God, world, and soul implodes and an absolute block, the "world" as such, vaguely and monolithically takes the place of the well-tempered distances between the poles of the threefold totality. To be sure, this block would be internally differentiated and would encompass in its unfathomable complexity our own, multidimensionally iridescent existence; however, it would not permit its being offset by anything other than itself, anything superior to itself, or anything held in reserve against itself. In this world block, everything falling under the names "God" and "soul" that was previously known and assumed joins the ranks of effects of the world. What matters now is that the world is everything that is the case. If God and the soul were really the case, they would have to be aspects of the world or attributes of world power; if they are not the case, they drop out[1] and remain non-cases and unrealities. As a consequence of the post-metaphysical radical secularization, the classic distinction between world and soul, as well as that between God and world, no longer functions. The world rolls up into a bundle in which all distinctions fall in on themselves. Under the banner of modern secularization – perhaps "widening" would be a more correct description – the all-encompassing world complex grows into an ontological monstrosity of hardly comprehensible form. Accordingly, secularization or becoming worldly would be the heading for a change in the image of the world – beyond the cultural-revolution implications of modernization. This is a change of disturbing proportions. With the adventure of secularization, the pioneer wings of current humanity, led by the Euro-American complex, have technologically, logically, and psychologically ventured into the new and the never before attempted. If we wish to bring to mind a rupture of comparable world-shaking power in the history of ideas, we must go back to the emergence of high cultures and to the crystallization of what Karl Jaspers once called the forms of thought of the axial age.

About 3,000 years ago, high cultures came on the scene as evolutionarily new sorts of complexes of political power formation and metaphysical interpretation of the world. From a logical perspective, we can understand them best as giant experiments on the difference between soul and thing, or rather between subjectivity and objectivity. Numerous oppositions that became decisive to the organization of spiritual–psychological life in various high cultures derive from this first-level difference, whereby bivalent thought became a world-historical power – oppositions such as the ensouled and the unsouled, the animate and the inanimate, the purpose and the tool, soul and mechanism, thinking and extended substance, mind and matter, the available and the unavailable. The more energy the early high cultures invested in the configuration of these differences, the more sharply did the cultural-revolution dynamics of bivalent thought find expression in them vis-à-vis earlier, animistic or panpsychistic, monovalent interpretations of the world – and the more emphatically did the fate of high cultures take effect in these differences. I mean here the fate of having to be the sovereign superstructure built on top of the older forms of life, which were sympathetic to nature and more impoverished in power and art. All empires that rose and fell into ruin were towers in a dual Babel; their successes were grounded in a technological and logical revolt against a nature that was once wholly uncontrollable but is now increasingly objectified. High cultures produced their triumphal constructions only by elevating subjectivity, the soul, and power – always in league with their gods and founders – over a non-psychic, instrumental, ancillary layer of objectivities. At work at the heart of high cultures is the irresistible awareness of the lordly rights of the subjective, ensouled, and divine over the objective, unsouled, and extra-divine. All the older tools, weapons, and machines are conceived of as unsouled objectivities in the hands of an ensouled lord.

High-culture dualism found its strongest expression in creation stories of the type of the Hebrew Genesis. Here the ontological divide between soul and thing, or between subject and object, is presented in the image of a god whose six- or seven-day work embodies the creator's radical superiority over his creation. Only the human being, as a third magnitude and ontological hybrid, relativizes the sharp asymmetry between creature and creator. She does so to the extent that, despite being a creature, she is furnished with a similarity to the creator in one aspect of his being. Incidentally, in the Hebrew Genesis, the classical metaphysical triangle God, world, and human being or soul is spelled out with great structural clarity. With perfect precociousness, this triangle makes clear how a dual theory of the totality of reality must proceed in accordance with its principle. It recognizes the powerful, creative subjectivity of God – who, as the highest manufacturer, remains also the absolute lord of all things – alongside the weak subjectivity of human beings, who are nevertheless emphatically called to subjugate the Earth to themselves. Without doubt, high cultures are distinguished in terms of their respective imperial styles – Peking is not Rome, Athens is not Persepolis, Memphis is not Mexico – and they do not reach everywhere the same degree of stringency in the objectification of things and people; yet everywhere they share a certain degree of imperial technicity that is based on dual or bivalent classifications. To be sure, tenacious stocks of animistic or monovalent worldviews continue to survive in all high cultures; and they look at the steep, rebelliously domineering unnaturalness of high forms of thought and power partly with overt animosity, partly with secret refusal. This anti-dualistic resistance appears not infrequently in the form of sublimation practiced among mystics who promote the doctrine of oneness. These mystics have developed in various parts of the world – the purest breed is to be found in India, Japan, and Europe – as a sort of animism of the educated. They teach, sometimes with great refinement, extreme monistic regresses behind the dualist interpretation of the world.

Yet high cultures converge most of all in their tendencies to ground commonwealth prosperity and the good luck of sovereigns in God's participation – or that of the world's intelligent base – in the fates of the imperial framework and of its leaders. As exemplary human beings, rulers of empires are drawn close to divine subjectivity, whether as sons of the heavens or as God's representatives. Ordinary mortals, by contrast, are readily downgraded for their vicinity to objects and tools. Human existence in high culture necessarily leads to a permanent anthropological crisis. In the historical world, the few soar up to the gods as though commanded by an invisible law, like victorious actors and mediumistic creators who dictate decrees and set benchmarks, while the many appear to be condemned to fall under the class of tools and things. The difference between souls and things, or subjects and objects, also splits the universe of relations among people, insofar as they encounter one another under the banner of inequality and class rule. From the perspective of what I am explaining here, this appears to be a necessary consequence of the fact that the right of the strongly ensouled to exercise power and the calling of subjectivity to dominate the non-subjective were universally conceptualized in the metaphysics of high cultures. Even the pedagogical idea of self-mastery is merely an application of the dualist slope to the human interior: an inner nobleman should show himself lord over an inner slave.

In animistic worldviews, the psychological space is omnipresent and appears to know no external opposition. By contrast, high-culture dualism leads to a radical truncation of soul, subjectivity, and power. Whoever possesses these lives on the sunny side of being; those who live in the dark are invisible. And, insofar as the age of classical metaphysics, taken cum grano salis, is coextensive with slavery and the exploitation of humans by humans, we have strong evidence of how a domineering subjectivity came to develop under this regime. This subjectivity knew no restraint in its effort to turn large majorities of human beings into things and to exclude them from the chances of higher subjectivation and ensoulment. It takes no effort to understand why the religions of redemption were provoked by the disensouling and desubjectivizing effects of the human use of high culture. Their only task was to hold open the chances of re-ensoulment for the victims of disensoulment.

From here, if we think back to a program of secularization in the strong philosophical sense of the word, we can understand better the stakes in the modern revolution of worldviews and life forms. What catches the eye first on the political mask of modernity is the democratization of the legal claim to subjectivity; connected with this is the god-free gospel of the will to power for all. Both axioms feed into the deep currents of individualism in the processes of modern civilization.

But when all the citizens who live in the modern period tend toward power, expression, and self-enjoyment, systems of expanded division of power are at hand. These systems must proceed democratically in form, but imperialistically in substance. Modern imperialism looks polycentric, technocratic, mediumistic, and diffuse. It is grounded in the pluralism of desires and in its economic medium, the market. It exceeds the Babylonian principle of the tower through the post-Babylonian principle of the network. Seen as a whole, modern civilizations leave behind the figure of the god-man standing at the tip of the power pyramid. Modern power is supposed to be grounded in agreement from below, not in charisma. Exceptions to this tendency can be found in papacy as an old imperial relic and in the spontaneous divinization of leaders in totalitarian cults.

Of course, in the absolutely firm world, the massively empowered modern subjectivities lose the ability to find support in a super-worldly authority; they must bank on self-protection through law, technology, and therapy.

Hence the second extra-worldly magnitude, the soul, is also stripped of its foundation in a partnership with God. When the world is everything that is the case, whatever was previously called soul becomes, by necessity, an effect of the world. Subjectivity descends into animated bodies, into institutions, perhaps even into higher machines; more or less explicitly, the soul steps back from its metaphysical ambitions and joins the ranks of natural mechanisms, even if it be as a super-complex neuro-informatic natural wonder. As a result, the classical high-culture dualities of soul and thing, subject and object, mind and matter must lose their usual draw. "Above" and "below" become indistinguishable. What appeared to belong to a "thither" gets reabsorbed into a further "hither." What the king desired is now desired by the democratic everyman. A confusing hyperimmanence opens up, in which the traditional discourses of transcendence have not kept pace with the world; today they sound like distant folk songs, or like table songs for lords and servants who no longer exist. An excited imbrication of idleness and the unfolding of power reigns in the hyperimmanent space. Nowhere is an objective goal set for powers; rather, goal-setting has itself become a function of powers. Everything wants to progress and enhance itself, but the steps of enhancement have no transcendent sense; at best, they form "histories." Thus one seems justified in thinking that in modern times human beings are less than ever able to state where they are sojourning when they claim to inhabit a place called "the world." The world – where is that?

Today astrophysicists and brain scientists are competing to answer this question; and they are seconded by psychologists and media theorists. But, no matter what answers they turn up, the place of the human being can no longer be defined as the midpoint between God and the world, as it was in the days of the triangular relations of classical metaphysics. Nor is the world any longer defined as what is penetrated by God and visited by souls. In a more radical sense than ever before, the human being finds himself "in the world" – more radical because today being in the world is always supposed also to mean being thoroughly of the world. As long as it was possible to set the world against an other and to set it apart from its creator, as a creature, the world was seen in the light of a transcendent arrangement. Like something written by God, it was a text composed according to the rules of heavenly grammar – or, to change the image, it was a house erected by a transcendent builder.

The grandeur of divine intellect gave created being a universal constitution, as it were. When something monstrous came into play, it had to be attributed to God himself; the god of the feudal soul could not fail to be majestic and formidable. If, however, the world is conceived of as a creatorless, self-authoring formation, as a lordless process that advances and topples ad hoc until it finally "yields" beings like us, then our place in the world can no longer be understood in terms of transcendence. No universally superior god grants us distance from the absolute world, as if we were transcendent allies; we fall prey to the world's gigantic activity. We are inserted into the monstrosity called "world" without a transcendent pillar to withdraw to. If we wanted to understand ourselves in the terms of this world, we would have to admit that we are ejections from an absolute explosion, the spawn of an infinitely daring development. If there is no transcendent god who confers shape and stands in solidarity with human beings, if this god has nothing in particular planned for us, then the world in and from which we exist is a hypermonstrosity that takes time and space for the display of its creations. From the monstrosity of all monstrosities, specific monsters crawl across the gooey switchback of evolution to the light of day – right up to *Tyrannosaurus rex*, *Homo sapiens*, and the Ebola virus.

We can measure the rank of philosophers in the process leading up to modernity by their role in the rise of the monstrosity that begins to show itself to radical thought as a completely self-secularizing world. Theologians still enjoy the privilege of being allowed to interpret the world as the institution of a god who gives shape to things. Thinkers of the modern period, however, must look at the world as a self-shaping whole. It thus becomes apparent that every semblance of order in the world springs from the world's endless experimentation with itself; a fundamental level of disorder and lack of structure is obvious in each experiment. "The monstrous" is the only concept or name used here that is suitable for an unstructured whole. It is the necessarily true name for a world whole that lacks an outside and is only inherently self-transcending. Therefore one may say that the process of secularization, understood radically, can be nothing but the revelation of that monstrosity that leads to success and catastrophe, that endows and consumes us. The authentic philosophy of modernity is the hermeneutics of the monstrous, as theory of the one and only world.

One of the characteristics of modernity is that its organ for logic – its head or brain, as it were – is, primarily, not a philosophical organ; rather it has taken the form of science and research. The typically modern enterprise of cognitively processing the world monstrosity is research in scientific style. It manages to investigate

the monstrosity without beholding it. It works on the world without
taking notice of its monstrous character. In this regard Heidegger
is right: science does not think – provided that we are justified in
taking thinking to mean nothing but an ecstatic meditation on our
own exposure to the open. Perhaps it would have been enough to
say that science does not tremble. This should not be understood
as a criticism of science, but rather as an indication of the shape-
conferring function of science and research in relation to the world
laid bare by God's rationality.

By virtue of the methods and habits of science, modernity has
indeed furnished a viable replacement for theology's assurances
of order. To this extent, it is justified, or at least understandable,
that a sort of scientist church developed in nineteenth-century
Europe; this church soothingly reassured contemporaries that it
was there to replace the faint old faith with a vital new one, with
the help of a scientific worldview. Functionally, "new faith" – to use
David Friedrich Strauß's notorious phrase – designates nothing but
science's and technology's achievement of order for the thoroughly
secularized world: like any old faith, the new one serves to make
the world safe for human beings. The first step toward establishing
the human being in the canny–uncanny world is to interpret the
secularized whole in advance as something that cannot in the long
run have any secrets that would remain hidden to scientific investigation. The second step is to consent to believe in the theorems of
evolutionist naturalism. The age of natural sciences is founded on
the devout compromise between physics and holism – a compromise
whereby the mechanistic credo of hard science is accommodated
without entirely losing the consolation of the classical doctrines
of world harmony. Whoever says "nature" and means "world" has
already done most of the taming of the monstrous; through naturalization, the monstrous world is subjected to a shape-conferring
act performed by the spirit of the sciences. After all, nature, the
mother, the bearer-builder can't be all that monstrous. In this way
God is sublated into the "nature" of the scientific worldview – if
not already as substance, then at least in his function as the world's
shape donor.

*

As for the secularization of the psyche, the nineteenth century saw
the arrival of a massive wave of scientific psychologies that begin to
translate psychological phenomena into the language of mechanism
in a significant way. Europe's German Friedrich Nietzsche and
New England's American William James occupy a prominent

position among nineteenth-century philosophical psychologists. Although they were deeply enmeshed in the project of a thorough-going naturalization of the psychological, their prominence lay in the fact that they were at the same time genuine thinkers of modernity, that is, interpreters of the monstrous. In the past, one would draw attention to parallels between Nietzsche's and James's intellectual and personal fates; people noticed their entanglement in the aliments of the nineteenth century, perceived their shared oscillation between sounding depressive and sounding heroic, and identified a deep similarity between them in their lifelong defensive battles against the specter of Victorian and Darwinian decadence and neurasthenia. Both were condemned to live with the hope that they could become their own doctors, and they slogged away for many years, with the patient impatience of people who await their convalescence.

That spirit and diet belong more closely together than the mindlessly healthful positivists realize – this was, for both of them, a certainty that was at once theoretical and personal. The parallelisms between their speculations on the life-serving functions of illusion and faith continue to be striking. Even more striking is the consonance between their doctrines on the secondary nature of logical representations in relation to energetic–affective primary processes. One may say that, with such doctrines, the psychologists Nietzsche and James have paid the most powerful tribute to the spirit of naturalism.

But their kinship reaches even more deeply. Nietzsche and James, each by his own means, carried out the naturalistic imperative of his time vis-à-vis the psychological, which, under the aegis of the artificial construct "psyche," was brought under investigation as a super-complex network of higher mechanisms. Yet what makes them such great thinkers is that they surpassed the scientific objectification of the psychological realm and pressed on to the demolition of naturalism through a philosophy of life and living. With this act of transcendence, they left behind the homely enclosure of steady and certain knowledge and ventured into a position in which the unconstituted world appeared to them as the monstrous. As psychologists, too, both were thinkers of the modern period. For in the object of their observation they perceived more than mere scientism was able to see. When they spoke of the psyche, they followed the rules of the art in presenting higher mechanisms, but in their exercises they did not forget that the very same psyche is the instrument of the monstrous. Even if the "soul" is just mechanical scenery, it is nonetheless the stage on which the world is performed for the very first time before every individual who comes to the world. In this accomplishment, the objectified psyche also remains, for both thinkers, the adventurous heart of existence. Consequently both push ahead toward an ethics of an experimental life: Nietzsche elucidated his notion of experiment with the help of aesthetic–political concepts such as the power of dreams and the will to power, whereas James meant by a life of experiment the living's moral and religious experience of themselves through the testing of their "live hypotheses."[2]

Nietzsche's and James's temperaments and paths part ways as soon as the passionately thoughtful interpretation of the monstrous begins. Where Nietzsche banks on solitude, elitism, and aggravation in order to goad the human being in the direction of the superhuman – since the human-weary Earth should ultimately be populated with self-generating gods – James behaves in a modernizing, conciliatory, appeasing, unselective, and republican manner as much as he can. The opposition between thinkers of aggravation and thinkers of mitigation is significant for the entire modernity. One could find a perfect illustration of this opposition in the difference of temper-ament between Nietzsche and James. To one, truth appears only at the peak of the climb; to the other, the descent is the king's road. While Nietzsche, bearing the mask of Zarathustra, would like to set himself up as educator of future princes and breed human beings by the measure or unmeasure of the monstrous, James, the Harvard professor, acts like the minister of an ontological republic in which everything there is, even the uncomfortable and the excessive, should enjoy at least a phenomenological civil right. This is the meaning of James's struggle for empiricism as a disposition of absolute openness vis-à-vis the expanse of the entire world of appearances. If we were to characterize Nietzsche's interpretation of the monstrous in one word, that word could only be "height." In James, it would undoubtedly be "variety." It is no accident that this word appears in the title of James's magnum opus on the philosophy of religion, *The Varieties of Religious Experience*. James was able to choose this title only later, by the way – when, looking back on his Gifford Lectures, held in Edinburgh in two cycles, in 1901 and 1902, he realized that he had produced a hit. Now he set his philosophical standard in the book's title and placed his confessional word "variety" over the undertaking; the title originally planned, *Man's Religious Appetites and Their Satisfaction through Philosophy*, was no longer considered, owing to its confining psychological strain.

It should not be overlooked that, when James speaks of varieties,[3] he means not so much the well-organized variety that is so dear to philosophers, and even less the notorious "manifoldness" of German idealism's officiants; he means rather the open assemblage

of the many, of – why not – things of all sorts, on a broad field
over which no effective arch-concept reigns. Jamesian variety is
no serious congress of appearances under the presidency of the
concept; rather it is a casserole of things that has to do more with
vaudeville than with systematic structure.

A program of ontological pluralism shines forth in the word
"varieties."[4] It is a part of William James's American aversion to
the old European absolute, which he reproaches for jamming all life
into the cage of the One. His claustrophobia vis-à-vis the absolute
went so far that he gave the greatest freedom to the monsters of
indeterminate variety rather than letting himself be embraced by
the unconditioned One. When James gives the most original interpretation to his experience of the monstrous, he confesses with
forced optimism that respect for the variety of the real belongs eo
ipso to genuine experience; for this reason empiricism can conform
to its definition only if it has a wide angle. This requires a certain
bravery in the face of the unusual, a readiness to endure in the face
of the strange, the excessive, the pathological. In his days of fame,
James was at once concerned and amused to see how some of his
more respectable colleagues would shake their heads as soon as
they noticed the suspicious amount of attention that he accorded
certain phenomena from the range of the paranormal – such as
telepathy, divination, or automatic writing. For James, this was no
more than a requirement of good empiricist manners – and at the
same time a chance to confess his pluralist credo against any sort
of coercion toward unity. It is precisely the ontological impropriety
of the paranormal that is sympathetic to James's pluralistic sensibility. One could say that James's empiricism was an American
way into phenomenology. As a free citizen, James wanted to live
in a republic of appearances that refused entry to no being – or at
least never refused it on a priori grounds. In this phenomenological
republic, ordinary and unordinary things immediately belong to the
monstrous.

*

If one looks back, from the end of the twentieth century, to the great
American's contribution to the revolutionary breaks in the thought
of the nineteenth century, the significance of William James as
sponsor of a transatlantic campaign deployed in parallel with those
of Nietzsche, Bergson, and Freud becomes obvious. His specific
effect should lie above all in the field where the Americanization
of the religious takes place. Two sorts of things can be connected
with this phrase. On the one hand, there is the pragmatic turn in the

psychology of religion, which insists, in the spirit of Jesus, on the fact that one does not know the good by its roots, but by its fruits. On the other hand, there is the tendency of Americans to develop ever more colorful syntheses of the most refined technology and of the most robust naivety. As a spokesman in the Americanization of the religious, James provided wide-reaching impulses toward the application of psycho-mechanical and psycho-technical procedures to the inner life of the individual. As James knew from his earlier experience of suffering, a tremendous potential for depression is unleashed when human beings reflect on their life using mechanistic and deterministic terms from natural science and take these terms literally. A fatal interaction between psychic depression and theoretical self-objectification can result.

Incidentally, in his popular writings from around 1800, Johann Gottlieb Fichte already expressed a similar idea with fanatic consistency: a person who understands herself, in the spirit of consistent, objective science, as a tiny, completely foreign-caused particle in the fabric of the world, who separates herself from her spontaneity, and who risks sinking into an incurable disensoulment – such a person would have to drift through a dead cosmos to the bitter end, like a piece of mentally ill matter. Fichte, too, already prescribed the break from determinism as a great therapy; his imperative, formulated in radical idealist terms, is healing through the self-positing of freedom.

Following the French Kantian Charles Renouvier, James, for his part, tested the effects of the freedom cure on himself, with varying degrees of success; later on he aligned himself with the modern thinkers of freedom, albeit no longer under the signs of idealism and absolutism. He knew from the experience of his own soul that self-objectification on mechanistic terms courts the risk of a motivational death in life. He anticipated somewhat the arrival of gigantic proletariats of depression, who are cut off from access to sources of self-motivation and have no other vital perspective than meager self-consumption. Early on, he warned about an AIDS of convictionlessness. James made himself useful and won great renown by making the theoretical surpluses of his self-therapeutic experiments known. He did so as an author and, even more, as a speaker. (This transmission of knowledge about self-healing has, by the way, remained an important mechanism in the modern market society for the formation of community and of a public, at least since the Protestant conversion literature of the seventeenth century.) And thus a not merely academic public got to know William James as the teacher of the right to life from an assisted élan and as the advocate of the "will to believe."

James's most famous texts can be read as though the author had wanted to translate Nietzsche's forceful doctrine of the will to power into a smart doctrine of the right to strength. For James as bearer of this energetic human right, a world-dominating, self-surpassing superman was out of the question; rather he had in view a bourgeois everyman, threatened by overload and demotivation, and whose heroism consisted in stalling his failure as much as he could. James's American or New England heroes are – as he himself was – heroes of the deferral of collapse. For James, a hero is anyone who braces himself up everyday in order to confess his chances. (We can, by the way, clearly see Arthur Miller's play *The Death of a Salesman* as a continuation of James's theory of human bravery in the face of trivial tragedy.) It was as though James wished to explain that being and remaining an American – or should we now simply say being and remaining a modern human being? – is possible only when one calls a capital of willpower and self-reliance [*Selbstvertrauen*] one's own. Of course, James had in his ear Ralph Waldo Emerson's magnificent hymn to the "categorical" American virtue of self-reliance.[5] The psychologist James was confronted with the task of transposing the song of the fabulous transcendentalist into an analytical key. What advice should one give, then, to human beings for whom the wellsprings of self-reliance have dried up? How can the philosopher speak to those who are psychically drained and at present find no access to visions and volitions?

In the answer given to this question we are able to see what the Americanization of religiousness ultimately means. Whoever finds no sparkling source of energy among her inner possessions should by no means give up; she must carry on searching within herself, until she touches the deep forces. This is precisely what Americanism is in religious matters: a union between prospecting mentality and devotion to success. Whoever seeks will find. In late twentieth-century America, that meant: even if you appear to be currently debilitated, a vibrant pool of motivations lies under you, too; you live at the top of an energetic netherworld that is waiting to well up in you. God is an inner Texas; the human being, a conveyor of deep energies. Americanism in spiritual matters means neo-mediumism. Anyone who lives in the New World always has the chance to make himself into a channel through which the drive for enterprise will flow from the spirit realm; every human being, the transatlantic human being above all, is a potential medium for the power to achieve from beyond.

Yet, because American religion is directly connected to the search for a successful life, faith becomes an experimental activity. Only now does the sentence that truth is what works hold without reservation. Thus, for the modern life of faith, the switches are set up for eclecticism: if it should prove that a belief did not turn out to be adequately effective, another one may and ought to be tried. From here, the road lies open to the postmodern supermarkets of religion; in less than a century, it was traveled full length by American and European religious experimentalists. They were quick to traverse all the stages, from syncretism through exoticism to banalization. Wherever the modern train to life showed an advantage for religious hypotheses, there was also a pragmatic motive in play, namely to give access to transcendent sources of energy within us. One understands quite well why there are retail stores on both sides of the Atlantic that carry on one shelf the entire gamut of publications on eastern and western religious studies and esotericism and, on the other, the entire gamut of vitamins in pill bottles. The same dietary pragmatism is at work in both offerings. Whether religions or vitamins, both serve the same metaconviction that every individual should figure out what convictions and what micronutrients work best for her and should ingest them on a regular basis. It is the modern and postmodern individual's duty to herself to operate her life motor with the optimal mixture of fuel that is unmistakably her own. Assertions plus vitamins: this is *vita vitalis*, "the lively life" – the healing at hand in the pragmatic pharmacy.

In his elegantly meditative address "The Will to Believe," delivered in the spring of 1896, William James explained to his colleagues in the Philosophical Clubs of Yale and Brown Universities that the human being, not least the scientist, has an unalienable right to lead his life on the basis of convictions that enable him even now to proceed to the highest deployment of himself. This right is valid unconditionally, because life is too short, indeed because it is perhaps altogether absurd to put on ice one's views and beliefs about everyday living until objective studies have perchance worked out the ultimate truths. Any human being always acts like an infallible pope when it comes to his vital instincts, and no one will blame him for it. Two or three generations later, the gurus were on the market with the very undistinguished slogan that enlightenment is the same, no matter how you get it.

Adherents of older forms of belief may find these remarks on the pragmatization of the religious shocking. And they are indeed offensive, to the extent that one struggles to admit that there is more intense cross-border traffic between the mechanical and spiritual.

In religion, Americanism presents the advantage of making no secret of its affiliation with the technological age. From its perspective, to believe ultimately means to experiment with a symbolic mind machine.[6] Moreover, one of the analytic strengths of pragmatism is that it puts a finger on the connection between faith and the will to success, which beautiful souls prefer to leave unnoticed. Pragmatized religiousness exhibits a fairly bald metaphysics of success in life, and it freely admits not to understand the things that don't pertain to it. If life based on conviction or, in pragmatist terms, life based on religion is in fact always already counted among the motivational secrets of success, then religious Americanism deserves the credit for having begun to bring light to the obscurity of a successful life. It seems to be saying frankly that what counts in the spiritual world is the law of the survival of those most capable of conviction.

Let's admit it: whoever is motivationally at the top has better chances of success. If Darwin had thought far enough, he would have spoken of survival of the fittest believer.[7] Of course, James made his own contribution by mitigating the brutality of this thesis. He outlined a sort of metatheory of convictions or theory of metaconvictions that allowed him to describe the life – and the successful life – of individuals through the lens of live hypotheses that are implemented in practice. In this we can see a metareligious remainder of respect for the vigor of belief of his fellow citizens from the republic of the persuaded – even if direct participation in the belief of the positive confessors is impossible. If one were to reconstruct James's scattered remarks on the logic of belief in a coherent thesis, one would arguably arrive at a theory of the circle of happiness. Anyone who runs in this circle is happy when in luck and happy when in misfortune; failure is success by indirect means. Faithful gamblers are always on a roll. In *circulus virtuosus*, the venture of belief gives rise to a self-awareness of success, and success gives rise to a self-awareness of confirmed belief. This "virtuous circle" can be interpreted as a self-reinforcing system or as a metamagical vortex; nothing in it is actually more successful than success – except the belief in the belief in success. It is a feature of William James's human and intellectual charm that he confessed his will to believe in the pluralism of happinesses with a magnanimity for which there are few examples. As his empiricism was able to appear as an American path to phenomenology, his metaconviction about the irreplaceable value of convictions and practices of belief can be characterized as the American path to ecumenism.

*

However, only a few paths of the American way of religious life[8] lead in ecumenical directions. As Harold Bloom undertook to show in his oppressive book *The American Religion: The Emergence of*

the Post-Christian Nation (1992), a gigantic metamorphosis of
mentality has taken place in the United States since the end of
World War I, under the cover of a civilizing secularism. In its wake,
the nation of "brave and free" citizens of an officially Christian faith
has metamorphosed into a pandemonium of freestyle prophetic–
spiritual confessions – among them powerful movements such as
spiritual healing, Mormonism, the Baptist Church, and Californian
neo-Orphism, aka New Age. Bloom's book reads like a direct reply
to the Gifford Lectures – displaced by a century. It deals with "the
varieties of American religious experiences"[9] at the open exit of the
American Christian age. It offers one of the few intellectually high-
ranking answers to the discovery, which is more than astounding
for Europeans, that according to recent polls over 90 percent of all
adult Americans claim to live in the belief that there is a relevant
higher being and that this being has shown itself to them in a special
love or in a choiceworthy attachment.

Harold Bloom blunders when he suggests the term "Gnosticism"
as a heading that sums up American syncretisms. According to
Bloom, the badges of American religion are the flag and the fetus
– that is, on the one hand the symbol of an American life that has
assumed global dominance and yet is at risk, and on the other
the symbol of an unborn American life whose salvation is under
threat. In reality, the neo-religious American syndrome is not a
case of Gnosticism, but a post-Christian national theosophy. Like
a Calvinist metastasis, it brings into play the religion of absolute
success in life; in terms of the concept of radical secularization
presented here, it is a religion gone worldly. In consequence it dallies,
with remarkable psycho-technic and media-technic ruthlessness,
in all the methods designed to make the beyond present in this
world. Its ultimate interest is to make god happen.[10] Wherever God
happens, my success is not far off. In American religion, everything .
is always given "already now."

Bloom's infelicitous talk of Gnosticism notwithstanding, *The
American Religion* leads to the victory of the opposite of the
Gnostic impulse, if by Gnosticism we mean the initiatives to
emancipate the soul from the pressure of the world that first became
manifest in late antiquity around the Mediterranean. By contrast,
the sects in *The American Religion* are nothing but schools of the
spiritually sustained yet mundane lust for success: they bank on
magical super-immanence; they all promise fitness[11] from within in
the run after the victor's prize in the real, in the all too real. For this
reason most of them are commercial, expressive, autohypnotic, and
interventionist; their adherents wear the little spark of the soul on
their sleeves and carry their hope in their checkbooks. They all take

God to be their sponsor. With them, irrationalism wreaks delightful vengeance on secular pragmatism. In view of such developments, the few European intellectuals who still have some idea of the concept of the Third Reich as a German national theosophy ought no longer to overhear the alarm that Harold Bloom has raised in his study of religious criticism.

*

As for William James, his religious–philosophical project of a liberal empiricism that would do justice to the entire republic of live hypotheses thus hovers far above the American tumult; his New England Protestantism of formative education, his scientifically minded Harvard discipline, his non-obtrusively impassioned individualism, and his euphoric prose remove him from the orbit of manic Americanism and its national–theosophical spawns. Thanks to his melancholic disposition, James was from the outset barred from any sort of flight into a positive faith. His path was one of empathic and excitable meta-religiousness, in which the interest in religion had to replace religion itself. This replacement was something that James in no way understood as an unfavorable exchange; interest, when it is a live hypothesis to a sufficient degree, can render a wholesale faith dispensable. Thus James is the natural ally of those who have reason to emancipate themselves from religion through interest in religion.

As an interpreter of the monstrous, James – unlike Nietzsche – held it necessary to shelter individuals from the disturbance that must result from the revelation of the fullness of the world before mere human intellects. He understood that it was one of the tasks of philosophy not to drive people to the madness that follows from ultimate philosophy. In this respect he hardly differed from the theologians of the Middle Ages, who thought they knew that God must be spoken of in such a way that the mortals' intellects would remain protected from his piercing revelation; as a rule, they thought little of mystical bedazzlement. Precautions about the bright–dark monstrosity of the world and its appearance in us are in place even more than about the overly beloved god. A wise measure was taken, it seems, with James's pragmatization of the concept of truth, according to which whatever bears fruit in life is true. Here the great American stands on the same side of the barricade as Nietzsche, the critic of knowledge.

If we were to name the theme through which something like a "must" or an irrevocable affirmation finds its way into James's interest in religion, we could not find a better word for it than "chance." It is William James's ownmost word concerning conviction, the stimulating sign that shows his intellect its tasks. Once one has heard this word uttered in James's unmistakable key, one will forever perceive in it a changed tone, no matter how stale it may appear everywhere else. When, in his hermeneutics of the monstrous, James emphasizes the aspect of variety, he thus interprets variety as the source of chances for individuals. In chances, the dark mass of things clears up for me; wherever chances make this clearing happen, I accept myself as the place in being where an upsurge is possible. Chance reconciles the individual with the monstrous by showing her where she should attempt anew to make the leap to success, even if she is surrounded by many failures. At times, James appears to go so far as to say that, for human beings, the chance of salvation is more important than salvation itself.

"The heart lives in chances." As a cautious pluralist who knows that not everything succeeds, but also that not everything gets lost, James encapsulates his existence in this careful formulation. In the will to believe in the chances of the individual, James expresses the sum total of his despair and certainties, as if in an exuberant confession.

Editorial Note*

"Is the World Affirmable?" Manuscript of a lecture delivered at Sankt-Matthäus-Kirche, Berlin, May 16, 2017.

"The True Heresy: Gnosticism." Preface to Peter Sloterdijk (ed.), *Weltrevolution der Seele: Ein Lese- und Arbeitsbuch der Gnosis von der Spätantike bis zur Gegenwart*. Munich: Artemis und Winkler, 1993, pp. 17–56.

"Closer to Me Than I Am Myself." Chapter 8 in Peter Sloterdijk, *Spheres*, vol. 1: *Bubbles: Microspherology*, trans. Wieland Hoban. South Pasadena, CA: Semiotext(e), 2011, pp. 539–618.

"God's Bastard: The Caesura of Jesus." Chapter 5, section 4 in Peter Sloterdijk, *Die schrecklichen Kinder der Neuzeit: Über das anti-genealogische Experiment der Moderne*. Frankfurt am Main: Suhrkamp, 2014, pp. 278–311. [An English translation by Oliver Berghof is forthcoming.]

"Improving the Human Being." Manuscript of a lecture given within the framework of the Studium Generale, Tübingen, winter semester of 2006/7 and subsequently printed in *Was bedeutet Leben?*, ed. Urs Baumann. Frankfurt am Main: Lembeck, 2008, pp. 149–68.

"Epochs of Ensoulment." Manuscript of a lecture delivered at Schloß Neubeurn/Inn, October 5, 2012.

---

* TRANSLATOR'S NOTE: This list, which appears at the end of the German edition of *After God*, contains pieces by the author himself that are referred to throughout this book; some of them are unpublished. These pieces are listed here in the order in which they are cited in the main text (and not chronologically or alphabetically).

"Latency." In Peter Sloterdijk, *Latenz: Blinde Passagiere in den Geisteswissenschaften*, ed. Hans Ulrich Gumbrecht and Florian Klinger. Göttingen: Vandenhoeck & Ruprecht, 2011, pp. 227–34.

"The Mystical Imperative." Preface to *Mystische Weltliteratur*, collected by Martin Buber, ed. Peter Sloterdijk. Munich: Hugendubel, 2007, pp. 9–44.

"Absolute and Categorical Imperative." Manuscript of a lecture held in French, Paris, June 15, 2009.

"News about the Will to Believe." Manuscript of a lecture delivered at Bochum, February 10, 2007, and subsequently printed in *Postsäkulare Gesellschaft: Perspektiven interdisziplinärer Forschung*, ed. Walter Schweidler. Freiburg: Karl Alber, 2007, pp. 76–93.

"Chances in the Monstrous." Preface to William James, *Die Vielfalt religiöser Erfahrungen*. Frankfurt am Main: Insel, 1997.

Notes

Notes to Chapter 1

1 *Nous autres, civilisations, nous savons maintenant que nous sommes mortelles.* [. . .] *Et nous voyons maintenant que l'abîme de l'histoire est assez grand pour tout le monde* ["We others, civilizations, we now know that we are mortal. [...] And we now see that the abyss of history is big enough for the whole world"]. Paul Valéry, *La Crise de l'Esprit* (Paris 1919), reedited in *Variété I* (Paris: Gallimard 1924), now in *Œuvres I* (Paris: Éditions de la Pléïade), p. 988.

2 See Raffaele Pettazzoni, *Der allwissende Gott: Zur Geschichte der Gottesidee* (Frankfurt am Main: Fischer Bücherei, 1960).

3 Peter Sloterdijk, *God's Zeal: The Battle of the Three Monotheisms*, translated by Wieland Hoban (Cambridge: Polity, 2009), pp. 140–2.

4 Friedrich Nietzsche, "The Case of Wagner," in Friedrich Nietzsche, *The Anti-Christ, Ecce Homo, Twilight of the Idols, and Other Writings*, edited by Aaron Ridley, translated by Judith Norman (Cambridge: Cambridge University Press, 2005), here p. 261.

5 See Jan Assmann, *Totale Religion: Ursprünge und Formen puritanischer Verschärfung* (Vienna: Pincus Verlag, 2016), pp. 58–9.

6 Friedrich Nietzsche, "Twilight of the Idols," in Friedrich Nietzsche, *The Anti-Christ, Ecce Homo, Twilight of the Idols, and Other Writings*, edited by Aaron Ridley, translated by Judith Norman (Cambridge: Cambridge University Press, 2005), here p. 155.

7 See *Lexikon der katholischen Dogmatik*, edited by Wolfgang Beiner, 3rd edn. (Freiburg: Herder, 1991), pp. 106–9, where the sixteen most distinctive attributes, from *Allgegenwart* [omnipresence] to *Zorn* [wrath] are enumerated under the entry "Eigenschaften Gottes" ["God's Attributes"], although the author – Wilhelm Breuning from Bonn – does not raise the issue of how to examine their compatibility.

8 On the Jewish side, the attribute of omnipotence has recently been revoked *expressis verbis*: see Hans Jonas, "The Concept of God after Auschwitz: A Jewish Voice," in Hans Jonas, *Mortality and Morality:*

A Search for the Good after Auschwitz, edited by Lawrence Vogel (Evanston, IL: Northwestern University Press, 1996), pp. 131–43.

9 See *Al Qaeda in Its Own Words*, edited by Gilles Kepel and Jean-Pierre Milelli (Cambridge, MA: Harvard University Press, 2008).

10 Max Bense, *Technische Existenz* (Stuttgart: Deutsche Verlags-Anstalt, 1949).

11 See pp. 10 and 67–8.

12 Cosima Wagner, *Die Tagebücher in 3 Bänden* (Berlin: 2006), entry dated August 3, 1872.

13 It is possible that Wagner took the expression not only from German translations of Nordic mythology, but also from the poem in Heinrich Heine's *Buch der Lieder* (1827) that bears the same name.

14 Peter Wapnewski, *Der Ring des Nibelungen: Wagners Weltendrama* (Munich: Piper, 2013; first published in 1995 under the title "Weisst du wie das wird...?"), here p. 304, in reference to Hans Mayer's analysis in *Richard Wagner in Selbstzeugnissen und Bilddokumenten* (Hamburg: Rowohlt, 1959), pp. 147–8.

15 Friedrich Nietzsche, "Richard Wagner in Bayreuth," in Friedrich Nietzsche, *Untimely Meditations*, edited by Daniel Breazeale, translated by R. J. Hollingdale (Cambridge: Cambridge University Press, 1997), ch. 11, here p. 253.

16 What is really fatal is the extinction of the gods as a result of the worldwide death of languages. Experts in this field contend that over a thousand minor languages will be made to disappear over the course of the twenty-first century. With every language that dies out, we also lose a mythology, a system of ritual, and a vocabulary of names for gods.

17 [TN: "Maker" in English in the original.]

18 See Paul Gerhardt's song "Ich bin ein Gast auf Erden" ["A Pilgrim and a Stranger"] (1667).

19 [TN: "Work in progress" in English in the original.]

20 Gotthard Günther, *Beiträge zur Grundlegung einer operationsfähigen Dialektik*, vol. 1 (Hamburg: Felix Meiner, 1976), p. 217.

21 Gotthard Günther, "Seele und Maschine," in Günther, *Beiträge*, p. 90.

Notes to Chapter 2

1 Dante placed hypocrites in the sixth circle of the penultimate levels of hell, where they circle about in gilded robes of lead (*Inferno*, Canto 23). A later Enlightenment will serenely note: "Hypocrisy is the mother of civilizations" (Régis Debray, *Dégagements*, Paris: Gallimard, 2010, p. 283).

2 Helmuth Plessner, *Die Stufen des Organischen und der Mensch: Einleitung in die philosophische Anthropologie* (Berlin: Walter de Gruyter, 1928).

3 [TN: This clause is in English in the original.]

4 See p. 11 here.

5 *Bonds: Schuld, Schulden und andere Verbindlichkeiten*, edited by Thomas Macho with the collaboration of Valeska Neumann (Munich: Wilhelm Fink, 2014).

6 Starting in 1860, the ethnologist Adolf Bastian developed an empirical universalism on the basis of so-called "elementary thoughts." See Adolf Bastian, *Der Mensch in der Geschichte*, 3 volumes (Leipzig: O. Wigand, 1860).

7 [TN: "Terms of trade" is in English in the original.]

8 See Heiner Mühlmann, *Die Natur des Christentums*, with a foreword by Bazon Brock (Paderborn: Wilhelm Fink, 2017).

9 Karl Jaspers, *The Origin and Goal of History* (Abingdon: Routledge, 2010).

10 See Jan Assmann, *Religio Duplex: How the Enlightenment Reinvented Egyptian Religion*, translated by Robert Savage (Cambridge: Polity, 2014).

11 Karl Jaspers, *The Question of German Guilt*, translated by E. B. Ashton (New York: Fordham University Press, 2000), p. 66.

12 Saint Augustine, *Confessions*, 3.6.11.

13 On the complex of axial-age world pictures shedding themselves of archaic cults, see Robert N. Bellah, *Religion in Human Evolution: From the Paleolithic to the Axial Age* (Cambridge, MA: Harvard University Press, 2011).

14 Søren Kierkegaard, *Either/Or: Part II*, edited and translated by Howard V. Hong and Edna H. Hong (Princeton, NJ: Princeton University Press, 1987), p. 349.

15 See Francesco Petrarca, *Secretum meum*.

16 Karlheinz Stierle, *Francesco Petrarca: Ein Intellektueller im Europa des 14. Jahrhunderts* (Munich: Hanser, 2003).

17 [TN: "Age of anxiety" is in English in the original.]

18 Lotario de Segni, *Vom Elend des menschlichen Daseins: Aus dem Lateinischen übersetzt und eingeleitet von Carl-Friedrich Geyer* (Hildeshim: Georg Olms, 1990). The introduction contains an overview of the literature of the Middle Ages on *conditio humana* that extends up to twentieth-century anthropology.

19 Ibid., p. 11.

20 Friedrich Nietzsche, *On the Genealogy of Morality*, revised student edition, edited by Keith Ansell-Pearson, translated by Carol Diethe (Cambridge: Cambridge University Press, 2007): "Third Essay," §11, p. 85.

21 Hugo Ball, *Byzantinisches Christentum: Drei Heiligen-Leben* (Göttingen: Wallstein, 2011 [1923]).

22 Ibid., p. 7.

23 See Peter Sloterdijk, *You Must Change Your Life*, translated by Wieland Hoban (Cambridge: Polity, 2013), pp. 271–2. Also Martin Riesebrodt, *Cultus und Heilsversprechen. Eine Theorie der Religionen* (Munich: Beck, 2007), chapter 6 ("Radikale Heilssuche: Praktiken asketischer Virtuosen"), here pp. 175–6.

24 Thomas Kaufmann, *Geschichte der Reformation* (Frankfurt am Main: Verlag der Weltreligionen, 2009), p. 718.

25 With this *et cetera* Luther brings to light a scholarly brutality that illuminates his later demeanor. The young scholar treats the first word of Christ testified to in the New Testament – which is a quotation from John the Baptist – as a truism that one can cite in an argument just

for the purpose of being right. The "etc." of the first thesis exposes the Reformation as a giant staging of "eccentric positionality" in the theological mode: penance as an attitude of being right.

26 [TN: Translation from *Martin Luther, 1483–1546*, edited by Kurt Aland (St. Louis: Concordia Publishing House, 1967).]
27 [TN: Ibid., translation modified.]
28 Albert Schweitzer, *Indian Thought and Its Development*, translated by Lilian M. Rigby Russell (New York: Holt, 1936 [1935]).

Notes to Chapter 3

1 Eric Voegelin, *Science, Politics and Gnosticism: Two Essays* (Chicago: Regnery, 1968), p. 83.
2 [TN: "Metaphysical fiction" is in English in the original]
3 [TN: "Fantasy" is in English in the original]
4 [TN: "Churchianity" is in English in the original]
5 [TN: *Pneuma* (originally "breath") was a crucial concept in Stoicism and in the medicine of Hellenistic and late antiquity, where it gave its name to a school – Pneumatism.]
6 "On the Cherubim," in *The Works of Philo Judaeus*, translated by Charles Duke Yonge (London: H. G. Bohn, 1854–1890), 24.120. [TN: Translation modified in accordance with Sloterdijk's German rendering.]
7 Hans Blumenberg, *Matthäuspassion* (Frankfurt am Main: Suhrkamp, 1998), p. 14.
8 [TN: "Appeal" is in English in the original]
9 [TN: "The Gospel of Truth," trans. Marvin Meyer, in *The Nag Hammadi Scriptures: The Revised and Updated Translation of Sacred Gnostic Texts*, edited by Marvin Meyer (New York: HarperCollins, 2007), p. 36.]
10 [TN: This is not translated from the Greek but from Sloterdijk's German, which seems to be a very loose paraphrase of passages from Book 1, ch. 36.]
11 [TN: This is an untranslatable wordplay on Wittgenstein's definition of the world as everything that is the case (*der Fall*).]
12 [TN: "Extracts from the Works of Theodotus and the So-Called Oriental Teachings at the Time of Valentinus," translation from http://gnosis.org/library/excr.htm.]
13 Martin Heidegger, *Contributions to Philosophy (Of the Event)*, translated by Richard Rojcewicz and Daniela Vallega-Neu (Bloomington: Indiana University Press, 2012), 256.
14 [TN: "Happy end" is in English in the original]
15 [TN: "Stories" is in English in the original.]
16 [TN: I have translated Sloterdijk's German directly, as it differs significantly from M. R. James's translation in *The Apocryphal New Testament* (Oxford: Clarendon Press, 1924), where this passage reads: "And if thou wouldst know concerning me, what I was, know that with a word did I deceive all things and I was no whit deceived. I have leaped: but do thou understand the whole."]

17 E. M. Cioran, *The Trouble with Being Born*, translated by Richard Howard (New York: Seaver, 1976), p. 15.

18 [TN: "Misfits" is in English in the original.]

19 [TN: "Stories" is in English in the original.]

20 Hans Jonas, *Gnosis und spätantiker Geist*, vol. 2: *Von der Mythologie zur mystischen Philosophie* (Göttingen: Vandenhoeck & Ruprecht, 1954), p. 62.

21 [TN: *The Poems of Heine*, translated by Edgar Alfred Bowring (London: George Bell & Sons, 1908), p. 130.]

22 [TN: "Stewardship" is in English in the original.]

23 [TN: Sigmund Freud, *Civilization and Its Discontents* (1930), in *The Standard Edition of the Complete Psychological Works of Sigmund Freud*, vol. 21: *1927–1931* (New York: Norton, 1961).]

24 Bill McKibben, *The End of Nature* (New York: Random House, 2006), pp. 67–8.

Notes to Chapter 4

1 Martin Heidegger, *Being and Time*, translated by John Macquarrie and Edward Robinson (New York: Harper & Row, 1962), p. 79.

2 Robert Musil, *The Man without Qualities*, translated by Sophie Wilkins and Burton Pike (New York: Vintage, 1996), p. 1497.

3 Heidegger, *Being and Time*, p. 79.

4 Gilles Deleuze took one step toward clarifying this matter in his final text "Immanence: A Life," in Gilles Deleuze, *Pure Immanence: Essays on a Life*, translated by Anne Boyman (New York: Zone Books, 2001), pp. 25–34.

5 Insofar as biblical theology teaches of a withdrawn or separate God, the immanence, *in* him, of everything that exists is modified into something that occurs *under* God, *with reference to* God, or *on the edge of* God, though never fully *outside* God. In a sense, classical theology was the first *analysis situs* [analysis of place = topology], for all the locations in that which exists constitute situations in relation to the absolute center. Radical ontology is therefore possible only as situsology, as a science of *situs* – and nowhere is this fact manifested more clearly than in Heidegger's early thought.

6 In the view of classical metaphysics, that is, absolute situsology, God is the unity of being with oneself and being outside oneself – a trait that can also be ascribed to finite existence [*Dasein*] if, in agreement with Heidegger, one understands it as insistent *and* ecstatic.

7 Alain Badiou, *Conditions*, translated by Steven Corcoran (London & New York: Continuum, 2008), p. 276. It is clear that this is not our own view, as Badiou's claim makes excessive concessions to the ideology of prior loneliness.

8 [TN: Fyodor Dostoyevsky, *The Idiot*, translated by Constance Garnett (Mineola, NY: Dover, 2003), p. 101.]

9 [TN: The words translated here as "recognition" and "misjudgment" are *Wiedererkennen* and *Verkennung*, both based on *kennen*, "to know."]

10 On Augustine's role as a portal figure of western Christian mysticism,

see Kurt Ruh, *Geschichte der abendländischen Mystik*, vol. 1: *Die Grundlegung durch die Kirchenväter und die Mönchstheologie des 12. Jahrhunderts* (Munich: 1990), pp. 86–7.

11 See Page DuBois, *Torture and Truth* (London: Routledge, 1991).

12 See Nicholas of Cusa, "Dialogue on the Hidden God," in his *Selected Spiritual Writings*, translated by H. Lawrence Bond (Mahwah, NJ: Paulist Press, 1997), p. 210: "For outside truth there is no truth [...] Therefore, truth is not found outside truth neither in some way nor in something else" (*extra veritatem non est veritas* [...] *Non reperitur igitur veritas extra veritam nec aliter nec in alio*).

13 For a macrospherological interpretation of apostleship, see Peter Sloterdijk, *Spheres*, vol. 2: *Globes: Macrospherology* (South Pasadena, CA: Semiotext(e), 2014): ch. 7, "How the True Spheric Center Has Long-Range Effects through Pure Media: On the Metaphysics of Telecommunication."

14 Augustine, *Confessions*, Book 10, ch. 2.2 (at p. 189 of Augustine, *Confessions*, 2nd edn., trans. F. J. Sheed, ed. Michael P. Foley, Indianapolis: Hackett, 2006). The formula *in te*, "in you," frequently used by Augustine, refers more to the topological or situsological structure of the ego–God relationship; in the passage *nec mihi nec tibi placeam nisi de te*, on the other hand, the phrase *de te* emphasizes the relationship with one's own ego in dynamic terms, as an internal relationship within the relationship with God: if I am something to myself, it is because I am something to you.

15 [TN: Here the author uses *Da-Sein* rather than *Dasein*. Like Heidegger, Sloterdijk here plays on the literal meaning of *Dasein* ("existence") as "being there." It should be noted that, as *Dasein* is also a conventional, non-Heideggerian word in German, it is sometimes translated here as "existence" rather than as "Dasein." Where Sloterdijk uses it in a Heideggerian sense without directly referring to Heidegger, the German term has been added in square parentheses, while for specifically Heidegger-related uses, the German word has been retained, in keeping with translation conventions.]

16 Augustine, *Confessions* 1.2.1 (at p. 4 in the Shed and Foley translation).

17 *Extra eam*: in other words, God is not found outside memory.

18 Ibid.10.24 (at p. 209). .

19 Ibid. 10.25 (at p. 209).

20 Ibid. 10.25 (at p. 210)

21 Ibid. 10.26 (at p. 210).

22 Ibid. 10.27 (at p. 210).

23 If this were the place to repeat the theological deduction of temporality, the difference between theodrama (God's process with the world) and affair (the soul's process with God) would need to be developed; for our purposes it is sufficient to foreground the aspect of the affair.

24 [TN: The original word *Kennenlernen* means "to become acquainted with"; it is translated differently here because it refers to the preceding quotation from Augustine, where the Latin *didici* was rendered as *kennen lernte* in the German translation used by the author and as "learned of" in the English translation used here. It is also worth noting that the literal meaning of *kennenlernen* is "to learn to know."]

25 Augustine, *Confessions* 3.6.11: "You were more inward than my most inward part, higher than my highest part" (*Tu autem eras interior intimo meo et superior summo meo*). [TN: The same passage is quoted and discussed in Chapter 2, p. 27 and n. 12.] This highest claim of Christian topological surrealism is explained with reference to its premises in the history of architecture in Sloterdijk, *Spheres*, vol. 2, ch. 3 ("Arks, City Walls, World Borders, Immune Systems: On the Ontology of the Walled Space"). Here the comparative sense of the inside emerges in the light of palace architecture in the Persian Empire: the inward is that which, in a system of nested spaces, does not simply lie *intus*, "inside," but is *interior*, "further inside."

26 [TN: "hot spot" is in English in the original.]

27 See Martin Buber, *Ecstatic Confessions*, translated by Esther Cameron (Syracuse, NY: Syracuse University Press, 1996). Cf. chapter 9 in this volume.

28 [TN: A reference to the "SWR Teleakademie," a television series produced by the SWR (Southwest German Broadcasting) featuring presentations by university lectures on various scientific, cultural and social topics.]

29 Marguerite Porete, *The Mirror of Simple Souls*, translated by Ellen L. Babinsky (Mahwah, NJ: Paulist Press, 1993), p. 83.

30 Ibid., pp. 192–3.

31 Ibid., p. 218.

32 In Islamic sources, the mythical founder of philosophy, Hermes Trismegistus, is called Idris.

33 Shihabuddin Suhrawerdi Maqtul [Shahab al-Din Suhrawardi], *Three Treatises on Mysticism*, edited and translated by Otto Spies and S. K. Khatak (Bonn: Selbstverlag des Orientalischen Seminars der Universität Bonn, 1935), pp. 25f.

34 See Seyyed Hossein Nasr, *Three Muslim Sages: Avicenna, Suhrawadi, Ibn 'Arabi* (Cambridge, MA: Harvard University Press, 1964), p. 76.

35 Alongside Christology, prophetology, pneumatology, and onto-semiology, or the doctrine of signs of being (meaning philosophical aesthetics).

36 Nicholas of Cusa, *Selected Spiritual Writings*, pp. 235ff. (with a slight alteration).

37 Ludwig Wittgenstein, *Culture and Value*, translated by Peter Winch (Oxford: Blackwell, 1980), p. 52.

38 [TN: In the original, the author comments here on the shortcomings of the German translation, which renders Cusa's *contractio* as *Verschränkung*, which normally means "interweaving or folding"; these remarks have been omitted.]

39 Nicholas of Cusa, *Selected Spiritual Writings*, p. 238.

40 [TN: The German word for "guilt" is *Schuld*; its plural can mean "debts," and the corresponding verb *schulden* means "to owe."]

41 On the modernization of guilt, see Sloterdijk, *Spheres*, vol. 2, ch. 8 ("The Last Orb: A Philosophical History of Terrestrial Globalization").

42 [TN: Although the author uses *verschränkt* [interwoven] rather than *zusammengezogen* [contracted] in these two sentences, he does so with reference to Cusa's *contractio* and its inadequate German translation (see note 38 above), which is why it is translated here as "contracted."]

43 Nicholas of Cusa, *Selected Spiritual Writings*, p. 240.
44 [TN: *Kleine Münze*, literally "small coin" or "small change," is a term from German copyright law that designates the minimal unit of creative work subject to copyright protection.]
45 Nicholas of Cusa, *De ludo globi*, translated by Pauline Moffitt Watts (New York: Abaris Books, 1986), p. 75.
46 Pseudo-Dionysius (Areopagita), "The Divine Names," in *The Complete Works*, translated by Colm Luibheid and Paul Rorem (Mahwah, NJ: Paulist Press, 1987), pp. 61–2.
47 See Blaise Pascal, *Thoughts*, translated by W. F. Trotter (New York: Cosimo, 2007), p. 180: "Jesus will be in agony even to the end of the world."
48 Saint John of Damascus, *Writings*, translated by Frederic H. Chase (New York: Fathers of the Church, 1958), p. 178.
49 Ibid., pp. 195–6.
50 See Albert Menne, "Mengenlehre und Trinität," in *Münchener Theologische Zeitschrift* 8 (1957), pp. 180ff.
51 Letter 38, written ca AD 370; in Saint Basil, *The Letters*, translated by Roy J. Deferrari (London: Heinemann, 1926), vol. 1, p. 209.
52 Gregory Nyssenus, *Adversus Macedonianos* (GNO III/1, 109 Müller), quoted here from Giulio Maspero, *Trinity and Man: Gregory of Nyssa's Ad Ablabium* (Leiden: Brill, 2007), p. 176.
53 In his book *Das seltsame Problem der Weltgesellschaft. Eine Neubrandenburger Vorlesung* (Opladen: Westdeutscher Verlag, 1997), Peter Fuchs provides a brilliant introduction to sociological systems theory, emphasizing the non-spatial character of "society" and giving the impression of attempting to approach a "perichoretic" sociology, i.e. a theory of society without drawing on images of spatial containers.
54 See Anaxagoras of Clazomenae, *Fragments and Testimonia: A Text and Translation with Notes and Essays*, edited and translated by Patricia Curd (Toronto: University of Toronto Press, 2007), fragment B12: "This revolution [*perichōrēsis*] caused them (the mixed qualities) to separate off. The dense is being separated off from the rare, and the warm from the cold, and the bright from the dark, and the dry from the moist" (p. 25).
55 Saint John of Damascus, "An Exact Exposition of the Orthodox Faith," in *Writings*, p. 177.
56 Ibid., p. 202.
57 Ibid., pp 197–8.
58 [TN: The last few lines of this paragraph play extensively with the prefix *um*-, which carries the meaning "around": *Umgeben-Sein* "being-surrounded," *Umfang* "magnitude," *Umwelt* "environment," *das Um* "the 'around,'" and, finally, the pairing of *weltlos* "worldless" and *umweltlos* "environmentless."]
59 See Cyril of Alexandria, *In Johannis Evangelium I, 5*, in Migne, *PG* [*Patrologia graeca*], 73, 81; quoted from Migne, *Encyclopédie théologique*, vol. C, p. 880.
60 Richard of Saint Victor, *De trinitate* 5.6. See Richard of Saint Victor, *La Trinité: Texte latin*, edited by Gaston Salet, S. J. (Paris: Les Editions du Cerf, 1959), 342. [TN: This is my translation of Sloterdijk's German rendering.]

61 See Richard of Saint Victor, *La Trinité*, 5.20, p. 351ff.: *quarta in trinitate persona locum habere non possit* ["a fourth person could not have a place in Trinity"]. Immanuel Kant's listless remark that it makes no difference whether an apprentice of faith believes that God comprises three persons or ten, as this difference has no effect on his behavior, merely shows that Kant had no idea of the difference between an ethics of following rules and an ethics of communal existence. A ten-person godhead would always be monstrous, either because the persons from the fourth to tenth, if equal, would be serially added or because, if unequal, they would set off a procession into the God-unlike. See Immanuel Kant, *The Conflict of the Faculties*, trans. Mary J. Gregor (Lincoln: University of Nebraska Press, 1992), p. 67.

62 "Hegel says somewhere that great historic facts and personages recur twice. He forgot to add: 'Once as tragedy, and again as farce'": Karl Marx, *The Eighteenth Brumaire of Louis Bonaparte*, translated by D. D. L. (New York & Berlin: Mondial, 2005), p. 1.

63 See Peter Stemmer, "Perichorese: Zur Geschichte eines Begriffs," in *Archiv für Begriffsgeschichte* 27 (1983): 32–4.

64 "Decree for the Armenians," http://www.clerus.org/bibliaclerusonline/en/dw3.htm; after Fulgentius of Ruspe.

65 Ibid.

Notes to Chapter 5

1 [TN: Here and in what follows, "Jesuanic" is used as an English equivalent of Sloterdijk's *jesuanisch* and carries the sense of "pertaining to Jesus."]

2 Joseph Ratzinger/Pope Benedict XVI, *Jesus of Nazareth: The Infancy Narratives*, translated by Philip J. Whitmore (London: Bloomsbury, 2012); Joseph Ratzinger/Pope Benedict XVI, *Jesus of Nazareth: From the Baptism in the Jordan to the Transfiguration* (London: Bloomsbury, 2007); Joseph Ratzinger/Pope Benedict XVI, *Jesus of Nazareth*, Part II: *Holy Week* (San Francisco, CA: Ignatius Press, 2011).

3 This reading of traces avoids invasive psychoanalytic assumptions of the kind that form the basis of Christoph Türcke's remarkable book *Jesu Traum: Psychoanalyse des Neuen Testaments* (Springe: Zu Klampen, 2009). It works instead only with pieces of genealogical evidence. Admittedly, these also have the status of "remainders of reality" that were handed down in the course of confabulation, but in pointing to them no claim to reconstruct the "dream work" of Jesus – or even the hallucinatory work of his disciples – is being made.

4 [All Bible quotations in this chapter follow the *New Jerusalem Bible* (Garden City, NY: Doubleday, 1985.]

5 See Gisbert Greshake, *Der dreieine Gott: Eine trinitarische Theologie* (Freiburg: Herder, 1997).

6 Albrecht Koschorke, *The Holy Family and Its Legacy*, translated by Thomas Dunlap (New York: Columbia University Press, 2003).

7 Pierre Legendre, *Les Enfants du texte: Étude sur la fonction parentale des états* (Paris: Fayard, 1992).

8 As for instance John Paul II, during a general audience in Rome on March 3, 1999.

9 Conquered by Pompey in 63 BC, during Jesus's lifetime the restive province had already been part of the Roman Empire for a hundred years; from 40 to 4 BC its Jewish ruler Herod ("the Great") had the function of a vassal king. If there really had been anything like a "Massacre of the Innocents" in Bethlehem, it would have had to have happened shortly before Herod's death and close to the birth of the chosen child.

10 "7 I will proclaim the decree of Yahweh: He said to me, 'You are my son, today have I fathered you. 8 Ask of me, and I shall give you the nations as your birthright, the whole wide world as your possession. 9 With an iron sceptre you will break them, shatter them like so many pots.'"

11 John 1:14. The phrase *monogenetos huios* in 1 John (4:9) underlines the privileged relationship between the divine father and the human son, regardless of whether one translates *monogenetos* as "inborn" (Luther) or "only born" (Jerusalem Bible). The phrase offers a point of connection for the later Gnostic theology of the equality of essence, which, later still, will be outdone by the classic doctrine of the Trinity.

12 Galatians 2:20.

13 Not to mention the chain of teachers and students in the sphere of Buddhism, which around the time when Jesus's drama was unfolding had already generated, for at least 400 years, cascades of succession that followed their own laws.

14 The Pauline formula "[t]here can be neither Jew nor Greek, there can be neither slave nor freeman, there can be neither male nor female" (Galatians 3:28) is said to have been pronounced at the first ceremonies of Christian baptism. Oftentimes the lifting of barriers to joining the Pauline commune has been interpreted as the foundation of a "Christian universalism" (most recently again in Alan Badiou, *Saint Paul: The Foundation of Universalism*, trans. Ray Brassier, Stanford, CA: Stanford University Press, 2009). However, there could not be a bigger misunderstanding. What Paul initiated was not a universalist project, but a community of the elect conceived of on a wide scale. Non-Jews as well as slaves and women were permitted to join without in the least causing the pneumatic commune to give up its strong characteristic: to be a highly selective organization that offered refuge to the few who could be saved ahead of the impending doom.

15 [TN: G. W. F. Hegel, *Lectures on the Philosophy of History*, trans. Ruben Alvarado (Aalten, Netherlands, WordBridge, 2011), p. 298.]

16 [TN: "Counter-culture" is in English in the original.]

17 These quotations are based on the modernized translation of the Bible by Martin Luther in the edition of the Württembergische Bibelanstalt, following the text of 1912. [TN: See n. 4.]

18 [TN: In German the part of the New Testament known in English as "Acts of the Apostles" is commonly referred to as "Apostelgeschichte" – literally "History of the Apostles."]

19 The later "philosophy of history" and its emasculation into "intellectual history" will increasingly cover up and formalize this initial

situation until it is no longer recognizable for what it is. In the twentieth century only a few historians, such as York von Wartenburg, Hans Urs von Balthasar, Friedrich Heer, and Eugen Rosenstock-Huessy, to name no others, continued to insist on the original unity between history and the history of the apostles, or between intellectual history [*Geistesgeschichte*] and the history of the Holy Spirit [*Heliggeistgeschichte*]. Most members of the fraternity participated willy-nilly in the secularization of history, which at the level of discourse appears as a transition from modernity to postmodernity. "Postmodernism" is a marker of the state of consciousness that has settled aggressively on the coexistence of cultures, in a sequence without sense of progress, in a juxtaposition without hierarchic implications, and in a multitude without sense of mission. On the structure of limited time in "essential" history, see Jacob Taubes, *Occidental Eschatology*, trans. David Ratmoko (Stanford, CA: Stanford University Press, 2009).

20 In his *Ecclesiastical History*, edited by Heinrich Kraft (Munich: Kösel, 1989), at 1.7 (= pp. 99–103 in this edition), Eusebius discusses the incompatibilities between the two "genealogical lines" of Jesus in Matthew and Luke and tries to reconcile them with the help of a distinction between "fathers according to nature" and "formal fathers." The logical impossibility of a simultaneous claim to virgin birth and to descent from David is being overlooked by Eusebius too.

21 [TN: In German *Pater* is still current in its meaning of "priest belonging to a religious order" (OED), a sense which is marked as rare in the Oxford English Dictionary for current English usage. "Pope" derives from post-classical Latin *papa* and Byzantine Greek πάπας, "father," "abbot" and *abbé* from Syriac *abbā*, "father" and Aramaic אבא (*abba*), "father"; the latter is transliterated in the Bible in Mark 14:36, Romans 8:15 and Galatians 4:6.]

22 [TN: Matthew 23:9.]

23 Koschorke, *Holy Family*.

24 [TN: "Laptop" is in English in the original.]

25 See Koschorke, *Holy Family*, pp. 48ff.

26 A pattern that transcends the Greek duplication of the role of the father in the biological father and the teacher.

27 Koschorke, *Holy Family*, p. 51.

28 Only Buddhism achieved a comparably powerful reversion of polarity in the conception of the self, when it admonished its students to correct all sensual, mental, conventional, and social "attachments" (*upadana*) by orienting themselves toward an all-dissolving Nirvana.

29 See also Louis Dumont, *Homo aequalis*, vol. 2: *L'idéologie allemande: France–Allemagne et retour* (Paris: Gallimard, 1991); Arno Bammé, *Homo occidentalis: Von der Anschauung zur Bemächtigung der Welt: Zäsuren abendländischer Epistemologie* (Weilerswist: Velbrück, 2011); David Gress, *From Plato to Nato: The Idea of the West and Its Opponents* (New York: Free Press, 2010).

30 See Peter Sloterdijk, *The Terrible Children of Modernity* (forthcoming), ch. 6.3 ("The Children of the Abyss: Mysticism as Anti-Genealogic Revolt").

31 After the rule of law had ceased.
32 Augustine, *De civitate Dei* 4.4.
33 Hans Joas, *The Sacredness of the Person: A New Genealogy of Human Rights* (Washington: Georgetown University Press, 2013).
34 In his main work *Totality and Infinity: An Essay on Exteriority*, translated by Alphonso Lingis (The Hague: M. Nijhoff, 1979, p. 279), Émmanuel Lévinas attempts to formulate a metaphysics of filiation that arrives at the same conclusion, albeit on a different path. "The son resumes the unicity of the father and yet remains exterior to the father: The son is a unique son. Not by number; each son of the father is the unique son, the chosen son [...] I am I and chosen one, but where can I be chosen, if not from among other chosen ones, among equals?" Lévinas keeps silent about the fact that these theses are not warranted by the Jewish stories of fathers; for what are they about, if not the preferential love of the father, to whom it would never occur to treat every son as his only son, and as the chosen one?

Notes to Chapter 6

1 [TN: "Political correctness" is in English in the original.]
2 [TN: "Vertically challenged people" is in English in the original.]
3 [TN: Pierre Beaumarchais, *The Marriage of Figaro*, in *The Barber of Seville and The Marriage of Figaro*, translated by John Wood (Harmondsworth: Penguin Classics, 1964), p. 199.]
4 [TN: "The Second Coming" is in English in the original.]
5 [TN: "High-tech" is in English in the original.]

Notes to Chapter 7

1 [TN: This is the English version used by David W. Smith in his introduction to Pierre Klossowski, *Living Currency* (London: Bloomsbury, 2017), here p. 18.]
2 Elements of logical training analysis are indicated above all in Peter Sloterdijk, *Weltfremdheit* (Frankfurt am Main: Suhrkamp, 1993) and Peter Sloterdijk, *Im selben Boot: Versuch über die Hyperpolitik* (Frankfurt am Main: Suhrkamp, 1993). Throughout these analyses we are dealing with a logic of pre-objective and pre-objectal intimacy; this is characterized by a threefold turn from the theory of the imaginary (i.e. the systemic barrier of psychoanalytic language) to psychoacoustics; from object relations theory (i.e. the logical barrier of psychoanalytic regress) to spherology; and from drive theory to excitement theory.
3 The long overdue critique of object relations theories would have to (and can) furnish proof that the so-called objects are actually occupants.
4 The quotation from Job in this chapter's epigraph signifies something of both; on the one hand, it recalls the old idea of genesis by means of coagulation – the primal model of the concrete created by concrescence;

on the other hand, its accusations against God bring to the fore in manifest speech what had previously remained unsaid.

5 These reflections have been developed more broadly in two treatises by this author; see Peter Sloterdijk, "Was heißt: sich übernehmen? Versuch über die Bejahung," and "Wie wurde der Todestrieb entdeckt? Versuch über seelische Endabsichten mit ständiger Rücksicht auf Sokrates, Jesus und Freud," both in Sloterdijk, *Weltfremdheit*, chapters 6 and 4.

6 From a postmodern position, the Canadian cultural theorist Arthur Kroker has reintroduced the motif of being possessed as the key to the psychosocial reality of the present. See Arthur Kroker, *The Possessed Individual: Technology and the French Postmodern* (Montreal: New World Perspectives, 1992).

7 On the complex of mesmerism, magnetism, and hypnosis, see Peter Sloterdijk, *Der Zauberbaum: Die Entstehung der Psychoanalyse im Jahr 1785* (Frankfurt am Main: Suhrkamp, 1985).

8 Hardly an author in our century has repeated the idealist autopsy of despiritualized human beings more rigorously than Theodor W. Adorno. In the famous thirty-sixth aphorism, "The Health unto Death," of *Minima Moralia: Reflections from a Damaged Life*, translated by E. F. N. Jephcott (London: Verso, 2005), p. 59, Adorno writes: "The very people who burst with proofs of exuberant vitality could easily be taken for prepared corpses, from whom the news of their not-quite-successful decease has been withheld for reasons of population policy. Underlying the prevalent health is death. All the movements of health resemble the reflex-movements of beings whose hearts have stopped beating."

9 On the difference between nugatory (narcissistic) and true (theonomous) inspiration in idealism and in other formations of manic motivation, see also Sloterdijk, *Weltfremdheit*, pp. 45–6.

10 See Arnold Gehlen, "Über die Geburt der Freiheit aus der Entfremdung," *Archiv für Rechts- und Sozialphilosophie* 40.3 (1952): 338–53; Odo Marquard, *Transzendentaler Idealismus: Romantische Naturphilosophie, Psychoanalyse* (Cologne: Verlag für Philosophie Jürgen Dinter, 1986); Thomas H. Macho, "Was denkt? Einige Überlegungen zu den philosophiehistorischen Wurzeln der Psychoanalyse," in *Philosophie und Psychoanalyse. Symposium der Wiener Festwochen*, edited by Ludwig Nagl, Helmuth Vetter, and Harald Leupold-Löwenthal (Frankfurt am Main: Nexus, 1990), pp. 191–204.

11 The loss of religious mediality is largely compensated in bourgeois culture by an aesthetic and entrepreneurial mediumism. One need not be a priest in order to become an artist; the nineteenth-century aesthetics of the genius interprets the artistic human being as medium and mouthpiece of the creative "nature." One need not be a priest or an artist in order to make it as an entrepreneur in the medium of a global process of gain, i.e. of progress in civilization. Whoever is incapable of being a priest or an artist or an entrepreneur is admittedly predestined to become a patient; a patient is someone who suffers without being able to relay his strain.

12 See, among others, Ludwig Janus, *Wie die Seele entsteht: Unser psychisches Leben vor und nach der Geburt* (Hamburg: Hoffmann und Campe, 1992).

13 [TN: "Jewish science" is in English in the original.]
14 On horde psychology, see also Sloterdijk, *Im selben Boot*, pp. 14–26.
15 See Ioan P. Couliano, *Out of this World: Otherworldly Journeys from Gilgamesh to Albert Einstein* (Boston, MA: Shambala, 1991), pp. 33ff.
16 Karl Jaspers, *The Origin and Goal of History* (Abingdon: Routledge, 2010). See p. 24 in this volume.
17 I discuss the calendar-constituting power of such watershed "events" in European antiquity in my unpublished lecture "Die physikalische Machtergreifung, Vortrag auf dem Kongreß 'Natur im Kopf,'" delivered in Stuttgart: on July 25, 1993.
18 It has been frequently remarked that classical psychoanalysis depended on a circle of patients that disappears toward the end of the twentieth century. This would indicate the conservative nature of the original psychoanalytic project: psychoanalysis would thus be an art of healing for the "world of yesterday"; it would discharge its tasks in relation to a dying high-cultural psychopathology. After the cultural revolution a therapy that already is, in part, utterly unprecedented is being established under old denominations.
19 See Sloterdijk, *Der Zauberbaum*, pp. 28ff.
20 This thesis would need to be rethought in light of Hinderk Emrich's remarks – in a lecture delivered in 2002 under the title "Wie kommt das Ich zum Du" ["How the I gets to the You"] – on the return of hysteria in the twenty-first century; if we understand hysteria as the effect of putting something on stage under the direction of a false self, then the entire field of symptoms of "coolness" can be understood as neo-hysterical, and in this sense as theatrical.

Notes to Chapter 8

1 See p. 231, note 6 in this volume.
2 [TN: Samuel Beckett, *Waiting for Godot: A Tragicomedy in Two Acts* (New York: Grove Press, 1954), pp. 57–8.]
3 Herodotus 1.98, in *The Landmark Herodotus: The Histories*, edited by Robert B. Strassler, translated by Andrea L. Purvis (New York: Anchor Books, 2009), at p. 58.
4 [TN: Xenophanes, Fragment 18, in *The Presocratic Philosophers: A Critical History with a Selection of Texts*, edited by G. S. Kirk, J. E. Raven, and M. Schofield, 2nd edn. (Cambridge: Cambridge University Press, 2007), p. 179.]

Notes to Chapter 9

1 This is why medieval epic and lyrical poets are bound to try to muffle the proper meaning of their texts by including Christian formulae at the beginning and at the end. Marsilio Ficino sees fit to mask his commentary on Plato's *Symposium*, a neopagan encomium on eros, with a concluding formula expressing thanks to the Holy Spirit. – We can see how far the medieval conception of inspirational monism

extends by considering, inter alia, the fact that even in our century the philosopher of religion Eugen Rosenstock-Huessy interpreted the European university as an apostolic institute that ultimately goes back not to the Athenian academy, but to the office of Pauline education.

2 Even medieval theologians were unable to cast off completely the specter of the non-sympathetic external observer. This is betrayed not least in the care that Saint Thomas Aquinas takes to formulate one of his "summaries" of Christian doctrine, namely the 1259 *Summa contra gentiles*; apologetics exposes the sensitive spot of monopoly.

3 Where such compromises were not aimed at or accepted, as in Islam and in old Catholic or fundamentalist–Protestant subcultures of the West, the structurally medieval monism of inspiration has continued, together with its concomitant diabolization of the external observer.

4 This formulation goes back to Max Weber, who characterized himself as "absolutely unmusical regarding religion"; see Max Weber, *Gesamtausgabe*, edited by H. Baier et al., Part I, Vol. 17: *Wissenschaft als Beruf* [1917/1919] (Tübingen: Mohr, 1992), p. 106.

5 For a typical document of the yearning for deliverance from mechanization by means of lived experience, see Walther Rathenau, *Zur Kritik der Zeit* (Berlin: S. Fischer, 1912).

6 Franz Rosenzweig, *The Star of Redemption*, translated by William W. Hallo from the second edition of 1930 (Notre Dame, IN: University of Notre Dame Press, 1985), p. 206.

7 Martin Buber, *At the Turning: Three Addresses on Judaism* (New York: Farrar, Straus and Young, 1952).

8 Martin Buber, *The Tales of Rabbi Nachman*, translated by Maurice Friedman (Amherst, NY: Humanity Books, 1988); Martin Buber, *The Legend of the Baal-Shem*, translated by Maurice Friedman, 2nd edn. (London: Routledge, 2002).

9 This is the title of the introductory essay in *Ekstatische Konfessionen*. Buber did not include this text in the edition of his collected writings.

10 Martin Buber, "Ekstase und Bekenntnis," in Peter Sloterdijk, ed., *Mystische Weltliteratur*, collected by Martin Buber (Kreuzlingen: Heinrich Hugendubel, 2007), p. 56.

11 In *Allgemeines Literaturblatt* 20 (1911), column 75, a Catholic reviewer named Wilhelm Oehl puts his finger on the critical point: "Most of all, it is probably a panpsychistic philosophy of identity that seems most deeply aligned with his thought. So is, by the way, the very monism that the publishing house Diederichs is promoting with such sense of purpose. B. is of course situated far from our Catholic thought, no matter how highly he estimates Christian – and in a narrower sense Catholic – mysticism. Harnack's line, 'A mystic who doesn't become Catholic is a dilettante,' hardly applies to B."

12 For the still current phenomenon of re-Judaizing Judaism, see the Gilles Kepel's book *The Revenge of God: The Resurgence of Islam, Christianity and Judaism in the Modern World*, translated by Alan Braley (Cambridge: Polity, 2007), chapter 4. I am indebted to the Hungarian translator of Franz Rosenzweig, the philosopher György Tatar, for the reference that the Jewish concept of conversion means

exactly this: to come back from the remoteness to one's faith and then to remain "at home."

13 The only person superior to him in this respect is Franz Kafka, whom Harold Bloom, following indications from Gerschom Scholem, attempts, not without good reason, to understand as the creator of a new heretical Kabbala. Buber's later formulation, "I have no doctrine, but I carry on a conversation," belongs together with Kafka's parable of the children's game King and Messenger: "They were given the choice of becoming kings or the kings' messengers. As is the way with children, they all wanted to be messengers. That is why there are only messengers, racing through the world and, since there are no kings, calling out to each other the messages that have now become meaningless. They would gladly put an end to their miserable life, but they do not dare to do so because of their oath of loyalty." Franz Kafka, *The Blue Octavo Notebooks*, edited by Max Brod, translated by Ernst Kaiser and Eithne Wilkins (Cambridge, MA: Exact Change, 1991), p. 28. Buber, like Kafka, embodies the dilemma of a "messenger religion" (Max Weber) at the zero point of the act of sending.

14 With his doctrine that the ability to be oneself comes from one's encounter with others, Buber reaches, from the premises of Judaism, what only Kierkegaard's Christology had contemplated before him: a concept of the chance to be oneself without hardening oneself – beyond the anathema of self-preservation.

15 Early readers of Buber already protested against the arbitrariness with which he ascribed the predicate "genuine confession"; among other things, one might find it strange that Buber decided to recast versified documents in prose, as though prose were closer to "genuine lived experience" than verse in all possible circumstances.

16 [TN: Exact source not identified.]

17 We are dealing of course with a barbed defenselessness. Since the seventeenth century, Christianity has trained specialists – especially in the Society of Jesus – to neutralize foreign descriptions. For a long time, such descriptions have formed their own genre: "criticism of religion." In 1979 the Jesuit Karl-Heinz Weger edited a dictionary of authors – *Religionskritik von der Aufklärung bis zur Gegenwart* (Freiburg im Breisgau: Herder, 1979) – that inventories "the criticism of religion from the Enlightenment to the present" in ninety-three articles, which range from Adorno to Wittgenstein. The work reads like a compendium of what one must immunize oneself against if one wishes to continue to "believe" as before.

18 Niklas Luhmann has used the phrase "differentiation of religion" to describe a development that makes sure this does not completely come to an end; see Niklas Luhmann, *Gesellschaftsstruktur und Semantik: Studien zur Wissenssoziologie der modernen Gesellschaft 3* (Frankfurt: Suhrkamp, 1989), pp. 249–357. "Differentiated" religion is church religion after the cold shock of modernity; it continues doing its own air-conditioning by concentrating on keeping the temperature constant in its spaces and keeping out drafts – as much as possible. For outside visitors the result is *prima vista* [at first sight] charming, in time becomes stuffy, and for long stays is hardly appropriate.

19 Whenever such mass deliveries are attempted, as in the case of the 1992 Catechism of the Catholic Church, conflicts are preprogrammed. What the Vatican presented as a "valid and legitimate instrument for ecclesial communion" had to be booed by the media of secular society as a compendium of dogmatic hubris: see Norbert Greinacher, "Römisch statt katholisch: Der neue katholische Weltkatechismus ist ein Desaster," *Süddeutsche Zeitung* 6, January 9–10, 1993.

20 [TN: "Mind machines" is in English in the original.]

21 Approaches to a theoretical consolidation of these mental exercises, which were highly experimental in their turn, can be found above all in the school of Milton Erickson's neo-hypnosis as well as in the metatheory of "positive thinking." See also Douglas R. Hofstadter, *Metamagical Themas: Questing for the Essence of Mind and Pattern* (New York: Basic Books, 2009). Serious metapsychiatric possibilities in connection with playful concepts of this sort can be found, among others, in Hinderk Emrich, *Psychiatrische Anthropologie: Therapeutische Bedeutung von Phantasiesystemen* (Munich: Pfeiffer, 1990), esp. pp. 141ff. ("Systemtheoretische Anthropologie: Auf dem Wege zu einer Strukturtheorie des Bewußtseins auf der Basis eines nichtreduktiven Monismus") and in John S. Kafka, *Jenseits des Realitätsprinzips: Multiple Realitäten in Klinik und Theorie der Psychoanalyse* (Berlin: Springer, 1991).

22 See Peter L. Berger, *The Heretical Imperative: Contemporary Possibilities of Religious Affirmation* (Garden City, NY: Anchor Press, 1979).

23 [TN: Compare p. 205 in vol. 1 of the *Encyclopaedia of Buddhism*, edited by Robert E. Buswell (New York: Macmillan Reference USA, 2004).

24 Other candidates for the role of "radicals" in the sense of basic building blocks or elementary functions of the religious realm, are dialogism, sacrificial operations, the establishment of corporate identity, missions, self-experience, humor, poetry, and the construal of catastrophes.

25 A typical title for the tendency to make mysticism easily accessible is, for instance, Michael Barnett's *At Heaven's Gate* (Zurich: Wild Goose Company Association, 1988). By contrast, a text from Martin Buber's post-mystical phase bears witness to the extreme scarcity of experiences that could be interpreted as direct manifestations of transcendence. See Martin Buber, *Eclipse of God: Studies in the Relation between Religion and Philosophy*, with a new introduction by Leora Batnitzky (Princeton, NJ: Princeton University Press, 2016).

26 [TN: "Apocalypse now" is in English in the original, then translated into German as *Offenbarung auch jetzt*.] Jacques Derrida has articulated in numerous versions his objection to the metaphysical prejudice that the absolute can become present in revelations. See, for example, his "Of an Apocalyptic Tone Recently Adopted in Philosophy," translated by John P. Leavey, Jr., *Oxford Literary Review* 6.2 (1984): 3–37; and his "No Apocalypse, Not Now (Full Speed Ahead, Seven Missiles, Seven Missives)," translated by Catherine Porter and Philip Lewis, *Diacritics* 14.2 (1984): 20–31.

27 See Heinrich Heine, *Germany: A Winter's Tale*, Chapter 1. Max Bense has given a quintessential characterization of the opening from consistent enlightenment into cosmological and existential atheism in

his essay "Warum man Atheist sein muß," *Club Voltaire: Jahrbuch für kritische Aufklärung* 1 (1963): 66–71.

28 Ludwig Wittgenstein, *Tractatus logico-philosophicus*, 6.44; compare also his *Lecture on Ethics*, where he speaks of "wondering at the existence of the world": Ludwig Wittgenstein, *Lecture on Ethics*, edited by Edoardo Zamuner, Ermelinda Valentina Di Lascio, and D. K. Levy (Chichester: Wiley Blackwell, 2014), p. 50.

29 Also here belongs the insufficiently explained circumstance that there is a "public" for mystical texts that consists of individuals who are not acquainted from their own experience with either the small or the great death of mysticism and yet assure us – correctly, from my perspective – that they feel addressed by the vibration of such communications.

30 On the elemental shift and profound movedness of humans, understood as their coming to the world, see Peter Sloterdijk, *Weltfremdheit* (Frankfurt am Main: Suhrkamp, 1993).

31 [TN: "Message" is in English in the original.]

32 Not without reason is the great mystical doctrine of India, the *Bhagavad Gita*, communicated in a war zone before battle – admittedly not with the moral punchline of making a peaceful yogi out of the warrior, but in order to transform the procrastinator into a fighter who has the comfort of not caring when he kills his next of kin in battle. Especially in the early period of mystical messages, remaining in a state of indifference amid bloody turbulence was regarded as important evidence of illumination, i.e. permanence of the other state – whence also the special attention paid to the serene death of masters.

33 The concept of enstasy serves to designate a particular sort of trance in the study of religion – especially the yogic trance.

34 See Alfred Tomatis, *Der Klang des Lebens: Vorgeburtliche Kommunikation: Die Anfänge der seelischen Entwicklung* (Reinbek bei Hamburg: Rowohlt, 2007).

35 The pathological disturbances of fetal and early symbiotic life can be reflected in the dark versions of mystical experience; in India as in the West, there is a type of isolating mysticism whose suicidal consequences can hardly be overlooked; it distills a superwitness or a mere observer completely distanced from the world, who experiences the cosmos as a monstrously indifferent life–death machine and does not even consider that she might belong to it. The mood of the complete meditative gaze upon the foreign whole oscillates between the threshold of great theater and the soul's landscape of death. This corresponds to the mysticism of schizoids, of those who, as it were, already died in the womb and remained stuck there – one thinks instinctively here of important mystical logicians, from Shankara to Wittgenstein. For the concept of "isolating mysticism" in contrast to the mysticism of all-encompassing unity, see R. C. Zaehner, *Mystik, religiös und profan: Eine Untersuchung über verschiedene Arten von außernatürlicher Erfahrung* (Stuttgart: Klett, n.d.), pp. 185ff.

36 This is why Ken Wilber's seemingly astute observations about the "pre/trans fallacy," i.e. the lack of distinction between transcendence and regression, in the spiritual psychology of the so-called New Age come to nothing. The possibility of the emergence of a "recollection"

of the state that precedes the differentiating experiences is, to be sure, not regressive; rather it presupposes significant accomplishments of personality and culture. Wilber's concern to separate sharply the transcending of the ego from regression before the ego reflects his evolutionistic positivism. For him, the human spirit must go through every grade of its schooling, from the fetal to the divine – so as not to repeat a year with the subtle ego. A less naive psychology of transcendence would assume a theory of progressive regression and a logic of the late emergence of what is earliest. See Ken Wilber, "The Pre/Trans Fallacy," ch. 7 in his *Eye to Eye: The Quest for the New Paradigm*, 3rd rev. edn., Foreword by Frances Vaughan (Boston: Shambhala, 2001).

Notes to Chapter 10

1 [TN: "The Urgency of Now" is in English in the original. Before it, Sloterdijk appends his German translation: *die Dringlichkeit des Jetzt*.]

Notes to Chapter 11

1 "The Will to Believe" [1896], in Henry James, *The Writings of William James. A Comprehensive Edition*, edited by John J. McDermott (Chicago, IL: University of Chicago Press, 1977), p. 717. [Quoted in English in the original.]
2 Ibid., p. 737.
3 Ibid., p. 724. [Quoted in English in the original.]
4 [TN: Sloterdijk uses the word *Ent-Einbettung* here and then writes in German, at the end of the sentence: "should this inelegant appropriation of the English term *disembedding* be allowed." I have left this out of the body of the text.]
5 For the expression "micro-evangelic," see Peter Sloterdijk, *What Happened in the Twentieth Century*, translated by Christopher Turner (Cambridge: Polity, 2018), pp. 116 and 125.
6 Heiner Mühlmann, "Die Ökonomiemaschine," in *5 Codes: Architektur, Paranoia und Risiko in Zeiten des Terrors*, edited by Gerd De Bruyn et al. (Basel: Birkhäuser, 2006), p. 227. One could perhaps clarify the meaning of this proposition by replacing "generation" with the sequence "learning phase in an individual life of average length"; from this would emerge, going back, the requirement to cooperate with the knowledge of predecessors whom one no longer knows (as a rule, predecessors from great grandparents on), and, going forward, the requirement to cooperate with descendants whose existence one no longer witnesses (beginning with great grandchildren).
7 We have the creationists to thank for the astounding idea that God created the world around the year 4000 before Christ in such a way as to make it seem infinitely older than it is (the theorem of the mirage of antiqueness). The spiritual costs of this ingenious reply to the evolutionist challenge are high: it makes God a *genius malignus* – a malignant

spirit who, during creation, left out nothing that would set the evolutionists on the wrong track.

8 Rudolf Otto, *The Idea of the Holy: An Inquiry into the Non-Rational Factor in the Idea of the Divine and Its Relation to the Rational*, translated by John W. Harvey, 2nd edn. (London: Oxford University Press, 1958), pp. 12–24.

9 [TN: Thomas Mann, *Joseph and His Brothers*, translated by John E. Woods (New York: Alfred A. Knopf, 2005), p. 538.]

10 See Peter Sloterdijk, "How the True Spheric Center Has Long-Range Effects through Pure Media: On the Metaphysics of Telecommunication," ch. 7 of *Spheres*, vol. 2: *Globes: Macrospherology* (South Pasadena, CA: Semiotext(e), 2014).

Notes to Chapter 12

1 [TN: German word play on the double meaning of *Fall* "case, instance"/"fall" in *der Fall sein* "to be the case" and *ausfallen* "to fail, break down, be cancelled."]

2 [TN: This is James's original term, rendered by Sloterdijk as *lebendigen Hypothesen*.]

3 [TN: "Varieties" is in English in the original.]

4 [TN: "Varieties" is in English in the original.]

5 [TN: "Self-reliance" is in English in the original.]

6 [TN: "Mind machine" is in English in the original.]

7 [TN: "Survival of the fittest believer" is in English in the original.]

8 [TN: "American way of religious life" is in English in the original.]

9 [TN: "Varieties of American religious experiences" is in English in the original.]

10 [TN: "To make god happen" is in English in the original.]

11 [TN: "Fitness" is in English in the original.]